Ballet and Dance

Auguste Vestris in *Les Amants Surpris*

A GUIDE TO THE REPERTORY

Ballet and Dance

PETER BRINSON AND CLEMENT CRISP

DAVID & CHARLES
Newton Abbot   London   North Pomfret (Vt)

British Library Cataloguing in Publication Data

Brinson, Peter
    Ballet and dance.
    1. Ballet – History
    I. Title   II. Crisp, Clement
    792.8'4   GV1787
    ISBN 0–7153–8114–8

Published in 1980 in conjunction with Pan Books Ltd.
This book incorporates material previously published in
Ballet for All (Pan Books, 1970, and David & Charles,
1971).

Printed in Great Britain
by Redwood Burn Limited, Trowbridge & Esher
for David & Charles (Publishers) Limited
Brunel House Newton Abbot Devon

Contents

Illustrations

Introduction and Acknowledgements

This is a guide to what can be seen on the dance stage today in Britain, Australia, Canada and New Zealand. By providing background information to over a hundred ballets we hope to increase the enjoyment of ballet-going as well as introduce a complex, fascinating art which has become one of Britain's chief cultural achievements in our time. Nowadays theatrical dance attracts hundreds of thousands of people every year in theatres throughout Britain, and many more in cinemas and on television; its history and practice have become subjects of school study in the General Certificate of Education. It is a form of theatre which combines music, literature, painting and dancing to create visual dramas which are the result of centuries of endeavour – as well as of public taste at this moment.

The perfect theatrical dance creation requires a perfect balance between each of its elements, and therefore a perfect collaboration between composer, designer, librettist and choreographer. Most often the choreographer is in control. Not only does he organize the performers on stage through his dances, but he usually supervises the production. He has been the central figure around which dance in the theatre has developed ever since it became able to tell stories in movement without the aid of words two hundred and fifty years ago. This book is about his work shown through the dance creations of thirty-eight choreographers, living and dead, who represent together what is called the international repertory and whose works are performed somewhere in Britain by a British dance company. In other words, we have been guided in what to include largely by whether or not the work of a choreographer can actually be seen on stage now and by whether that choreographer has, or seems likely to acquire, an international reputation.

When we wrote the first edition of this book and titled it *Ballet for All* in 1970, it was still appropriate in Britain, Australia, Canada and New Zealand to concentrate on classical ballet. This was the dominant dance style of our theatres, as it was in Europe. Today, not so. Already at that time in Britain the London Contemporary Dance School and Company were four years old and were beginning to make an impact on the British dance scene.

In Canada, so close to American modern dance sources, modern dance had begun to grow during the same period, but spread across Canada's vast territory in small, uncertainly financed groups. The reports of the Canada Council and a study conducted for the Council by the McKinsey Company, record their growth and chart their location. By the 1971–2 season there were nine companies, one each in Vancouver, Winnipeg and Edmonton; two in Toronto; and four in Montreal. None could offer more than sporadic employment to their dancers although the Toronto Dance Theatre had begun to attract subsidies which before long made it the most firmly based modern dance company in Canada. This was the beginning of a modern dance explosion in Canada which has continued throughout the 1970s, particularly attracting young people. In Australia the same trend was discernible in 1970 in the work of some teachers and some choreographers returned from Europe, although it would be some years before this new interest became translated into the development of professional modern dance companies. In New Zealand the trend is more recent but equally unmistakable.

'Contemporary dance' is the name given in Britain to that branch of modern dance which derives from the school and company of Martha Graham in New York. The London Contemporary Dance School and Company derive directly from Martha Graham through their artistic director and principal choreographer, Robert Cohan. For many years a dancer in the Graham Company, he became one of the company's associate directors and teachers before accepting Robin Howard's invitation in 1965 to help found a contemporary dance organization in London. Almost at the same time, Ballet Rambert, Britain's oldest classical ballet company, abandoned its allegiance to traditional classicism in favour of a style of modern dance which though classically based was greatly influenced by the practices of leading modern dance choreographers in the United States, especially Graham and Glen Tetley (q.v.). Thus modern dance was introduced to British choreography from two directions.

In Canada the influences were similar. David Earle and Peter Randazzo, two of the three initiators of the Toronto Dance Theatre in the spring of 1968, were disciples of the teaching of Martha Graham. So, too, was Patricia Beatty who joined them later the same year to establish the company. Earle had also gained experience with the London Contemporary Dance Theatre. He was a member of the company on its formation in

2

1967, and the British première of his *Witness of Innocence* formed part of its opening programme in October that year. Other Canadian modern dance companies equally reflect the dominant influence of a major American teacher or choreographer.

In Australia the American influence is much less marked and modern dance is closer to the classically based Rambert model. Jonathan Taylor, director of the Australian Dance Theatre which serves the states of Victoria and South Australia, is a former leading dancer of Ballet Rambert who took with him to Australia a number of dance works from Rambert's early modern repertory. Graeme Murphy, artistic director of the Sydney Dance Theatre, is classically trained and gained his first experience of contemporary dance through working with the French Ballet Felix Blaska. His predecessor at the head of the company was Jaap Flier of the Nederlands Dans Theater. Australia also has a long connection with the Central European tradition of modern dance through Gertrud Bodenweiser, the Austrian teacher, dancer and choreographer who settled in Sydney in 1938, where she opened a school and formed a company of dancers, many of whom are teachers today. Australian modern dance thus reflects European influences and may in time develop a style very different from the leading styles of America.

Modern dance now accounts for a substantial part of new choreography in the dance theatre of all three countries and hence also for much new music and theatrical design. The London Contemporary Dance Company and Ballet Rambert remain its creative centres, but there are also other influences from across the Atlantic. It is no longer possible, therefore, to speak only of classical ballet in any national dance theatre. Hence our new title and new approach. Our starting point is what is danced by British companies, embracing many works by American, Dutch and other choreographers, as well as British. Much of the living repertory of dance theatre thus assembled is common to Canada, Australia, New Zealand and the United Kingdom. Through this approach and by concentrating on choreographers with an international reputation we hope we have produced a repertory guide which has a wide interest and application.

Such a guide, of course, can range more widely in choreographic scope than it could do in 1970. Indeed, the decade has seen a choreographic expansion which we examine in more detail in the pages which follow. These pages present synopses and commentaries on over one hundred and fifty dance works from Galeotti in the eighteenth century to Frederick Ashton, Robert Cohan and Richard Alston today. Many other dance works and choreographers are mentioned in passing. All those treated in detail, selected according to our own prejudice and enthusiasm, are discussed in three parts: production credits – synopsis – commentary. They are grouped under their choreographers arranged in roughly chronological order. A narrative links each period with the one preceding, and introduces the leading choreographers, thus providing a compressed history of dance theatre in Britain. At the end is a short reading list to guide further study.

Our thanks are due to the editors of the *Financial Times* and the *Spectator*, the general administrator, Royal Opera House, Covent Garden and the Friends of Covent Garden, for permission to reproduce material originally published by them. Although we have seen for ourselves every ballet we discuss, except one (and therefore the opinions expressed are our own), we have checked our research of detail against recognized sources and must particularly record our indebtedness to Mr Cyril Beaumont's monumental *Complete Book of Ballets* and its supplements; *A Dictionary of Modern Ballet*, edited by Francis Gadan and Robert Maillard; Mr G. B. L. Wilson's *A Dictionary of Ballet*; Mr Horst Koegler's *The Concise Oxford Dictionary of Ballet*; and *The Choreographic Art* by Peggy van Praagh and Peter Brinson. Notices and production details in *Dance and Dancers* and the *Dancing Times* have also proved invaluable sources of reference. We owe particular debt to all dance companies for permission to reproduce synopses and other details from their programmes.

Our thanks are due also to Dame Peggy van Praagh and Mr Edward Pask for much helpful advice about repertories in Australia; to Mr P. J. Brooks of the Commonwealth Secretariat, London, and the Queen Elizabeth II Arts Council of New Zealand for advice about New Zealand; to Miss Mary Skeaping for historical information in Chapter Two; to Mr Alan Fridericia for additional information on *Konservatoriet*; to Miss Mary Clarke of the *Dancing Times* for the loan of photographs from her collection; to Mrs Claire H. de Robilant, former librarian/archivist of the London School of Contemporary Dance, for helpful advice and detail in the contemporary sections; to Mrs Dora Lewis for much assistance; and to Miss Claire Seignior, our secretary, without whom the work would never have reached the publishers.

PETER BRINSON
CLEMENT CRISP
London, 1980

ONE

The Background

Since modern dance in all its styles belongs only to the twentieth century any earlier dance work for the European theatre was likely to have been created using the style and technique of classical ballet. Classical ballet, therefore, has both an historical image and a contemporary image. It is, for example, *The Sleeping Beauty*, opulent, spectacular, a fairy tale told in dance, known to most people through the version presented by the Royal Ballet at Covent Garden; or it is the clean lines of Balanchine's *Serenade* from America, no story, just dancing to music (see plate section). It might also be something which uses bodies rather differently, combining the clean lines of Balanchine with other modern influences to produce a contemporary work like *Embrace Tiger and Return to Mountain*.

Whatever it is, the dancers' movements, their training and the ballets in which they appear on stage are the product of two things, like any other art: first, the past; second, the ideas and pressures of people today.

If you study the pictures of *The Sleeping Beauty* and Balanchine's *Serenade* you will notice a similarity in the way the dancers dance and hold themselves. This is because the dancers are classical dancers in ballets which are expressions of *classical* style – classical because the body is held as a central upright while arms and legs move always in balance and harmony around it. In architecture, painting, music, every art in fact, classicism implies these same qualities of balance and harmony. So in ballet.

The foundation of classical ballet and classical dancing is the academic vocabulary of what dance teachers call the *danse d'école*. This vocabulary of steps, always developing and changing, is what dancers learn in the classroom. It is their language, as words are the language of an actor. For historical reasons its terminology is French, and the steps, too, are the product of history. So to enjoy ballet in the fullest possible way one needs to know something of how it began.

The *danse d'école* is the product of five hundred years of study and creative work by dancers, teachers and choreographers. It is also a part of social history because, throughout this long period, dancing, like other arts, has always been an expression of the ideas of the time. Any movement we make as individuals reflects some idea or intention in our minds; in the same way dancing is human movement organized to music reflecting the ideas of a group or class of people.

Five hundred years ago such 'organization' produced the first ballets. These were nothing like ballets today, but elaborate combinations of music, singing, poetry, 'machines' (i.e. stage effects), costumes and dancing to praise in allegory the qualities of some prince or important guest. They were a product of court life with all the performers drawn from the same circle – kings, princes and courtiers – often very good at dancing or singing, but essentially amateurs. Professionals were used only as dancing masters, to arrange and produce the whole show, or as dancers in burlesque interludes which it might be undignified for a nobleman to perform. Men were the founders of these grand court ballets, dancing also the feminine roles, much as boys performed female roles in Shakespeare's plays. Women might dance privately at court, but never in the more public performances which were given to impress the king's subjects and the world at large with his wealth and importance.

Such ballets arose five hundred years ago as a result of the Renaissance, the great social and intellectual movement which freed European thought from the restraints of medieval Christian philosophy. Parallel with this intellectual liberation went a political liberation. Individual kings and princes allied themselves with the lesser nobility and merchant class in order to end the power of the great nobles, concentrate state power in the king's hands and so enable him to organize the social peace necessary for the expansion of trade and social wealth. It was important, therefore, to establish the king publicly as the centre of the life of the state in every sense, not just politically and economically, but artistically and intellectually. The princes realized this too, gathering around their persons as many artists as they could afford, to embellish their homes and their reputations. Court ballet assisted this political use of the arts in two ways. First and most obviously it combined many arts for a single purpose, the impact of such a combination being more powerful and immediate than the impact of a single art alone. From the combination arose almost incidentally a new art, greater than its individual parts: court ballet. Second, the new art was flexible enough to be adapted easily to particular themes, important at the time. Hence court ballet, new in form and flexible in content, became a leader of the arts and to some extent their principal influence in the service of the monarch.

6

The idea began in Italy because the Renaissance began there, and it was there that the concept of the absolute prince first established itself. In very early days – the late 1400s – the entertainments were combined with meals, as dinner ballets, each course being accompanied by an entry, or new scene, to carry forward the story. A reminder of this beginning still appears in the term 'entrée' on menus today.

When Charles VIII of France invaded Italy in 1494 to claim the throne of Naples, he and his nobility were astonished at the size and quality of the 'balli' they saw there, and the fact that so many leading artists contributed to them. Back in France the French copied the Italians and developed their own court ballets, often assisted by Italian dancing masters and by the taste of Italian princesses marrying into the royal house. A hundred years after the French invasion of Italy Catherine de Medici, Queen Mother of France, inspired the *Ballet Comique de la Reine*; largely created by her Italian dancing master, Belgiojoso. Accounts of its splendour were distributed around Europe resulting in the greatest period of court ballet, when every European monarch of any standing included ballet among his entertainments. In England ballet took the form of the masque, popular under Henry VIII, and rising under James I, through Ben Jonson and Inigo Jones, to become briefly the envy of Europe.

Court ballet, however, belonged absolutely to the monarch and existed solely for him. Restrain the monarch, or curb his absolutism, and the reason for court ballet would disappear. This happened in England under Charles I. Conversely, if the monarch grew in glory and power so did court ballet. Thus it was Louis XIV of France, most absolute monarch of his time, who raised *ballet de cour* to the heights and gave it thenceforth a French image.

Because of this the French have tended to overshadow the Italians in their contribution. Yet the Italians invented the idea of ballet as a combination of all the arts, have been largely responsible for its spectacular tradition; and inspired since very early days the virtuoso element in its dancing with ingenious rhythms and originality of steps. For two centuries before Louis XIV's time Italian dancing masters played the leading part in most European court entertainments, and it was an Italian, Lulli (or Lully) who translated Louis XIV's love of dancing into the court ballet's most splendid form.

France contributed to the new art the prestige and wealth of the most influential court of Europe, plus French qualities of grace and charm in executing steps and in the performance as a whole. Since the French court was the European centre of manners and polite society, it was here, rather than Italy, that the *danse d'école* grew up. Until Louis XIV's time there did not exist any formal vocabulary of steps such as professional dancers learn today in the classroom. Dancing masters had always used the steps of ballroom dances fashionable at court – which every courtier knew – and arranged them to make groups and patterns across the floor much as formation dancers do now. Pattern, in fact, was more important than step, because court ballet was often performed in a large hall, the audience looking down upon the performers from tiers of seats round three sides of the room.

In time, as the new art developed under Louis XIV, and heavier demands were made upon the performers by Lully and others, it became impossible for the noble amateurs to achieve the necessary standard. Louis XIV, moreover, 'growing portly', danced less often so that his courtiers, sycophantically, took less interest in ballet. Hence, in 1661, the king established an Académie Royale de Danse 'to increase the said art as much as possible', followed in 1669 by an Académie Royale de Musique, now the Paris Opéra. It was this latter academy, to which a dancing school was added in 1672, which produced the professional dancers Lully needed. Their studies embraced manners as well as dance steps, because ballroom dancing has always involved the niceties of social behaviour. In the seventeenth century these niceties required knowledge of social ceremonial to the smallest detail: how to walk elegantly with feet and legs turned out (though not as fully turned out as a dancer's today); how to raise the hat; and how to bow. Behind all this lay the mastery of posture, dignity in the carriage of the body, and grace in the deportment of the arms. When the steps of dancing began to be codified around the 1660s by Pierre Beauchamps, the king's dancing master, and his colleagues, the rules and style of aristocratic bearing were naturally included. Thus today's classical ballet steps are descended largely from ballroom dance steps fashionable at the courts of Renaissance monarchs, while their style is developed from the manners of polite society in Louis XIV's time. Together, steps and style make up the vocabulary of the *danse d'école* whose growth can be traced through the ballets of three hundred years.

The first edition of this book was able to record the existence in 1970 of five short dance works which illustrated the early years of this historical development. One work, still performed at the Royal Theatre, Copenhagen, dates from 1786 and has been staged continually ever since. The other four works were recreations by Mary Skeaping for the Royal Ballet's

Ballet for All company between 1964 and 1979. They were: an extract from *Le Ballet Royal de la Nuit* showing the style of French baroque ballet in 1653; a part of *The Loves of Mars and Venus* illustrating the style of the first *ballet d'action* in 1717; a solo from *Les Petits Riens* in the style of the French choreographer, Jean-Georges Noverre at the Paris Opéra 1778; and *The Return of Springtime*, a recreation of a ballet by the romantic choreographer, Filippo Taglioni. First staged in 1818, *The Return of Springtime* illustrated the transition of classical ballet from eighteenth century rococo to the romantic style of the 1830s. *The Return of Springtime* soon entered the repertory of the Royal Swedish Ballet in Stockholm and is thus preserved. The other works were lost when the Royal Ballet dissolved its Ballet for All company in 1979. The costumes, however, remain in the possession of the British Theatre Museum as memorial to a valuable enterprise in the presentation of dance history.

Since then the presentation and interpretation of dance history to the general public has been greatly assisted by television programmes which have variously explored the dance world and stimulated public response to live performance. The Ballet for All productions, however, were the only stage recreations regularly seen in British theatres over many years. We included them for this reason in our first edition and recall them here because they illustrate important moments in dance history.

The extract from *Le Ballet Royal de la Nuit* showed not only the dance style of court ballet in the early years of Louis XIV's reign, but also the political significance of this art form with the king at its centre. The years 1648–53 were marked by civil wars of the Fronde, in which first the Parliament of Paris, then the nobility, challenged the power of the Crown and of Mazarin, its chief minister. In 1652, led by Condé and supported by Spain, the rebel nobles had even occupied Paris, although the king returned to his capital by the end of the year. Early in 1653 it was clear the rebellion was failing and the last strongholds of the Fronde were being crushed.

With victory in sight the court resumed its normal life and lavish arrangements went forward for the *Ballet de la Nuit*. Mazarin's political purpose in presenting the young king, aged fifteen, in such a role and such a ballet at this point becomes clear in the extracts recreated by the Royal Ballet's Ballet for All company – the first time, so far as we can discover, that any part of this important production has been seen or heard since 1653. A long recitative between Sleep and Silence at the opening of the fourth part begins the build-up to the arrival of the Sun.

Musically, this recitative is very interesting as well as being very beautiful. It is one of the first examples of its kind and reflects the influence of Italian opera vigorously championed by Mazarin. As a result of this influence ballet began to be performed publicly in France by professional dancers and courtiers towards the end of the 1640s (the first public opera house had been opened in Venice in 1637), but Italian opera never achieved the same popularity.

Except in such recitatives, the texts of *ballets de cour* were usually not delivered from the stage area at this period; the ballets were intensely visual with magnificent costumes and effects, and many changes of scene. To follow the events depicted, the audience were given printed booklets from which have been drawn the words which introduce the Sun in the Ballet for All production, and which still express Mazarin's political purpose in Fergus Early's translation.

On mountain tops glowing with my first fire
Already I shine for the world to admire.
On my vast course have I far to run
But already to all things I have begun
To give form and colour. And who does not meet
My light with homage, shall feel its heat.

Louis XIV had danced in his first ballet two years earlier, but this is probably the first time he danced the role of the Sun from which he acquired his famous title *Le Roi Soleil*. Already, at fifteen, an excellent dancer in the noble style, his skill and interest gave to dancing the decisive influence which insured its triumph over Mazarin's interest in opera. Louis was aware of the political value of his allegorical roles and continued, like Mazarin, to use his writers to convey the propaganda message of the crown against any rival. Hence many ballets ended with an apotheosis of the king which had the useful effect of renewing the homage of the nobility who took part.

The Loves of Mars and Venus sixty-four years later was a very different kind of work. Created by John Weaver in six scenes at Drury Lane Theatre, London, on 2 March 1717, this first ballet without words (*ballet d'action*) emphasizes that there is a long dance history in Britain which includes significant contributions to the development of classical ballet. *Le Ballet Royal* showed the essential characteristics of all the theatre arts in which words were essential to convey the meanings. In France, once the monarchy had become firmly established, and a number of Royal Academies had

10

been founded for different arts to guide them in their service to the king, court ballet largely lost its political function. Its aesthetic value as an art form, however, was unquestioned, encouraging development into opera-ballet under Lully's guidance, and its transfer from palace hall to public stage performance by professional artists. The title 'opera-ballet' arose because it was a combination of Italian opera and French ballet in which words remained essential to explain the story and the feelings of the characters. Dance steps were still those fashionable in the ballroom. Modern formation dancing shows how adequately such steps can create pattern and spectacle but how lacking they are when it comes to portraying finer emotions. Hence dancing masters early began to tackle the problem of making dance steps expressive enough to tell a story without the aid of words.

Although a mimed representation of a scene in Corneille's *Les Horaces* had been given at Sceaux in France in 1708, the credit for the first major attempt to solve the problem belongs to John Weaver, one of the leaders of a brilliant group of dancing masters in London during the reigns of Queen Anne and George I. Weaver argued that words could be replaced by gestures. He demonstrated his idea in *The Loves of Mars and Venus* by giving to each feeling expressed by his characters – Neglect, Coquetry, Contempt, etc. – an appropriate gesture. From his own description, this first *ballet d'action* 'which drew the whole town after it', seems to have had mimed passages of 'conversation' alternating with danced passages which still used the ballroom steps of the period. The result must have been a production of great novelty, although it failed to catch on because experimental theatre always needs a patron. The England of George I was not interested in theatre which could not pay its way. Nevertheless, this addition of gestures to ordinary dance steps marks the beginning of ballet as we now know it.

The event also emphasized that the traditions of 'the dancing English', for which Elizabethans were noted, were not yet lost in early eighteenth-century London. Weaver himself danced Vulcan, and all the named cast but one were English, including Venus, 'danced by Mrs Santlow'. The exception was Mars, danced by M. Dupré, most famous French dancer of his day, and subsequently a teacher of Noverre, founder of the *ballet d'action* in France. Through Dupré, Weaver's ideas may have influenced Noverre.

We know little of the style of Noverre's choreography – only what can be learned from his important theoretical writings, especially *Letters on*

11

Dancing and Ballets, and what can be divined from caricatures of the time. *Les Petits Riens* was as light-hearted as its title implies and thus rather out of the mainstream of Noverre's major choreography which seems to have been dramatic, even melodramatic. In three scenes, linked only by the slenderest theme, it is chiefly notable for its music, illustrating in Noverre's choice of Mozart his maxim that music for ballet should be specially composed by the best composers. In fact Mozart composed exactly two-thirds of the music, the other six pieces, he said, consisting of 'trumpery old French airs'.

The solo recreated by the Ballet for All company was useful mainly to show how *ballet d'action* had progressed in the generation since Weaver's day. It used one of Mozart's pieces to illustrate the development of choreography and dance technique by 1778. Women at this time were still hampered by long skirts, wigs and heeled slippers, but whereas Weaver had separated mime and dance passages, Noverre and choreographers like Angiolini were now combining these two elements into expressive choreography. And dance steps were no longer just ballroom steps but the beginnings of classical technique capable of expressing simple feelings with a skill beyond anything the most gifted amateur could achieve. In the interval since Weaver, the singing and dancing of Louis XIV's opera-ballets have begun to form separate arts. Singing becomes opera; dancing becomes ballet, because dancing at last was learning to speak without the aid of words. Rather unfairly, Noverre has been given most of the credit for this important advance because his *Letters on Dancing and Ballets*, published in Stuttgart in 1760, became the first really widely read book on the theory and practice of *ballet d'action*. But many other ballet masters had dreamed and worked to the same end since Weaver's day. Among them the Austrian Hilferding van Wewen, and the Italian, Gasparo Angiolini, deserve at least as much honour. The first worked mainly in St Petersburg; the second collaborated with Gluck in Vienna.

Thus the development of classical ballet was never the work of one particular country. It was a European art fostered by the courts of Europe, albeit French and Italian ballet masters exerted dominant influences, working wherever royal patrons engaged them. Hence ballet took root in Russia, Sweden and Denmark as well as in Southern Europe. The contribution of the Italian choreographer, Vincenzo Galeotti, to the expansion of Danish ballet illustrates the process.

Galeotti's *Les Caprices du Cupidon et du Maître de Ballet* was performed first at the Royal Danish Opera on 31 October 1786 and remains in the repertory of the Royal Danish Ballet today, the oldest ballet still danced in its original choreography. Never long out of the repertory since 1786, it is safe to say the choreography has been preserved largely as Galeotti created it. Thus the work is an important indication of the technical level of one genre of ballet just before the French Revolution, and also of Galeotti's quality as a choreographer, although he never regarded it as anything more than a trifle. It is indeed a trifle, albeit a charming one, intelligently conceived, with well-observed comments on a succession of married states easily recognizable today, and with an inventive use of dance material carefully contrasted to obtain maximum effect. Styrian, Norwegian and Amager couples appear in adaptations of folk dances. An old-people's dance burlesques eighteenth-century court dance. A French dance is created in terms of academic ballet of the period; and a Greek dance is presented as an academic *pas de deux* in a version of ancient Greek costume. Best is the American dance of the Quaker couple, a witty joke at the expense of starchy respectability.

Equally important is the reminder, through Galeotti, of Italy's profound contribution to the development of *ballet d'action*. Galeotti was born in Florence in 1733 and studied principally under Angiolini, absorbing the principles of *ballet d'action* mostly from that master, although he worked later with Noverre and saw the results of the work of both choreographers during wide travels throughout Europe. By the time he was appointed ballet master to Copenhagen in 1775, at the age of forty-two, he was established as a dancer and choreographer with a reputation among the highest in his profession. He found in Denmark a well-established theatre and company, trained in the French style and deriving some tradition from the court ballet of the Danish kings in the previous century. There were many such ballet companies in Europe at that time, all operating under some form of royal patronage and tracing their existence from the days when Renaissance princes had felt it necessary to demonstrate their importance through suitable court ballets. Although he continued as a dancer, Galeotti's principal contribution in Copenhagen was as teacher and choreographer. He created a wide range of ballets, using Danish composers like Jens Lolle to write his music, and in his own style developed the *ballet d'action* much as others were doing elsewhere. More important still, the regular classes he conducted for his dancers established the school which became the foundation of Bournonville's company during the nineteenth century.

By the period of the French Revolution when Galeotti was at work in Denmark the most important centre of classical ballet training in Europe was the studio of Auguste Vestris in Paris. Here were drawn together and combined the traditions of Italian brilliance in dance technique with French elegance and style, laying the basis for romantic ballet. Filippo Taglioni, choreographer of the first romantic ballet, *La Sylphide*, had made his début at the Paris Opéra in 1799, and by 1818 was working in Stockholm as chief dancer and ballet master, much as Galeotti had done in Denmark. Filippo Taglioni, then aged thirty, was too ambitious to remain in Stockholm as Galeotti did in Copenhagen, but the Swedish engagement provided important choreographic experience. Part of this experience was an invitation from the Spanish ambassador to compose a short ballet to be given in the embassy at a party attended by the crown prince of Sweden. The occasion represented a considerable compliment to Taglioni. In response he produced *The Return of Springtime*.

Today, the only record of this little work is the libretto which Taglioni wrote, adapting the classical myth of Flora, Zephyr and Cupid which had been popular for many years among ballet masters in Europe. Mary Skeaping, the well-known English producer and choreographer in historical genres, found this libretto in Stockholm and was commissioned by Peter Brinson, director of the Royal Ballet's Ballet for All, to create a ballet which would show the link between theatrical dance in the late eighteenth century and romantic ballet of the 1830s.

The most famous ballet of that period on the same theme was *Flore et Zéphyr*, created at the King's Theatre, London, in 1796 by Charles Louis Didelot. Didelot, great French ballet master and pupil of Noverre, had been born in Stockholm and went on to become a founder of ballet in Russia. Into his *Flore et Zéphyr* Didelot introduced for the first time dancers of the *corps de ballet*, made to fly with the aid of wires. Taglioni omitted from his libretto all such provision for a *corps de ballet* and concentrated only on the three principal characters. The result was a distillation of eighteenth-century Anacreontic ballet, that is a ballet which was required to show 'free, joyous and erotic' qualities – personified as Zephyr, Flora and Cupid respectively.

This was a period of intense change, a preparation for the triumphs of romantic ballet launched fourteen years later in Paris by Filippo Taglioni's *La Sylphide*, with his daughter Marie in the leading role. Themes like *The Return of Springtime* were still variations of eighteenth-century mythological formulae, as were music, stage lighting and production techniques. But costumes, especially for women, had abandoned eighteenth-century restrictions and now allowed a much wider range of movement, to the feet

14

in soft heel-less slippers, and to the body in flowing empire-line draperies. Dance technique followed suit. Men still dominated the ballet stage, as they had done since ballet began, but the dancing of men and women now commanded resources of technical display and expression which were the fruit of new exercises in the classroom and new, more advanced methods of teaching.

The choreography of *The Return of Springtime* draws on these period resources. Since Taglioni was Italian-trained – although, like all other leading professional dancers of the day, he studied in Paris and made his début at the Opéra – Mary Skeaping based her work entirely on Italian technical dance manuals of the late eighteenth and early nineteenth centuries, up to and including Carlo Blasis' *Treatise on the Dance*. Published in 1820, this early manual, by a man who became the greatest teacher of the nineteenth century, can safely be assumed to summarize technique and training methods at that time, and therefore represents the knowledge upon which the Italian-trained Taglioni would draw.

TWO

Romantic Ballet

AUGUST BOURNONVILLE (1805–79)

Of the two great choreographers of romantic ballet, August Bournonville and Jules Perrot, Bournonville's work has been preserved more completely and becomes the best guide today to the style and quality of a movement which revolutionized choreography in the mid-nineteenth century. Born in Copenhagen, trained there first by his father, Antoine, and by Galeotti, both pupils of Noverre, he became a student of Auguste Vestris in Paris in 1820. Thus he inherited the best classic traditions of the eighteenth-century French and Italian schools. The French tradition was one of grace and style, epitomized in the teaching and ballets of Pierre Gardel, chief ballet master at the Paris Opéra from 1787 to 1827. The Italians contributed virtuosity in performance, invention of steps and a more thorough academic approach. It is notable that all the technical manuals which have descended to us from the late eighteenth and early nineteenth centuries are Italian, so that we have no very clear idea of Gardel's teaching methods. We can be more certain of Vestris', partly because he inherited Italian traditions from his father and because Carlo Blasis' *Treatise on the Dance* of 1820 sums up the best of these traditions; partly because August Bournonville has left a choreographic portrait of a Vestris class in his ballet, *Konservatoriet* (q.v.).

Vestris, born in Paris in 1760, *premier danseur* at the Paris Opéra for thirty-six years – and even, for one performance at the age of seventy-five, the partner of Marie Taglioni, then aged thirty-one – thus became the undisputed master and guardian of the best traditions of both schools. On the basis of his teaching, further explored by younger masters like Filippo Taglioni and Carlo Blasis, was created the whole technical edifice of romantic ballet. Here began its exploration of the air through all kinds of jumps, the unprecedented lightness its female dancers achieved through the new skill of dancing on *pointe*, the qualities of its *port de bras*, and the grace of its movement.

In 1820, of course, much of this was still to come, although the exercises and training methods were there already and feminine fashion, in the flowing empire line and new kinds of shoe, had begun to free body and feet for a much wider range of dance movement than was possible before. Filippo Taglioni, too, was busy on the harsh regime of training – six hours a day – which by 1832 produced in his daughter, Marie, the new image of ballet which has lasted to our own day.

As always, the technical discoveries of teaching in the classroom could not be considered complete until adapted and developed by choreographers on stage. It was the choreographers of romantic ballet – Taglioni, Bournonville and Perrot – who gave the movement the directions which have passed into history. Bournonville in Copenhagen is unique for the balance he maintained between the male and female dancer, where all other choreographers of romantic ballet emphasized the woman at the expense of the man. Such an emphasis proved fatal in the end, almost destroying ballet as an art because it destroyed the balance between the sexes on which dancing depends. By contrast, Bournonville's work has survived not only because of the particular isolation of ballet in Denmark but because all his ballets challenge male dancers as strongly as they challenge the female. To this day his choreography remains the basis of the style and school of Danish dancers.

After becoming soloist at the Paris Opéra in 1826 and dancing a season in London, Bournonville returned to Copenhagen in 1829. Here he created his first ballet and was appointed ballet master soon after. Except for short interludes of absence, he retained his position until his retirement in 1877. In his half century of life-work was created the Bournonville style, based on the style of Vestris. It was evolved through methods of teaching whose principles are described in his technical notes, *Etudes Chorégraphiques* published in 1861, and through the creation of thirty-six ballets and *divertissements*, a valuable group of which remain in the Danish repertory.

La Sylphide

Ballet in two acts. Libretto: Adolphe Nourrit. Choreography: August Bournonville after Filippo Taglioni. Music: Løvenskjold. First performed Royal Theatre, Copenhagen, 28 November 1836. Lucille Grahn: the Sylphide and Bournonville: James Taglioni's version – music: Schneitzhöffer; décor: Ciceri; costumes: Lami. First performed Paris Opéra, 12 March 1832, with Marie Taglioni in the name role and Joseph Mazilier as James.

ACT I: The interior of a farmhouse in Scotland. At dawn on his wedding day, James sits asleep in a chair in front of the fire with Gurn, a friend, also

17

Contemporary engraving showing Ciceri's décor for Act I of Taglioni's *La Sylphide*, with Marie Taglioni as the Sylphide and Joseph Mazilier as James

asleep in a corner. Around him are the things he loves: the panelled walls of his Scottish home, warmed and lit from the great fireplace; in an upper room his mother and fiancée, Effie, also asleep. Beyond the farmhouse door lies the forest, 'green, mysterious, silent'. He ought to be happy, yet he is troubled. In his dreams, a white figure has appeared between him and his betrothed, a Sylphide, an ideal of love and beauty out of the forest and the Scottish mist. She is beside him as the curtain rises, kisses him lightly and disappears through the chimney as he wakes. He rouses Gurn, but at that moment Effie and his mother enter. Gurn protests his love for Effie, but she declares for James and kneels with him to receive his mother's blessing.

Effie's friends bring her presents while James, still looking for the Sylphide, suddenly finds old Madge, a witch, beside the chimney. The girls beg him to let Madge tell their fortunes, but Madge reads in Effie's hand that it is Gurn, not James, she will marry and James orders Madge away. Effie retires to prepare for the wedding and the Sylphide appears to James a second time, confessing her love for him. At the wedding celebrations the Sylphide flits in and out among the guests, seizes James's wedding ring and finally induces him to follow her into the forest. Effie, in despair, hears Gurn again protest his love.

ACT II: In the forest at night. Old Madge and her attendant witches cast a spell upon a scarf. At dawn they vanish. James enters, searching for the Sylphide who appears beside him. She brings him water from a stream, fruit from the forest. James wants her to remain always with him instead of disappearing among the other Sylphides. Seeing Madge cross his path, he begs her forgiveness and she offers him help by means of a magic scarf which, she says, will make the Sylphide his for ever. When the Sylphide returns, James puts the scarf about her. Instantly her wings fall off and she dies while Madge gloats over the results of her work. The Sylphides carry their sister into the tree tops while below them James sees in the distance the bridal procession of Gurn leading Effie to the altar.

In Filippo Taglioni's original version, at the Paris Opéra in 1832, *La Sylphide* became one of those unique ballets which change choreographic history and introduce a new era. Its significance lies in the influence and philosophy of the Romantic Movement which altered the arts of Europe as

An engraving from Gautier's *Les Beautés de L'Opéra* of Act II of *La Sylphide*

19

decisively as the Renaissance had done three centuries before.

The social upheavals manifest in the French Revolution and the Napoleonic regime gave a new perspective to man's thought. He moved beyond eighteenth-century rationalism to look deeper into the emotions. Foreshadowed in the writings of Rousseau and Madame de Staël, this romanticism found expression in France in a passionate interest in the writings of Walter Scott and Goethe, in the early poems of Lamartine, the paintings of Delacroix, Hugo's *Hernani*, and the music of Berlioz. So profound a change in the arts of Europe reflected in turn the change in social relations caused by the Industrial Revolution, including the relationship of artist and patron. A new bourgeois audience, which knew nothing about the theatrical conventions of the past, came into the theatre. Outside the theatre a world of dirt, smoke and industrial squalor had arisen in which the artist found himself equated with the worker. No longer able to expect the patronage of the rich, the artist must sell the fruits of his labour or starve.

To help forget the harshness of this new world and as a manifestation of the new romantic ethos, public and artist alike sought colour, fantasy and delight. They tried to evoke in art the creatures they would like to be, or to dream about – faraway exotic peoples with strange customs; spiritual beings from the occult and the supernatural; history become romance. People asked to see, in fact, a different, idealized world. This was the impulse behind the Romantic Movement, new, rebellious, led by young people who resembled, in outward forms at least, young critics of society and the arts today. They wore their hair long, upset their elders with strange ideas of behaviour and dress, experimented with drugs. 'Our cry,' declared Théophile Gautier, the poet and one of their leaders, 'was liberation from the past, the bonds of classical restraint and all restriction!'

In ballet the new themes demanded by the new audiences gave inspiration and direction to the work of teachers, dancers and writers of ballet libretti. In 1831, Meyerbeer's *Robert le Diable* owed much of its success to a ballet of nuns who were summoned from the grave by the opera's hero. Their ghostly shapes on stage inspired the tenor in the opera, Nourrit, to propose the following year a libretto for a ballet which became *La Sylphide*. This responded so perfectly to the feeling of the time that it established a formula for all romantic ballet during the next forty years. Its story mirrored the tragic conflict between ideals and reality, which runs through all romantic art. The ending of this story, like the end of most romantic ballets after it, was unhappy because romantic art carried within itself its own fatal end. Dealing only in dreams and fantasies, its ideals (*right*) Karen Kain in the National Ballet of Canada's production of *Giselle*. (*below*) Peter Schaufuss and Eva Evdokimova with London Festival Ballet in *La Sylphide*

(*above*) Vergie Derman as the Lilac Fairy with a group of fairies from the Prologue to *The Sleeping Beauty* as presented by the Royal Ballet. (*below*) A group of soloists from the Royal Danish Ballet in *Napoli*, Act III

could never be realized; there had to be the moment of awakening and return to reality.

Marie Taglioni was schooled exactly to create the image of the Sylphide. Her father's choreography of the ballet exploited the gifts she had developed in the classroom, and those gifts established her in the hearts of her audience as the image of the new style. The great and essential feature of this style was the exploration of the air through all kinds of steps of elevation. In other words, the lightness and grace on which Vestris had insisted as attributes of female dancing were developed to exploit the special qualities which women could bring to ballet. These qualities were emphasized further by new gas lighting and the simplicity of the Sylphide's costume, which began the gradual introduction of a silhouette quite different from the high-waisted Empire line of the preceding period. Of white muslin, leaving neck and shoulders bare, the skirt reaching midway between knee and ankle, it became the prototype of romantic ballet costume, providing in its later bell-shaped form an image retained until today. Similarly with Taglioni's utterly simple hair style, parted down the centre and gathered tight around the head to be tied at the back; and with Ciceri's farmhouse and forest bringing reality on to the ballet stage.

All this was continued and preserved in Bournonville's *La Sylphide*. The two versions cannot be compared since no choreographic record remains of Taglioni's staging, but Bournonville rejected Taglioni's mime-and-partnering conception of James ('In addition,' remarked Gautier of Taglioni's *Sylphide*, 'there are hardly any dances for men, which is a great comfort') in favour of the more lively conception which has descended to us, including a great deal of dancing in the first act and excellent male solos in the second. Very probably, Bournonville's whole treatment of Nourrit's libretto was fresher and less sophisticated than the original treatment. His was a younger approach, with a 17-year-old Sylphide in Lucille Grahn, compared with Marie Taglioni who was 28; a 21-year-old composer in Løvenskjold compared with the older Schneitzhöffer; and Bournonville himself, aged 31, at the height of his dancing career, twenty-seven years younger than Filippo Taglioni. Nevertheless, the style of choreography, costume, scenery and, of course, libretto closely follow Taglioni's original. Thanks to Bournonville and the Danes, we have a simile of one of the most influential ballets ever created.

Napoli, or The Fisherman and his Bride
Romantic ballet in three acts. Libretto and choreography: August Bournonville.

Music: Paulli, Helsted, Gade and Lumbye. Scenery: Christensen. First per-
formed Royal Theatre, Copenhagen, 29 March 1842.

ACT I: The square and beach of Santa Lucia, Naples. To the left, the
house of Veronica, a widow. To the right, a palace. In the square, people,
children, macaroni and lemonade stalls, and so on. Enter Teresina with her
mother, Veronica. It is clear that Giacomo and Peppo, the macaroni and
lemonade sellers, are in love with Teresina, but she waits only for the return
of the fisherman, Gennaro. The fishermen return. After some quarrelling
over division of the catch, which Gennaro solves by giving a major portion
to the Madonna, he offers Teresina an engagement ring. She accepts,
Veronica giving them her blessing. To be alone, the young couple decide
to go out in Gennaro's boat but a storm arises, Teresina is lost overboard
and Gennaro, rescued by his friends, is blamed for her death. He appeals
to the Madonna, and Fra Ambrosio, a monk, advises him to search the sea
for his beloved, giving him an amulet of the Madonna for protection.

ACT II: The blue grotto on the Island of Capri. Golfo, a sea-sprite,
appears and Tritons attend to receive his commands. Naiads bring in the
lifeless form of Teresina. Captivated by her beauty, Golfo restores her to
life, but when she begs to return to her betrothed he turns her into a Naiad
so that she loses all memory of human existence. Even so, she cannot
reciprocate Golfo's affection. Gennaro enters the grotto searching for
Teresina and finds the guitar she had carried with her, but when Teresina
herself appears she fails to recognize him. He remembers the amulet and
prays that Teresina be restored to him. Gradually her memory returns.
Golfo, enraged, orders the Naiads to seize Teresina and the Tritons to
crush Gennaro, who again raises the amulet. Golfo submits to its superior
power and Teresina and Gennaro depart, their boat loaded with riches.

ACT III: Noon. An open space below a bridge connecting two hills outside Naples.

The bridge's centre pillar displays a picture of the Madonna, before
which pilgrims come to kneel. Teresina arrives with her mother and
Gennaro, but the people, encouraged by Peppo and Giacomo, think
Teresina has been rescued by witchcraft and separate the couple. Fra
Ambrosio, sent for to cast out the evil spirit, tells the crowd that Teresina
was rescued by the divine power of the Madonna. Fear changes to joy and
the return of the couple is celebrated with dances.

This, the most popular of Danish ballets, illustrates particularly well the
direction which Bournonville's own talents and interest gave to romantic
ballet. A distinguished male dancer – he was the first Gennaro in *Napoli*,

22

the first James in his own *Sylphide* – he never accepted the secondary role ascribed to men by French romantic ballet, a fashion copied almost everywhere else. All his ballets include challenging dances for men but nowhere more than in the brilliant Tarantella which is the principal item in the celebrations at the end of *Napoli*. Dances of this kind sustained public interest in male dancing and provided essential proof – at a time when such proof was lacking everywhere else – of the male dancer's importance.

Napoli's theme stresses Bournonville's abiding interest in the folk genre. It shows how he added the gaiety of folk characters to the mystery and melancholy of Paris romanticism, building a Danish form of *ballet d'action*, the romantic folk-life ballet. His work favoured the real-life element of romantic ballet rather than the supernatural element fashionable in Paris; and Bournonville reaches the summit of his art as the scenic narrator of genius who gives dance form to the romantic-bourgeois outlook of his time.

Konservatoriet eller et avisfrieri (The Dancing School, or A Proposal by Advertising)

Ballet in two acts. Libretto and choreography: Bournonville. Music: Paulli. First performed Royal Theatre, Copenhagen, 6 May 1849. Revised and revived as Konservatoriet (The Dancing School) *by Harald Lander and Valborg Borchsenius, using extracts from the original music. First performed Royal Theatre, Copenhagen, 24 October* 1941.

Only the Lander-Borchsenius one-act version of Bournonville's original two-act work now survives. Set in a classroom of the 1820s, it recalls and recreates Bournonville's classroom experiences under Vestris in the Paris of that time. Its principal character is the ballet master, violin in hand, who sets the exercises, demonstrates and controls everything. The *corps de ballet* and principal dancers comprise his pupils – from the youngest to the oldest. The result is an elaborate and charming *divertissement* linked by the exercises and rivalries of dancers in class.

Konservatoriet is one of the few – and perhaps the first – choreographic memoirs. Slonimsky, the Russian critic, recalls how in 1900 *Les Millions d'Arlequin,* also known as *Harlequinade,* came to enshrine the octogenarian Petipa's memories of his young days in Paris. So *Konservatoriet* recalls the forty-three-year-old Bournonville's memories of Paris; first when he was taken by his father to study under Vestris at the age of fourteen, then four years later when he settled there with the help of a royal subsidy from Copenhagen. Subsequently, he visited Vestris' classes every time he returned to Paris for as long as the old man was teaching.

Nor is this 'choreographic memoir' based only on a memory dimmed after twenty years. At the age of eighteen Bournonville made a complete scheme of the Vestris *enchaînements*, many of which he used in his daily lessons, and so preserved them. Besides this, and his booklet *Etudes Chorégraphiques*, there remain two further manuscripts, unprinted and unfinished, dealing mainly with notation problems and the classification of dances and steps. Some of these latter were innovations by Bournonville, others were named as being particularly characteristic of leading contemporary dancers or ballets, such as Taglioni, Elssler, *La Sylphide*.

All this material indicates how aware Bournonville was of the value of what he learned in Paris and the care he took to preserve his knowledge in easy reference form. *Konservatoriet* remains the purest choreographic expression of the school of Vestris so that its historical importance is enormous. It illustrated the French-Italian style which evolved over the hundred and fifty years since Louis XIV formed his Royal Academies: lightness, grace and charm from the women; elegance, strength and a virile nobility from the men; from both, a considerable technical virtuosity.

It is worth recording that Bournonville's influence was to be strongly felt in Russia. His pupil, the Swedish Per Christian Johannson (1817–1903), was invited by Marie Taglioni to accompany her to Russia as a partner on her visit there in 1841. Johannson opted to stay on in St Petersburg, where he was appointed a principal soloist, and while still active as a dancer he became a teacher in the Imperial School. Following his retirement in 1869, he was appointed chief teacher at the Imperial School, and his inspiring classes became a vital force in developing the abilities of Russian dancers. Among his pupils – notably in his 'perfection class' – were Pavel Gerdt, Lev Ivanov, Mathilde Kshessinskaya and the brothers Nikolay and Sergey Legat. In his memoirs, N. Legat pays eloquent tribute to Johannson's greatness as a pedagogue, and records that Petipa would attend the boys' classes in search of ideas for male variations. We see, here, how essentially a part of the great fabric of the Imperial Ballet were to be the style and technical attitudes of the Danish school: the pre-eminence of the Bournonville manner can still be traced in the purity and elegance of the Leningrad style. Outside Scandinavia, the Australian Ballet was the first company to receive permission to dance this work, staged by Paul Gnatt and presented at Her Majesty's Theatre, Adelaide, 5 February 1965, with décor and costumes by Desmond Digby.

La Ventana

Ballet in two scenes. Choreography: August Bournonville. Music: H. C. Lumbye and V. C. Holm. First performed Royal Theatre, Copenhagen, 1854. Revised by the choreographer in 1856. Juliette Price: the Señorita.

A room in a Spanish house. A señorita enters her room; she fans herself, and dreams of a gentleman she has met at the Alameda. She dances with her image reflected in a looking glass, and then hears the sounds of guitars below her window. It is her admirer, come to serenade her, and taking up her castanets she dances to the guitar's music. She then approaches her window, and throws him a bow from her hair.

A public place. The señorita has left her room and joined her admirer and his friends. There ensues a *pas de trois*, a male solo, a *seguidilla* with the two lovers as its central attraction.

The Romantic Age found much to charm it in the Spanish dance – from Fanny Elssler's *cachucha* to the more authentic offerings of such brilliant exponents as Manuela Perea (*La Nena,* a huge favourite in London) and Petra Camara who brought a troupe of twenty-eight dancers to delight Paris and London.

Bournonville, who had already used Spanish themes in his *Toreadors* of 1840, often considered Spanish dancers too provocatively sensual, and in creating a role for Juliette Price, whom he thought his favourite ballerina, he aimed at a manner more graceful and charming. *La Ventana* shows his skill in creating a harmonious style from the classic vocabulary and Spanish steps, and in the *pas de trois* he produced one of his most delightful compositions.

Today Bournonville is increasingly represented in the British repertory. The Royal Ballet at one time owned a *divertissement,* mounted for them by the great Danish dancer Erik Bruhn, which included the *pas de deux* from *Flower Festival in Genzano* and the variations from *Napoli* and an interpolated number from *Abdallah*. Ballet Rambert had a delightful *La Sylphide*, staged for them by Elsa Marianne von Rosen in 1960, which was abandoned when the company was reorganized as a more modern troupe in 1966. It is the Scottish Ballet which has done most to bring Bournonville to the British audience, with exemplary productions of *La Sylphide*, *Napoli* and *La Ventana* staged during the past decade, while London Festival Ballet acquired a production of *La Sylphide* in 1979 in which Peter Schaufuss, notable young Danish star, incorporated music long since dropped from the Danish production, which he fleshed out with dances using only the Bournonville vocabulary of steps.

JEAN CORALLI (1779–1854)
JULES PERROT (1810–92)

These joint creators of *Giselle* span in their careers the ambitions and weaknesses of romantic ballet. Coralli, born in the early years of Louis XVI, Italian of Bolognese extraction but trained at the Opéra in what was then the best school in Europe, never acquired distinction as a dancer. He aimed always at choreography. In this he displayed competence with occasional distinction as in *Giselle*, but never that creative originality which distinguishes the important artist. His strength lay in the arrangement of *corps* dances, a certain gift for spectacle and a grasp of what was appropriate to public taste at a particular moment.

Perrot, son of a carpenter who became chief machinist at the Grand-Théatre, Lyons, began to study dancing there, then worked in the boulevard theatres and the Porte-Saint-Martin of Paris. Later, through his own ambition, he became a pupil of Auguste Vestris who instantly recognized his talent. Thus *Giselle* jointed two opposite talents: Coralli, by that time *maître de ballet en chef* at the Opéra, achieving through *Giselle* his small place in history; and Perrot, self-made, a natural theatre man of enormous talent. Already established as a distinguished dancer, he was the lover of Carlotta Grisi, the first Giselle, and collaborated in the production entirely on her account, having left the service of the Opéra in 1835 after disagreement with Véron, the director. How great a loss to the Opéra this was became clear only after 1841 when Perrot was ballet master at Her Majesty's Theatre, London, where he created most of his greatest works.

Giselle, ou Les Wilis

Fantastic ballet in two acts. Libretto: Théophile Gautier, Vernoy de St Georges and Jean Coralli. Choreography: Coralli and Perrot. Music: Adam, and some numbers by Burgmüller. Décor: Ciceri. First performed Paris Opéra, 28 June 1841. Carlotta Grisi: Giselle. Lucien Petipa: Albrecht. Adèle Dumilâtre: Myrtha.

ACT I: Outside Giselle's cottage. 'We set the action,' said Gautier, 'in some mysterious corner of Germany, among hillocks weighed down with russet vines: those beautiful vines from which hang the amber-coloured grapes which produce Rhine wine, these form the background.' In the distance, 'at the summit of a grey and bare rock stands like an eagle's nest one of those castles so common in Germany, with its battlemented walls, its pepperbox turrets and its feudal weathercocks. It is the abode of Albrecht, young Duke of Silesia.' Here, on the edge of the forest, 'half buried among the leaves, cool and clean, is Giselle's cottage. The hut facing is occupied by Loys; Loys whom Giselle loves as much as she loves dancing; Loys whom she believes to be a village boy of her own kind; Loys who is, in fact, Duke Albrecht in disguise.' Betrothed already to someone else, he is not free to marry the peasant girl Giselle, however much he loves her. But as yet Giselle knows nothing of this. She loves Loys and she loves dancing, until one morning Hilarion, a gamekeeper, discovers Loys' secret.

Hilarion, who is deeply in love with Giselle, comes to lay flowers at her door and sees 'Loys' hiding a cloak and sword in his cottage. His suspicions aroused, Hilarion warns Giselle against Loys, but Giselle is sure of Loys' devotion. She disregards Hilarion's suspicions and the worries of Berthe, her mother, and joins happily with 'Loys' in the celebrations which mark the end of the grape harvest.

Horns sound faintly in the distance, and Albrecht's squire, Wilfrid, comes to warn his master that a hunting party is approaching. Albrecht retreats into the forest, but Hilarion observes this encounter and breaks

Giselle, by Jean Coralli and Jules Perrot; Paris, 1841. Giselle is crowned Queen of the Harvest. From the wood engraving in Gautier's *Les Beautés de l'Opéra,* 1845

into Loys' cottage to try to uncover the mystery of the cloak and sword.

The hunting party arrives led by the Prince of Courland and his daughter, Bathilde, betrothed to Albrecht and staying at his castle. They ask for rest and refreshment at Berthe's cottage; Bathilde is charmed by Giselle and gives her a necklace on discovering that she, too, is betrothed. The Prince and Bathilde retire to rest in the cottage leaving orders that a hunting horn be hung outside so that they may be summoned in case of emergency. At this moment Hilarion appears from Loys' cottage with Albrecht's sword. Its crest tells him what he suspected – Loys is only trifling with Giselle's love. Choosing the moment when Giselle has been crowned Queen of the Vintage he unmasks Loys, but Giselle refuses to believe him, until he blows the horn. Bathilde appears with the Prince and claims Albrecht as her fiancé. The shock of such duplicity, unsuspected even by Hilarion, unhinges Giselle's reason. In her madness she enters another world between reality and unreality. She recognizes no one, but relives for herself the happiness she knew with Albrecht, the way they danced, until, heartbroken, she dies.

ACT II: Beside Giselle's tomb in the forest. 'The heart of our ballet,' said Gautier, 'lay in its second act. There is the poetry. It is where I began . . . A world of which the German poet speaks, where maidens who have died before their wedding day, because of faithless lovers, return as Wilis to dance by night.'

First Hilarion, then Albrecht, come to keep a night time vigil of penitence beside Giselle's grave. Meanwhile the Wilis appear, led by Myrtha, their Queen, and summon Giselle to join their band. Giselle must obey the Queen, but when she sees Albrecht she is moved because he is so sad. The Wilis return, pursuing Hilarion, who is driven to death in the lake. Next they capture Albrecht and the Queen commands him to dance to his death. Giselle urges him to the protection of the cross on her grave. He is safe from Myrtha's power until the Queen compels Giselle to dance and thus entice Albrecht from the cross. But Giselle dances with him and for him until dawn breaks; the power of the Queen of the Wilis over Albrecht evaporates with the sun, and Albrecht is saved.

Coming nine years after *La Sylphide*, *Giselle* perfected the romantic formula. As Gautier said, each collaborator – composer, designer and choreographer – raised to a higher sphere what had been achieved before. This was especially true of Jules Perrot, 'the greatest male dancer and choreographer of his day', who devised most of the dances for Giselle herself. In these dances he combined acting with dancing so closely as to create danced action which was a more expressive kind of ballet, and 'a new development in the art of choreography'.

In fact, the role of Giselle represented not only a great advance in choreography when Perrot created it, but a great advance in the demands it made upon the dancer. It is one of the most emotionally exhausting roles in classical ballet today because of the contrast it requires between realism in Act I and fantasy in Act II and because the dancer must be able to mime joy and sorrow while dancing. 'Perrot,' said Gautier, 'had dreamed of combining the two sides of romantic ballet – the real and the supernatural – in one person. And he did. In Carlotta Grisi, the first Giselle.'

Never before had character been explored so deeply in dance form. Perrot achieved this through the combination of dance steps with acting; through a contrast of choreography between the two acts – bright, quick, folk-inspired steps for the peasant Giselle in the first act compared with a larger, more remote and joyless style requiring exceptional elevation in the second act; also through the use of elementary motifs in movement similar to Adam's elementary motifs in the score. These motifs were phrases of dancing given to the leading characters and repeated with variations to show their dramatic development. Because Albrecht remains the same living, human person throughout the ballet, his motif remains the same in both acts.

Hilarion, a mime role, receives only a motif in the music. But for Giselle it is different. As a ghost in Act II, her dancing moves into a different key, while in Act I, she has two motifs, sometimes danced alone sometimes with Albrecht, to show her happiness and love of dancing. Both these return in distorted form to reflect her pain and madness when Albrecht's duplicity is revealed.

Choreographically and in every other way, as Gautier pointed out, *Giselle*'s greatness lies in its second act. The conception was Gautier's, whereas St Georges was responsible for the skilled carpentry of Act I. In Act II, all the innovations of music, costume and lighting, style and theme, all the technical developments introduced through *La Sylphide*, were perfected and used at their highest level to evoke a world of spirits. Perrot's choreography, in particular, reveals the purest romantic feeling through movements in a different key, with the music taken more slowly.

In this act Coralli had been responsible for the organization of the *corps de ballet* and its dances – as he had been in Act I, enjoying particular success with an interpolated peasant dance for two principals and *corps de ballet* to music by Burgmüller – but *Giselle* owes its excellence to Perrot's genius reflected especially in the choreography for the title role in Act II.

For so significant a ballet it was created in record time. Adam sketched the score in just a week, producing music which was a considerable advance on previous ballet music. At the same time Ciceri set to work to design the scenery and the whole was completed in little more than two months. Its triumph was absolute, 'the greatest success of a ballet at the Opéra since *La Sylphide*', said Gautier. 'After it even *La Sylphide* seemed but a beginning.'

Versions were staged throughout Europe. Perrot produced it for London on 12 March 1842, again with Carlotta Grisi as Giselle but with himself instead of Lucien Petipa as Albrecht. In 1848 he produced it in St Petersburg (which had already seen a garbled version by the old ballet master Titus) with Elssler as Giselle and Marius Petipa, Lucien's brother, as Albrecht. Two years later he produced it again in St Petersburg, this time for Grisi.

Appointed as a ballet master to the Imperial Theatre in 1862, Petipa maintained *Giselle* in the repertory during the remaining forty years of his career as master of the Russian ballet, making a series of alterations and emendations to the text, notably in 1884. He retained, for example, Elssler's acted version of the mad scene at the end of Act I in preference to Grisi's original danced version because Elssler was the more popular of the two ballerinas in Russia. He also blended, naturally and rightly, the simple, charming French style of Perrot's *Giselle* with new dance developments of the period, particularly the more brilliant technique and greater virtuosity acquired by the Russians from Italy. That is why the Queen of the Wilis now moves with greater jumps than Perrot ever knew, sharper and quicker turns, a longer line of the leg in arabesque, stronger use of the *pointes*, and shoes with blocked toes to make such things possible. In this way the Russians preserved *Giselle* while retaining the essential qualities of Perrot's choreography. It is the same with Gautier's theme. The story remains but the Russians have added a deeper dramatic truth, emphasizing Giselle's pathetic dilemma, that Myrtha can force her to destroy the man she loves; and, especially, the triumph of Giselle's love over the vengeance demanded by the Queen of the Wilis.

Elsewhere in Europe, *Giselle* slipped into oblivion. It was not until 1910, when Diaghilev presented it in his second Paris season, with Karsavina and Nijinsky, that this romantic masterpiece was rediscovered by audiences in its original home. Subsequent stagings of the ballet have all stemmed from the St Petersburg version descended to us in a direct link from Perrot through Petipa and Nicholas Sergueyev's productions based on his Stepanov notation of the Maryinsky repertory.

The first modern British production was staged by Sergueyev for Olga Spessivtseva during the Camargo Society's season at the Savoy Theatre, London, in June 1932. It was revived two years later for the Markova and Vic-Wells Ballet at Sadler's Wells and has remained in repertory.

Other productions in Britain include the careful recreation of the romantic text by Mary Skeaping for London Festival Ballet, which includes the restoration of the first-act solo for Giselle and Albrecht in the *pas des vendangeurs*, and the second act fugue, in which lines of Wilis attack the cross where Albrecht seeks protection from Myrtha. The Scottish Ballet has a staging of *Giselle* by Peter Darrell, first produced 1971, setting the action clearly and sensitively within a village community; Northern Ballet Theatre has a production by Robert de Warren and Peter Clegg, adapted to the relatively small forces of this Manchester-based company. In Australia *Giselle* was first seen in 1855 at Melbourne's Theatre Royal. Its most recent production was in 1965 by Peggy van Praagh for the Australian Ballet. In Canada it is in both the National Ballet and Grands Ballets Canadiens repertories. It was first staged in full for the New Zealand Ballet in 1965.

ARTHUR ST-LÉON (*c.* 1821–70)
Coppélia, ou La Fille aux yeux d'émail
Ballet in two acts and three scenes. Libretto: Charles Nuitter and Arthur St-Léon. Choreography: St-Léon. Music: Delibes. Scenery: Cambon, Despléchin and Lavastre. Costumes: Paul Lormier. First performed Paris Opéra, 25 May 1870.

ACT I: A square in a little town on the border of Galicia. To the left, an inn with Swanilda's house upstage in the background. To the right, opposite, Coppélius' house with a large dormer window.

As the curtain rises Coppélius pushes into the dormer window his newest and best creation – Coppélia, a mechanical doll so lifelike that he wants to see who will believe she is real. The first person to fall for the trick is Swanilda who comes into the square and is very annoyed when the beautiful girl in Coppélius' window seems to ignore her. The second person to be taken in is Franz, Swanilda's fiancé, who tries to flirt with Coppélia and is caught doing so by Swanilda. During a general dance the burgomaster announces a fête to celebrate the presentation of a new bell to the

31

town. All who are betrothed at that time will receive dowries from the Lord of the Manor. He asks Swanilda if she is to be among them. To test Franz's faithfulness Swanilda takes an ear of corn. If it rustles, then Franz *does* love her. But however much she listens, and her friends listen, the ear of corn is silent. She is comforted when Franz assures her all is well. Everyone dances for the burgomaster, then leaves as evening falls. Coppélius, pleased at the success of his trick, comes out of his house for an evening stroll. Teased by a crowd of youths, he is rescued by the innkeeper but drops the key of his house in the scuffle. Swanilda and her friends find the key and use it to enter the house to discover more about Céloppia. Coppélius returns to look for the key, finds the door of his house open and steals in to surprise the intruders. Franz also determines to meet Coppélia. He brings a ladder and is climbing to her window as the curtain falls.

ACT II: Dr Coppélius' workshop. Inside the workshop Swanilda is urged by her companions to approach the alcove where they think Coppélia must be. They are astonished to discover she is only a doll. The other mechanical dolls are set in motion and the girls dance round them. Coppélius bursts in and drives them all out except Swanilda, who hides in the alcove and disguises herself by dressing in Coppélia's clothes. Franz appears at the window and Coppélius, pretending to be one of his own dolls, allows him to enter before seizing him by the ear and threatening punishment. Then Coppélius has an idea. Inviting Franz to share a bottle of wine, he drugs the wine and, using a book of magic, tries to bring Coppélia to life by transferring Franz's spirit to the doll. Swanilda, disguised as the doll, pretends to come to life. The old man is delighted, but the doll becomes more and more difficult and demanding. Coppélius teaches her a Spanish dance and a Scottish dance, but, finally, Swanilda's friends return, Franz regains his senses and the old man realizes he has been tricked.

ACT III: The square of the town. Next evening, at the presentation of the bell, the Lord of the Manor bestows purses of gold on all the betrothed couples. Coppélius arrives and complains that his dolls have been ruined. Swanilda offers her dowry as compensation, but the Lord of the Manor gives one of his own purses to Coppélius and so placates him. As part of the celebrations the young people of the town dance 'A Masque of the Hours'. Franz and Swanilda are forgiven and their marriage is made the crowning event of the occasion.

Just as romantic ballet required a sad or fatal ending to most of its stories, so romantic ballet itself suffered from a fatal weakness. It relegated male

32

dancers, first to become partners, foils and *porteurs* for the all-important ballerina, then mimers and dancers in speciality spots. By the time of *Coppélia*, in 1870, leading male roles were often danced by women *en travesti* and regiments of women could be seen on London and Parisian stages at the turn of the century impersonating soldiers and sailors. Thus the Romantic Movement nearly destroyed the art of ballet by destroying the balance between the sexes upon which all dancing depends.

In its historical development *Coppélia*'s significance is twofold: with Franz danced by a woman and the production itself being the last new ballet before the closure of the Opéra in the siege of Paris in 1870, it marks the end of romantic ballet; at the same time the positive elements of the production, especially Delibes' score, serve as a link between romantic ballet and the new classical style arising under Petipa in Russia.

The ballet was the work of three people in collaboration – Arthur St-Léon as choreographer, Léo Delibes as composer and Charles Nuitter, librarian of the Opéra, as the librettist. Of these, St-Léon and Nuitter were close friends, well established in their professions; Delibes, then aged thirty-four, was still building his reputation. Each of them, through *Coppélia*, enhanced the separate arts of their contribution to create a work which remains a model of ballet construction. The basis of *Coppélia*'s success – and the reason it has survived – is the music of Delibes. Delibes was a dancer's composer with the gift of illustrating action, creating atmosphere and inspiring movement. He attempted in the music of *Coppélia* what the impressionists had achieved already in painting – to make colour the thing that mattered most. The result was the first symphonic ballet score, developing many of the devices which composers like Adam in *Giselle* had tried tentatively already. The colour in the music is a development of the descriptive passages introduced in most romantic scores. The rudimentary use of leitmotiv, initiated in *Giselle*, is developed here and woven into the score to describe the principal characters – old Coppélius, Swanilda and, of course, Franz, who has two themes, both very suitable for a woman playing a man's role.

St-Léon, the choreographer, had been born in Paris and studied under his father while he was ballet master at Stuttgart. Becoming an excellent dancer, actor and choreographer, he appeared subsequently all over Europe dancing and mounting his ballets. His taste was somewhat erratic and inclined to be commercial, reflecting also the wide interests of the man as teacher, historian, author, violinist – and one of the best choreographers of his time. In 1870, he was *maître de ballet* at the Opéra as well as having fulfilled much the same function in St Petersburg for the previous ten years, commuting between the two capitals. His health was now failing, and the creation of the new ballet was spread over three years.

Nuitter's contribution was a libretto which helped to restore the fading reputation of the *ballet d'action* as well as being almost unique in its time. No supernatural beings or ethereal heroines like Giselle. Instead, real people, both nice and nasty. But it was St-Léon's professional expertise which drew everything together. At his suggestion, Delibes included a Hungarian Czardas for the first time in any theatre score. And he made certain the libretto had all the elements which would allow him to hold the interest of audiences, especially through national dances with plenty of spectacular effects. In this way choreography reflected the rising nationalism of the time and gained an extra variety of steps.

None of St-Léon's dances for the ballet remain today in a direct line of performance although Pierre Lacotte, a French choreographer greatly interested in the dance of the nineteenth century, has restored and revived the ballet at the Paris Opéra (as he has done *La Sylphide*) and recaptured much of what we can feel is the original manner – in which he is aided by the use of the original sets and costumes. It offers an intriguing comparison with the versions known elsewhere in the West which stem from the version of the ballet mounted in Russia.

The first Russian production was in Moscow in 1882 by Joseph Hansen, who was responsible for the first staging seen outside France – in 1871 at the Théâtre de la Monnaie, Brussels. His Moscow version remained popular until it was superseded by a staging by Gorsky in 1905. In Petersburg, Marius Petipa first mounted the ballet in 1884. Ten years later, the ballet was revised by Enrico Cecchetti, and it is this staging – in which the role of Franz was danced by a man – which was thereafter reproduced in the West, notably for the Vic-Wells Ballet in 1933 (with Lydia Lopukhova as Swanilda). The production was by Nicholas Sergueyev from his Stepanov notations of the Maryinsky Theatre version, and it remains the basic text for later Royal Ballet productions. In Australia the ballet was first seen at Her Majesty's Theatre, Melbourne, on 21 June 1913, opening a tour by Adeline Genée and members of the Imperial Russian Ballet. The most recent production is by Peggy van Praagh for the Australian Ballet, scenery and costumes by Kristian Fredrikson. In Canada *Coppélia* is in both the National Ballet and Grands Ballets Canadiens repertories. It entered the repertory of the young New Zealand Ballet in 1955.

THREE

The Imperial Russian Ballet

MARIUS PETIPA (1818–1910)

Marius Petipa is the colossus of nineteenth-century ballet. Other choreographers may well have rivalled him for genius, or have had as great – or greater – influence on the art of ballet; but none rivalled him for productivity; none achieved the creation of a monument so grand or influential as the Imperial Russian Ballet, of which he was effective master for more than forty years. This ballet was created out of the combination of French style, traditional in Russia, with newly imported Italian technique expressed through Russian bodies and Russian temperament. The result was a new national school of ballet which remains a yardstick for dancers today. Over the birth of this school Petipa presided; it is his principal legacy.

Marius Petipa was born into a family of itinerant dancers in 1818 in Marseille, where his father was at that time ballet master. Like many of the dance families of that day, the Petipas were ever on the move. By the time Alphonse Victor Marius was three years old, his father was in Brussels with his wife, elder son Lucien and elder daughter Victoria. They stayed there until 1831 – Marius started dancing lessons with his father at the age of seven, and first appearing on stage at the age of nine. Revolutionary activity in 1830–31 drove them to Antwerp, then back to Brussels. They next went to Bordeaux for four years, and at the age of sixteen Marius launched out on his own, obtaining work in Nantes where he was called upon to compose a few short ballets. While there, he broke his leg and was obliged to return to his family who, in 1839, set out for New York. Their stay was brief. Jean Petipa staged some ballets (including Taglioni's *Jocko, the Brazilian Ape*), but a manager absconded with their funds and the Petipas hastened back to Europe.

Lucien was already *premier danseur* at the Paris Opéra, and Marius joined the classes given by the eighty-year-old Auguste Vestris. He also partnered Carlotta Grisi at a benefit gala, and then was offered a post as *premier danseur* at Bordeaux where he danced in *Giselle*, *La Péri* and *La Fille Mal Gardée*, as well as staging four ballets of his own. After a year he was engaged to go to the Royal Theatre, Madrid, creating four more ballets and dancing leading roles during the next four years. A duel with an aristo-crat over an affair of the heart necessitated his fleeing Spain, and in 1846 he was back in Paris, out of work. He was saved, so to speak, in 1847 by an invitation from the veteran ballet master Titus (*maître de ballet* in St Petersburg) to go to that city as *premier danseur*, arriving there in May. Since his father, Jean, was a professor at the Imperial School, one may well assume a certain parental influence in the offer of the post.

His experience as dancer and choreographer stood him in good stead. In his first season he staged three ballets: *Paquita, Satanella* and *La Péri*, for himself and the principal ballerina, Andreyanova, as well as dancing Albrecht in *Giselle*. (Marius, incidentally, was very much under the shadow of his more famous brother Lucien, who was one of the great dancers of the Romantic Age and the first Albrecht.)

Any hope of his further developing as a choreographer was killed by the arrival in St Petersburg of Jules Perrot, who remained as ballet master until 1859. During this time Petipa danced leading roles, but his choreographic output amounted to a few brief works, staged principally for his first wife, Marie Surovschikova, whom he married in 1854. Even with Perrot's depar-ture Petipa was not to be given a real chance to stage ballets. Arthur St-Léon was appointed, an accomplished and prolific choreographer, whose ballets were often described as protracted *divertissements*. He could invent charming solos and duets, but he was less accomplished at the dramatic ensembles which so distinguished the work of Perrot. Despite St-Léon's attempts to prevent Petipa being entrusted with any creative work, the director of the imperial theatres offered him a ballet in 1861. The fact that the work was to star the fading technical abilities of the Italian guest ballerina, Carolina Rosati, who was past her prime, may have accounted for Petipa's being given what was, in effect, a very difficult task. But he realized that an important chance was being offered him. With a clear sense of occasion – which never deserted him throughout his creative life – he realized, too, that things Egyptian were the current fashion (Russia was at that time fascinated with the news of archaeological excavations in Egypt). Accordingly he went to Paris to consult Vernoy de St Georges, the most accomplished ballet librettist of the time, and together they con-cocted an intrigue of massive complication, based upon Gautier's *Le Roman de la Momie*. On his return to Petersburg, Petipa was told that the ballet had to be completed within six weeks, in time for Rosati's benefit performance. He agreed, and while Pugni ran up the score, Petipa laboured and completed three acts with prologue in an unprecedentedly short time. *La Fille du Pharaon* was a huge success, and Petipa's reputation was made.

Tamara Karsavina and Adolf Bolm in *The Firebird*, 1910

(*above*) Colleen Neary and Heather Watts with members of the New York City Ballet in *Serenade*. (*below*) Robert Helpmann as the Rake in the first scene of *The Rake's Progress*

The work was a grand spectacular – indeed it is the first of the ballets *à grand spectacle* that were to delight audiences for the next forty years. Petipa was a genius, of that there can be no doubt, and his genius lay not only in his sheer ability to make dances, but in his power to absorb ideas, to accept influences from other choreographers. In *La Fille du Pharaon*, he was making use of everything he had learned while working with Perrot and St-Léon, and he shaped these elements into the massive work that won him acclaim.

Six weeks was, in fact, the period in which the piece was staged; it had been gestating for much longer. The skill with which Petipa built each act, balancing solos with ensembles, processions with set pieces, was the result of a profound and lengthy consideration.

The next forty years present the picture of a career that was filled with disappointments as well as triumphs; from 1862 until 1869 when St-Léon left, Petipa laboured as second ballet master, producing (almost alternately it now seems) flops and successes. With St-Léon's departure he was named chief ballet master, responsible for the imperial theatres in St Petersburg and Moscow and the imperial schools. His duty was 'to produce a new ballet at the beginning of every season'. This Petipa did, offering his audiences the sort of grand and complicated productions which had first won him fame. Alas, his audiences became bored, attendances fell off at the ballet performances, but Petipa had to go on producing spectacle after spectacle: *Don Quixote* (1869), *Trilby* (1871), *Camargo* (1872), *The Butterfly* (1874), *The Bandits* (1875) and many more.

That he was not happy with the need to turn out spectacle after brilliant spectacle we know from the testimony of August Bournonville, who visited St Petersburg in 1874 and commented on the hollow magnificence of these dance extravaganzas. Petipa agreed but pointed out that the public expected them and were not to be weaned from them. In 1881, however, the imperial theatres were placed under the direction of Ivan Vsevolozhsky (for further details about this admirable man see *The Sleeping Beauty* note), and it is to his guidance that Petipa's later career owes its greatness. He supported and advised the choreographer, gave him a new long contract as ballet master-in-chief and helped in the reorganization of the imperial theatres. With the arrival of a troupe of visiting Italian dancers in a summer theatre in St Petersburg in 1885, a new interest in ballet arose. The Italians were led by Virginia Zucchi, and danced in a farrago called *A Flight to the Moon*. What gripped the Russian audiences was their technical brilliance and Zucchi's dramatic power. She was promptly invited to appear at the Maryinsky, and during the next two years her great gifts lured back an audience to the theatre. She was followed by a series of Italian virtuosi: Pierina Legnani, Antonietta dell'Era, Carlotta Brianza, Enrico Cecchetti. They offered the most stimulating example to the Russian dancers, who sought to emulate and rival their prodigious brilliance. (Cecchetti stayed on in Russia to teach for some years and created both the first Bluebird and Carabosse in *Beauty*.)

In the late golden years of the century when the Imperial Ballet knew its apogee, Petipa continued producing ballets – notably the last two great works of his career, *The Sleeping Beauty* and *Raymonda*. In 1899 Vsevolozhsky resigned, to be succeeded by an equally amiable and charming aristocrat, Prince Volkonsky. But his tenure of office was short, and following a disagreement with the ballerina, Kschessinskaya, he was forced to resign. His successor, Colonel Telyakovsky, was inimical to everything Petipa stood for. The old ballet master's memoirs recount insults and reproaches, and his final ballet, *The Magic Mirror* in 1903, was a tragic and terrible débâcle. Petipa had outlived his own career; Telyakovsky was intent upon change – much influenced by the new artistic world of Moscow – and Petipa represented the old establishment. The première of *The Magic Mirror*, with the Imperial family present, was to be Petipa's benefit; it turned into a madhouse of hooting and catcalls. Soon after, Petipa retired, and the Imperial Ballet (though not the imperial schools), left without a major choreographer, went into a decline from which it was only to be saved by the Revolution.

Petipa made the Imperial Ballet. With an audience bent on spectacle and splendour, he provided all the requisite magnificence and technical dazzle. He had at times to sacrifice his own tastes to those of his audience; he was a purveyor of pleasures, and fortunately his genius was such that he could produce magnificent ballets to order. He insisted, above all, on the supremacy of dancing, and under his rule the imperial schools produced and went on producing many of the finest artists of their time, whom the new Russian school made supreme. He constantly sought to extend the range of his dancers – and at the same time was extending his own powers. In sum, he made the Imperial Ballet great at a time when ballet in the rest of the world was sunk into depths from which it was soon to be rescued by the next generation led by Diaghilev and Fokine.

La Bayadère

Ballet in four acts and seven scenes. Libretto: Khudekov. Choreography: Petipa. Music: Minkus. First performed Bolshoy Theatre, St Petersburg, 4 February 1877.

The libretto of this Indian extravaganza in romantic style tells of Solor, a warrior, who falls in love with a temple dancer (a Bayadère), Nikiya. A Brahmin priest loves her too, but she rejects his attentions. Solor is offered the hand of Gamsatti, daughter of a Rajah, and he is unable to refuse. Gamsatti learns of his love for Nikiya, and quarrels with her. Eventually Nikiya is given a basket containing a poisonous snake which bites her, and she dies. Solor dreams that he has followed her to the Kingdom of Shades and there dances with her and begs her forgiveness. (In the now suppressed fourth act Solor marries Gamsatti; the temple is struck by lightning and crashes to the ground in ruins, killing everyone beneath it, including Solor and Gamsatti.)

When the Kirov Ballet made their first London appearance in July 1961, they brought nothing more beautiful or exciting than the Kingdom of Shades scene from *La Bayadère*. As the first of the thirty-two Bayadères appeared on the ramp and began that slow unfolding of arabesque penché after arabesque penché, we became aware of something novel and beautiful. To realize that this choreography was nearly a hundred years old was to be reminded once again of Petipa's genius. As given subsequently by the Royal Ballet (27 November 1963) – staged by Nureyev and decorated by Philip Prowse – the sequence of dances is as follows: entry of the *corps de ballet*; *pas de trois* for three soloists; entry of Solor and appearance of Nikiya; *pas de deux*; entry of *corps de ballet* and solos for Nikiya; solo for Solor; variations by three soloists; duet for Solor and Nikiya; solo for Nikiya; *pas de trois* with *corps de ballet*; *pas de deux* for Solor and Nikiya; solo for Nikiya; solo for Solor; finale.

The Kingdom of Shades is a masterpiece of choreography; it relies entirely upon its dancing – drama is minimally present – but what delights is the superb fashion in which Petipa has manipulated his forces. One Soviet critic has called it 'symphonic' in structure, and this is certainly true in the way the *corps de ballet* echoes or enhances the work of the principals. It recalls, too, the second act of *Giselle*, but the profusion of dances are here far superior to the choreography of *Giselle*. Each of the variations for the three soloists is a gem and the work for Nikiya (particularly) and Solor is by turns dazzling and moving – because Petipa was writing Nikiya for his favourite ballerina, Vazem. Perhaps the most extraordinary thing about the ballet is its modernity; it looks far less dated and old-fashioned than many another piece half its age: a witness, were witness needed, to the enduring freshness of the classic dance, of which *La Bayadère* is a glorious example.

The entire ballet has been restaged and revised by Natalya Makarova for American Ballet Theater. In her version Makarova makes use of the text of the ballet as she knew it from her years with the Leningrad Kirov Ballet, but she made the important and wise decision to recreate the missing final act. By reordering the ballet's action in accordance with Petipa's original scheme – in Leningrad the ballet had been much altered by Lopukhov and, later, by Chabukany – Makarova has restored the dramatic progress and the proper climax of the work.

The Sleeping Beauty

Ballet in prologue and three acts. Choreography: Marius Petipa. Libretto: I. A. Vsevolozhsky after Perrault. Music: Tchaikovsky. Scenery: Levogt, Botcharov, Shishkov, Ivanov. Costumes: I. A. Vsevolozhsky. First performed 15 January 1890, Maryinsky Theatre, St Petersburg. Carlotta Brianza: Aurora. Paul Gerdt: the Prince. Cecchetti: Carabosse. Cecchetti and Varvara Nikitina: Bluebirds. Marie M. Petipa: Lilac Fairy.

PROLOGUE: The christening. In a hall of King Florestan XXIV's palace the courtiers are assembling for the celebration of the christening of the King's infant daughter, Aurora. Catalabutte, the Master of Ceremonies, marshals the guests; the King and Queen arrive to receive the greetings of their court, and soon a group of five fairies arrive with their cavaliers, to be followed by the Lilac Fairy. Each fairy dances a variation but just as they have presented their gifts to the infant princess, a roll of thunder announces the appearance of another fairy. It is Carabosse, who comes in with attendant creatures; she is furious at having been forgotten when the invitations to the christening were sent out. She mocks the other fairies and announces that her gift to Aurora is death: when the Princess grows up she will prick her finger on a spindle and die. As she bursts into peals of evil laughter, the Lilac Fairy steps forward; she has yet to make her present to Aurora and she says that, though she cannot remove all of Carabosse's curse, she can save Aurora's life. Instead of dying, Aurora will sink into a hundred years sleep, from which she shall be awakened by a prince's kiss. Carabosse exits in a furious temper, and the relieved court turn and pay their respects to the infant princess.

ACT I: The spell. It is Aurora's twentieth birthday and, in a garden of the palace, peasants and courtiers are assembled to celebrate the happy day. Although anything sharp-pointed has been banned from the kingdom, three knitting women are discovered by Catalabutte, who seizes their needles and threatens them with punishment. When the King and Queen enter, with four Princes who are suitors for Aurora's hand, they are furious at the sight of the needles, and the King condemns the three old women to death; the Queen intercedes for them and, because it is Aurora's birthday, the King forgives them. The peasants dance a joyous waltz, after which, heralded by a group of her friends, Aurora appears. She greets her parents, who present the four princely suitors to her; Aurora dances for them, accepting the roses that they offer. As she dances, an old woman mysteriously comes forward, offering her a curious gift the like of which Aurora has never seen before. It is a spindle. Her parents are horrified, but Aurora has already pricked her finger with it. She sinks to the ground in a faint, then revives and seems fully recovered; but as she starts to dance again her head swims, she circles round in a series of dizzying turns and collapses. At once the old woman throws off her cloak and reveals herself as Carabosse. The courtiers try to seize her, but she vanishes in a cloud of smoke, leaving the distraught assembly contemplating the body of Aurora which lies on the ground at the Queen's feet. Now the Lilac Fairy arrives to fulfil her promise; Aurora is carried away, and the Lilac Fairy casts a spell of sleep over the scene, causing a forest of trees and twining brambles to rise up and hide the entire palace and gardens.

ACT II, *Scene 1*: The vision. A hundred years later Prince Florimund is out hunting with his court in this same forest. His companions dance and sport, but when beaters enter announcing that a wild boar has been sighted, Florimund stays behind, urging his whole retinue to go after the animal, while he remains alone. The Lilac Fairy now appears to him, telling him of the enchanted forest and the sleeping Aurora. She shows him a vision of Aurora and the Prince is immediately struck by her beauty. The vision appears surrounded by a group of nymphs, and dances with the Prince before melting away into the night. Florimund, by now in love with Aurora, begs the Lilac Fairy to take him to the spot where she sleeps, and they move off in the Lilac Fairy's boat to the palace of the Sleeping Beauty.

Scene 2: The awakening. The Lilac Fairy guides Florimund through the forest and the cobwebby palace to the room where Aurora sleeps. The Prince awakens her with a kiss.

ACT III: The wedding. Characters from all the fairy tales come to the wedding of Aurora and Florimund and pay their homage to the newly-wed pair: a quartet of fairies; a Bluebird and the enchanted Princess Florisse; Puss in Boots and the White Cat; Red Riding Hood and the Wolf; Cinderella and Prince Fortuné; these and many more, with the Lilac Fairy and her attendants, dance in celebration. Aurora and Florimund dance, too, and the whole court joins in a general mazurka which leads into an apotheosis of happiness as the curtain falls.

There is a name missing from the credits for *The Sleeping Beauty* on our ballet programmes, and ironically it is that of the man who planned, guided and inspired its creation, and in no small measure made possible the very existence of this masterpiece.

Ivan Alexandrovich Vsevolozhsky (1835–1909) was director of the imperial theatres from 1881–99, and during his eighteen years of service, ballet in Russia flourished as never before – just how much we may judge from the crowning achievement of his regime, *The Sleeping Beauty*. The Maryinsky Theatre was a direct adjunct of the imperial court and it reflected, probably better than anything else, the taste of that closed, aristocratic world; appropriately enough its director was appointed either from the higher ranks of the army or from the diplomatic corps. Vsevolozhsky, who succeeded the penny-pinching Baron Kister (Petipa records that his insistence on reusing rickety old scenery occasioned an incident when a set collapsed in pieces during a performance, and the stage manager 'lost his reason right there on stage') was a diplomatist who had been *en poste* in Paris and was considered very francophile by his contemporaries. A man of wide culture, a playwright and essayist, he was also a talented amateur artist, sufficiently gifted to design costumes for the theatre. But his claim to fame and to our gratitude rests on the very considerable impact he had on the Imperial Ballet.

Natalia Roslavleva's valuable *Era of the Russian Ballet* records that within a year of his appointment his salary had been doubled 'for excellent management'; that he instituted the rehearsal hall in Theatre Street that is still in use today; that at his instance the first syllabus of the ballet school was drawn up, and that he created a system of advisory panels – comprising composer, librettist, choreographer, designer and stage manager – to ensure the highest standards of collaboration in the creation of ballets, in which he seems a notable forerunner of Diaghilev.

In 1886, in an act which we can still applaud even at this distance in time, he abolished the post of official ballet composer – alas, poor Minkus – as part of his scheme to encourage better music in the theatre; and it is significant that as early in his official career as 1883 he had championed Tchaikovsky. In that year the composer had written in amazement to Mme von Meck:

Without any advances on my part, Petersburg and Moscow contend for my work [the opera *Mazeppa*] . . . I cannot understand the reason for such attentions on the part of the theatrical world – there must be some secret cause for it, and I can only surmise that the Emperor himself must have expressed a wish that my opera should be given as well as possible in both capitals.

The 'secret cause' was Vsevolozhsky, whose admiration for Tchaikovsky was to manifest itself in even more practical form five years later when he obtained an annual pension of 3000 roubles for the composer from the Emperor. In 1886 he had already made his first attempt to get a ballet score from Tchaikovsky, whose diary for the October of that year records a couple of visits to Vsevolozhsky's home and then on 8 November:

> At home, where everything was packed [for his return home to Maidanavo] found a letter from Vsevolozhsky with an invitation for Sunday to talk over ballet. Fell into despair but decided to stay and made arrangements accordingly. Ran to Vsevolozhsky's where both Petipa and Frolov [a critic] turned up. Immediately started discussions. My rejection of *Salammbô*. *Undine*.

Nothing came of the projected ballet, in part because, reportedly, Modeste Tchaikovsky's libretto was found unsuitable, but two years later Vsevolozhsky tried again. In May 1888 he wrote to Tchaikovsky:

> It wouldn't be a bad idea, by the way, for you to write a ballet. I have been thinking of writing a libretto on Perrault's *La Belle au Bois Dormant*. I should like the scenery to be in the style of Louis XIV, and in this setting one could stage a magical fantasy and compose melodies in the style of Lully, Bach and Rameau, etc. . . . In the last act we must have a quadrille of all the Perrault fairy tales: *Puss in Boots*, *Tom Thumb*, *Cinderella*, *Bluebeard* and so on.

The style of this proposed ballet was clearly inspired by the theatrical fashion of the time for extravagant, complicated *féeries*, whose chief attribute was a profusion of *divertissements*. The inspiration for this type of gorgeously undemanding entertainment may well have been the success of Manzotti's *Excelsior* (Milan, 1881), which sparked off many imitations, and which itself was seen in St Petersburg in 1887 in two separate but simultaneous stagings in one of which Cecchetti appeared. The *ballet féerie* had become *de rigueur* at the Maryinsky – it was both Petipa's strength and his weakness that he could so successfully turn out ballets to suit the vagaries of public taste, and ignore his personal feelings as to what his ballets might

43

be – and in *The Sleeping Beauty* its limitations are more than transcended by Petipa and Tchaikovsky, who transformed it into a great work of art.

On receipt of Vsevolozhsky's scenario, Tchaikovsky replied: 'I have just seen the scenario of *The Sleeping Beauty* . . . and I should like to tell you straight away how charmed and enthusiastic I am. The idea appeals to me and I wish nothing better than to write the music for it.'

This last remark is revealing, since he had earlier in the same year completed his fifth symphony, and after its first two performances had written to Mme von Meck: 'I have come to the conclusion that it is a failure. There is something repellent, something superfluous, patchy and insincere which the public instantly recognizes . . . Am I really played out as they say ?'

But Tchaikovsky's enthusiasm for his new project may well have been somewhat dampened in the late autumn when he received Petipa's immensely detailed working draft of the action. This fascinating document is preserved in the Bakhrushin Museum, Moscow, and we are indebted to Joan Lawson's important translation (published in the *Dancing Times* between December 1942 and March 1943) for quotations from it. It was Petipa's habit to draw up a complete plan of a ballet before appearing in the rehearsal room, thus furnishing his composer with fullest details of his musical requirements. (He also on occasion provided notes for the designer and costumier.) His notes for *Beauty* indicate just how precise were his preliminary ideas. The draft sent to Tchaikovsky comprises duplicate notes for each section: the first contains the plans for the dance/mime action, the second (bracketed with it) gives minute indications of the type of music, its duration in bars, tempo, rhythm, even in certain instances, orchestration. We can assume from this that Petipa went into rehearsal with certain of the dances already partially composed in his head – as evidenced by the Fairy Variations in the Prologue.

The Fairies descend from the platform. Each in turn, they go to bless the child. (A little introduction for a pas de six.) Pas de six. *A sweet* adagio. *A little* allegro. *Variations: Candide. Fleur de Farine (flowing). Kroshka (Breadcrumbs). (Which interweaves and twines?). Canary (who sings). Violante (2/4 animated). (Plucked strings). The Lilac Fairy (A sweetly happy variation). Coda (3/4, fast and stirring).*

In his *The Story of the Russian School* Nicolai Legat gives a fascinating description of Petipa at work:

Whenever Petipa set about producing a ballet he waited till absolute silence reigned in the hall. Then, consulting the notes he had composed at home, he would methodically begin work. He worked out many of his groupings at home, where he used little figures like chess pawns to represent dancers, arranging them all over the table. He would spend long hours studying these groupings and write down the successful ones in his note book. Separate numbers, solos and *pas de deux* he composed at rehearsals.

First he had the music played through. Then he would sit for a time in deep thought. Then he would usually ask for the music to be played through again, imagining the dance, making little gestures, and moving his eyebrows. In the middle he would jump up and cry: 'Enough'. He would then compose the dance in eight bars at a time, call the dancer to him, and explain the movements at first in words rather than gestures. The whole dance having been explained, the dancer began again from the beginning, while Petipa frequently stopped, corrected or modified the movements. In the end he would cry: 'Now try nice,' which meant that the artist might try to execute the finished dance.

. . . The most fascinating moments of all were those when Petipa composed his mimic scenes. Showing each participant in turn he would get quite carried away by the parts, and the whole hall would sit with bated breath, following the extraordinary expressive mimicry of this artistic giant. When the scene was set there would be a terrific outburst of applause, but Petipa paid little attention. He would return quietly to his seat, smiling and licking his lips in a characteristic gesture, lighting a cigarette, and sitting silent for a time. Then the whole scene would be repeated while Petipa put finishing touches to the actions of the individual artists.

A study of Petipa's notes reveals just how thrilling these 'mimic scenes' must have been – and how much of the dramatic detail, dramatic logic even, we no longer see properly. The celebrated note to Tchaikovsky concerning the knitting women gives some idea of the minutiae of the mime between the King and Catalabutte:

Four beats for the questions and four for the answers; this to be pronounced four times. A broad 2/4, i.e. Questions: 'Where are you taking the women?' four beats. Answer: 'To prison' four beats. Question: 'What have these peasant women done?' four beats. Catalabutte shows the evidence (from 32–48 all together). The King's anger is now aroused. 'Let them be punished for their offence.' Energetic music. But the princes plead for clemency since no tears must be shed on Aurora's birthday.

With all this Tchaikovsky proved he could cope, even with the constricting requirements for the most dramatic moment in the ballet, when one might expect genius to need a somewhat freer rein. Listening to the vivid writing of the end of Act I, so effortlessly brilliant in its theatrical effects, it is hard to believe that Tchaikovsky was working to the following notes:

Suddenly Aurora notices the old woman who beats the time of her dance with her spindle – 2/4 which develops. It is beaten out all the time, into a 3/4 tempo, gay and very flowing. When the 3/4 begins, Aurora seizes the spindle, which she waves like a sceptre. She expresses her delight to everyone – 24 bars valse. But suddenly (pause – the pain – blood flows!) Eight bars, tempo 4/4 – broadly. Full of terror, now it is not a dance, it is a frenzy, as if she had been bitten by a tarantula. She turns and falls senseless. This will require from 24/32 bars. A few bars tremolo, with sobbing and cries of pain. 'Father! Mother!' Then the old woman with the spindle throws off her disguise. At this moment the entire orchestra must play a chromatic scale. Everyone recognizes the Fairy Carabosse, who laughs at the sorrow of King Florestan and the Queen. Short masculine-like music, culminating in a diabolical laugh tempo, when Carabosse disappears in a flurry of flame and smoke. The four princes run away in terror. At this moment the fountain in the centre stage is illuminated: here, tender, fantastic, and magical music. This passage must be long, as it has to last until the end of the act.

Tchaikovsky settled down to his extraordinary task in December 1888 and by great good fortune his diary for the next six months has been preserved (we quote from Vladimir Lakond's translation), and through it one can chart the composer's progress. He was at this time living at Frolovskoye, some distance from Moscow, but during the time he was writing *Beauty*, Tchaikovsky also undertook his second lengthy European concert tour as a conductor, appearing in Germany, Switzerland, Paris, London and proceeding thence, via the Mediterranean, to Tiflis and St Petersburg. Some of the relevant entries read as follows:

1 Jan. Celebrated so much that, in due time, I did not even remember. Worked all morning (Entrance of Aurora) [Petipa's note asked for from 16 to 24 bars which develops into another tempo. For Aurora's entrance – abruptly coquettish 3/4. 32 bars. Finish with 16 bars, 6/8, *forte*].

2 Jan. The day went by, as always, when I am absorbed in work. Was writing the grand adage *in the second scene, and it came hard.*

3 Jan. The work went so-so. But I did not strain myself too much and for that reason my head did not hurt.

4 Jan. How beautiful the days continue! Not very frosty, bright, and, starting at about 3 or 4 o'clock, the moon! . . . worked, as always now, beyond my strength. It seems to me I am played out!! . . . after dinner, walked long and was down by the river. Wonderful! Worked after tea, but very differently. It's not the same!

5 Jan. Still the same amazing, beautiful, bright weather. Worked well today on the whole. Finished the second scene. Played it through (lasts half an hour).

10 Jan. The work went well: wrote the entire entr'acte to the Sleep scene, and I think it's all right . . . In the evening played the overture to The Voyevode *and examined the orchestra score of the ballet (given me once upon a time by Gerber)* [music supervisor at the Bolshoy Theatre].

11 Jan. The work went especially well today, as of old. Did many things. Finished the second scene of the second act.

14 Jan. Worked still as painstakingly. Hope arises of finishing the first four scenes before my departure.

16 Jan. . . . worked till I was tired out. A passion for chocolate.

17 Jan. Worked beyond my strength. How very tired I am.

18 Jan. It seems to me that never has there been such a divine, beautiful winter day. The beauty was truly stunning. Finished the work, i.e. the first four scenes.

On 19 January Tchaikovsky went to Petersburg for consultations with Petipa and Vsevolozhsky, and within a week had set out on his concert tour. During his travels he completed part of the fifth scene (Act III of the ballet) and by the time he had reached Tiflis on 26 April he wrote to Petipa (a letter which is to be found in Lilian Moore's edition of Petipa's *Memoirs*) announcing that the sketches for the ballet were complete, and hoping that a newspaper report which suggested that *Beauty* was to be postponed for a year was true, so that he might have more time to undertake the orchestration of the work. The rumour was not true; on his arrival in St Petersburg in May he found Vsevolozhsky engaged on designing the costumes for the ballet and had further consultations with Petipa, before returning to Frolovskoye to complete the actual composition and start on the task of orchestration. By 26 May he had finished the writing, after working 'strenuously and successfully' and reading the orchestral score of *Giselle*, and from 30 May until the end of June when the diary ends, there are entries which detail Tchaikovsky's sheer slogging hard labour at orchestrating the ballet. The entries contain phrases like 'worked, worked and

47

worked – nothing unusual' or 'I worked all day like a madman', and at the same time he was obliged to indicate the markings in the score for his friend the pianist Alexander Siloti who was undertaking the preparation of a piano transcription for publication in the autumn.

Tchaikovsky's most revealing comment on his labours during the period comes in a letter he wrote to Mme von Meck on 25 July:

> My ballet will be published in November or December. Siloti is making the pianoforte arrangement. I think, dear friend, that it will be one of my best works. The subject is so poetical, so grateful for musical setting, that I have worked at it with all that enthusiasm and goodwill upon which the value of a composition so much depends. The orchestration gives me far more trouble than it used to do; consequently the work goes slowly, but perhaps all the better. Many of my earlier compositions show traces of hurry and lack of due reflection.

The ballet was put into rehearsal in September, and Tchaikovsky was on hand to assist, and even play the piano – so says Kschessinskaya – at rehearsals. He was equally prepared, as we have seen, to make alterations to the score, even excising the beautiful entr'acte before the Awakening (a lengthy section whose dominant violin part had been intended for the great virtuoso, Leopold Auer). An important alteration was the suppression of two characters in the *pas de quatre* for Cinderella, Prince Fortuné, Princess Florisse and the Bluebird, which, to make a better vehicle for Cecchetti's virtuosity, was set as the *pas de deux* we know today. (Cecchetti's mimic skill was displayed in the role of Carabosse.) One other change has become famous: that of the panorama music. Petipa's notes read: 'The duration of the music depends on the length of the panorama'; when the vast roll of the panorama's painted canvas was unwound, so that the audience might see the fantastic world of Perrault's tales unfolding before their eyes, it was found that there were several yards of canvas without accompaniment. To cut the canvas was unthinkable, so Tchaikovsky very obligingly wrote the extra music needed, which became known as the 'Yard Music'.

The actual first performance was on Tuesday 2 January 1890, o.s. taking the form of a *répétition générale* in the presence of the Emperor Alexander III and the whole court.

The reception was far from the triumph Tchaikovsky might have expected. His diary for 2 January and 3 January records, baldly, the events:

2 Jan. Rehearsal of the ballet with the Emperor present. 'Very nice'!!!
His Majesty treated me very haughtily. God bless him.

3 Jan. First performance of the ballet.

That is all. The ballet's reception by the critics was as dispiriting as the Tsar's comment. Stasov referred to Vsevolozhsky as 'that insipid Frenchman' who thought of nothing but French operettas and 'Tchaikovsky's music for them'. Some found the work 'much too serious', or dismissed the ballet as 'not a ballet at all, but a fairy tale, a whole *divertissement*' or thought Tchaikovsky's music was 'for the concert hall, serious and heavy'.

Despite this carping, the ballet swiftly won its public. In November 1892 it had achieved fifty performances, an occasion marked by the ballet's artists giving a crown to Tchaikovsky on stage at the Maryinsky, and Nicolai Legat states that by 1914 the work had reached nearly 200 performances.

Tchaikovsky in particular won devotees for the ballet: his score, Bakst tells us, was exciting admiration in Siloti's transcription even before the première, and its effect on a group of young artists and writers was to have a profound influence on ballet itself. The 'Neva Pickwickians', a band of young artists and intellectuals, led by Benois, with Nouvel, Bakst, Filosofov, and eventually their most junior member, Diaghilev, were all enthusiasts for the work. During one carnival week, Benois and Nouvel managed to see *The Sleeping Beauty* six times, and this inspiration was to reach an extraordinary fruition in the Diaghilev Ballets Russes movement of twenty years later. Benois even remarks that had it not been for *The Sleeping Beauty* it is much more difficult to envisage the birth of the Ballets Russes.

But the ultimate triumph of *The Sleeping Beauty* is as much due to Vsevolozhsky as to Tchaikovsky and Petipa. Vsevolozhsky aimed at the creation of a *Gesamtkunstwerk*, and in the original staging it must seem that he succeeded. He intended the ballet to show a fascinating contrast in historical styles in its two halves: he placed the prologue and first act in the middle of the sixteenth century, which was to be designed in a fantastically stylized manner, while the awakening and wedding were to be seen in an historically accurate evocation of the golden years of the young Louis XIV.

Of course, *Beauty* is markedly a work of its time and place, one of the highest theatrical achievements of the westward-looking culture of Imperial St Petersburg, reflecting the aristocratic spirit of the court and the pomp, luxury and opulent grandeur of its ultimate master, the Emperor, who made up the imperial theatres' annual deficit of two million gold roubles (£200,000) from his privy purse.

It is no accident that the finale of *The Sleeping Beauty* is a hymn to the monarchic ideal as seen in its most glorious and absolute form: Petipa's

49

apotheosis showed *Apollo, in the costume of Louis XIV, lighted by the sun's rays and surrounded by fairies.* The style and grandiose decoration of the ballet (for which silks and velvets were imported from Lyons) reflected Vsevolozhsky's own taste very clearly, since he designed all the costumes and suggested the type of setting. But as organizer of the court entertainments – in which, perhaps, he saw himself as the equivalent of Louis XIV's *maître des menus plaisirs du roy* – he showed considerable elegance, and a supreme skill for getting the best out of people in the nicest way. Tactful, persuasive, 'a great charmer' according to Benois, he inspired real affection, and as we have seen from his efforts on Tchaikovsky's behalf and in his ideals for the development of the Imperial Ballet itself, possessed a strong artistic conscience.

Petipa, who dedicated his memoirs to him, wrote glowingly of his gifts: 'During the long years of Vsevolozhsky's management, all the artists, without exception, adored their noble, kind, cultured director. This kindest of men was a real courtier, in the best sense of the word.'

That *The Sleeping Beauty* so far transcends the limitations of its form – and even of the world that created it – is in no small measure due to Vsevolozhsky. His personal involvement in the work, which went far beyond designing the costumes and devising the scenario, resulted in a masterpiece that is not only a telling portrait of a vanished world, but also a tribute to Petipa's 'noble, kind and cultured' master.

But let the last word be Tchaikovsky's. Writing to his publisher, Jurgenson, he said, 'I dedicate this ballet to Vsevolozhsky. Do not forget to put this on the title page in large letters. He is extremely proud of the dedication.'

The Sleeping Beauty was first seen in the West in 1921. In that year Diaghilev was without a choreographer, and so he decided to show his European audiences something of the splendour of the Imperial Ballet. *The Sleeping Beauty* was thus staged by Nicholas Sergueyev, who had been *régisseur* at the Maryinsky Theatre during 1904–17. He used the priceless Stepanov notations in which most of the St Petersburg repertory was recorded and which he had brought with him when he left Russia. The ballet was decorated in superb style by Léon Bakst; the finest St Petersburg ballerinas – Spessivtseva, Trefilova, Egorova – were seen as Aurora; Lopokova was first Lilac Fairy and later danced Aurora; Vladimirov was the Prince; and Brianza, the first Aurora, was lured out of retirement to dance Carabosse (though Diaghilev had at first tried to persuade her to dance Aurora again). The production opened at the Alhambra Theatre,

London, on 21 November 1921, but the audience were incapable of responding to its magnificence of music, design and dancing. After 105 performances, it was withdrawn, at enormous loss, never to be revived in full by Diaghilev again.

The Royal Ballet gave their first performance at Sadler's Wells Theatre, London, on 2 February 1939, with Margot Fonteyn and Robert Helpmann in the leading roles. With this production the company also reopened the Royal Opera House, Covent Garden, after the war, on 20 February 1946, and it has been associated ever since with some of the company's most triumphant moments – notably the first New York appearance in 1949.

In 1975 Rudolf Nureyev mounted his own idiosyncratic version for the London Festival Ballet – a staging which he had already produced at La Scala, Milan, in 1966, and for the National Ballet of Canada in 1972. At Covent Garden the Royal Ballet has had productions by Peter Wright and by Kenneth MacMillan, but in 1977 an attempt, successful in the main, was made to restore the manner and the 'feel' of the production by Ninette de Valois which, in 1946, reopened the Royal Opera House Covent Garden as the home for Britain's national ballet. The ballet is also in the repertory of the Australian Ballet in a production by Peggy van Praagh and Robert Helpmann first presented at the Sydney Opera House, 7 December 1973, with décor and costumes by Kenneth Rowell.

LEV IVANOV (1834–1901)

The Nutcracker

Ballet in two acts. Choreography: Lev Ivanov. Libretto: Marius Petipa. Music: Tchaikovsky. Décor: Botcharov and Ivanov. First performed Maryinsky Theatre, St Petersburg, 17 December 1892. Antonietta dell' Era: the Sugar Plum Fairy.

ACT I, *Scene 1*: The President Stahlbaum is giving a Christmas party for his son and daughter, Clara and Fritz. The guests arrive and dance, and the children are given presents from the Christmas tree; suddenly, mysterious chords announce the arrival of another guest: Herr Drosselmeyer, an eccentric old gentleman. He produces four clockwork toys: a Vivandière and a soldier; and Harlequin and Columbine, who dance for the children. Then Drosselmeyer brings out a special present for Clara – a Nutcracker. She is enchanted with it, but her brother interrupts the girls' games with their dolls by leading on his young companions in a mock cavalry charge in which they all brandish the swords and toys that they have been given. Jealous of the Nutcracker, he snatches it from Clara and breaks it; Clara is disconsolate, but Drosselmeyer repairs it, and the guests all join in a final *Grossvatertanz*, before the over-tired children and their parents take their leave. The Stahlbaums now retire for the night with their children, but Clara cannot sleep for thinking of her Nutcracker whom she has left in the drawing room. She comes down to fetch it, but as she clasps it to her, midnight sounds. Drosselmeyer seems to be peering from the clock, and suddenly the room is invaded with mice. There follows a battle between the mice and the toy soldiers who have magically come to life; Clara's Nutcracker is their commander, and, as he is about to be attacked by the king of the mice, Clara throws her shoe and fells the Mouse King. This devoted act causes the Nutcracker to be transformed into a Prince and he invites Clara to accompany him on a journey to the Kingdom of Sweets.

Scene 2: Their way to the country of sweets lies through an enchanted snow-covered forest where they see a swirling, dancing group of Snow-flakes.

ACT II: Clara and the Prince arrive at the Kingdom of Sweets, and are greeted by the Sugar Plum Fairy. The Prince tells of Clara's bravery, and in her honour a grand *divertissement* is presented. There are dances by Chocolate – *Danse Espagnole*; Coffee – *Danse Arabe*; Tea – *Danse Chinoise*; there is a Trepak (a Russian dance); Mère Gigogne appears with her troupe of children peeping from under her skirts; there is a *Danse des Mirlitons*, a grand *pas de deux* by the Sugar Plum Fairy and her Cavalier and a final 'Valse des Fleurs', and the ballet ends with an apotheosis.

In February 1891, Tchaikovsky received a commission from the imperial theatres to write a double bill for the Maryinsky; this was to comprise the one-act opera *Iolanthe*, and the two-act ballet *Casse Noisette*. The director of the imperial theatres, I. A. Vsevolozhsky had already decided on the theme for the ballet: a story by Alexandre Dumas (*père*) based on E. T. A. Hoffman's tale of the *Nutcracker and the Mouse King*. Marius Petipa was to create the choreography and, in March, Tchaikovsky received the usual immensely detailed plan of the stage action which was to serve as a working plan for the score. This scenario had caused Petipa some difficulty; Vsevolozhsky had rejected a first draft, but Petipa's notes, preserved in Russia, commend at the end of the second draft: '*J'ai affranchi, j'ai écrit cela, c'est très bon.*' Très bon it certainly is not; the dramatic weakness of the plot is plain for all to see. Tchaikovsky was impelled to write that he 'liked the plot of *The Nutcracker* very little', and he found that the second act was particularly feeble: 'I feel a complete impossibility to reproduce musically the *Konfiturenberg* (The Kingdom of Sweets).' Even when he had completed the score he was still seized with doubts (and who should blame him?). 'The ballet is infinitely worse than *The Sleeping Beauty*.' What Petipa would have made choreographically of the score we shall never know, for shortly before rehearsals were due to begin he fell ill, and the task of creating the choreography went naturally to the second ballet master, Lev Ivanov. It was too late for him to make any changes in either libretto or in style of staging; his task, as so often throughout his career, was to do the best he could. Only in the Snowflakes scene, in which Tchaikovsky's genius had been given its head, and where there were none of the detailed requirements that abounded in the rest of the ballet, did music and choreography meet to create something very beautiful. It became the most admired section of the ballet, surviving in a slightly altered form in the Sergueyev staging for the Royal Ballet in 1934. With the *grand pas de deux* of the second act, this is all that remained of the original choreography, but it insisted upon the merits of Ivanov as a creator.

The ballet was a failure. Despite the splendour of its staging, 'it can under no circumstances be called a ballet', wrote one paper. 'The production of such "spectacles" on our stage is an insult of sorts . . . this may soon and easily lead to the ruin of our ballet troupe,' wrote another. Abuse was heaped on the ballet, and certainly it is a hugely flawed piece. Its faults include a total absence of logical plot; a heroine – or no heroine if you prefer – who is a child; the appearance of the ballerina to dance one *pas de deux* in the second act; a profusion of *divertissements*, and a dramatic action in the first act that is hardly compelling. Its merits (such as they are) are of a nostalgic kind; we can accept the ballet as a look back at the magic world of childhood at a time more innocent than our own. It might be made to work as a magical fantasy, rather after the fashion of *L'Enfant et les Sortilèges*; certainly the music might sustain this.

Tchaikovsky's score has great moments, and is never less than marvellously assured, but it lacks both the splendour and opulence of *Beauty* and the elegiac tragedy of *Swan Lake*.

Despite the failure of the work, it is (as we know to our cost) impossible to keep a good Tchaikovsky score down. The ballet has been constantly restaged, both in Russia (by Vainonen) and in Europe. Festival Ballet mounted a version early in their existence, and later invited Alexandre Benois to supervise and decorate a staging which has remained remarkably true in essence (though not in choreography) to the original. Sergueyev staged the ballet for the Sadler's Wells company in 1934 and it did yeoman service before the war and gave Markova a role which she danced to perfection. After the war it was not revived – though Sir Frederick Ashton supervised a staging of the second act for the Sadler's Wells Theatre Ballet; and in 1968 Rudolf Nureyev also mounted a version. This, with designs by Nicholas Georgiadis, was first seen at Covent Garden (it had earlier been given in Sweden), on 29 February 1968. Entirely rechoreographed by Nureyev, the ballet offered a complete rethinking of the dramatic structure in an attempt to give cohesion to the piece. With an intrigue that is best described as sub-Freudian, the ballet starts conventionally enough with the party, but after receiving the Nutcracker doll, Clara falls asleep in midparty and dreams of the battle of mice, now aggrandized into bloated and repellently frightening rats; she rescues the Nutcracker who reveals himself as a Prince and they journey through the kingdom of snow. But once arrived at the second act, we find Clara attacked by bats (who turn out to be members of her family) and Drosselmeyer reappears to reveal himself as the Nutcracker Prince. The *divertissement* is given by the dolls from Clara's toy theatre: it comprises the Spanish dance, Russian dance, a dance for three Chinese acrobats, a porcelain *pas de trois* for a man and two girls (to the Mirliton's music) and a singularly unconvincing domestic scene for the 'Danse Arabe', after which Clara and Prince Drosselmeyer (what else is one to call him?) dance the *grand pas de deux*, and there follows the 'Valse des Fleurs'. Suddenly we are back at the party; Clara awakes from her sleep, the guests depart and Clara rushes to the door of the house to watch Drosselmeyer departing into the snowy night.

The London Festival Ballet maintained for many years a more traditional version, until in 1976 Ronald Hynd provided a new approach to the ballet (designed by Peter Docherty) in which he sought to revivify its action by considering its first sources. This implied a return to the original story of the *Nutcracker and the Mouse King* by E. T. A. Hoffman, and the devising of a stage action which accepted the emotional power of Tchaikovsky's score. In a programme note Hynd wrote:

Towards the close [of Hoffmann's original tale] the Prince (who in the child Clara's dream is the Nutcracker come to life) declares himself to be the nephew of Drosselmeyer, Clara's godfather who had given her the Nutcracker. Here is a character who could accompany Drosselmeyer to the Stahlbaum's Christmas Eve party. But would he fall in love with a child? Hardly with the passion Tchaikovsky suggests. But what about Louise, the elder sister who barely exists in Hoffman. In elevating her to the romantic heroine, she would then be a constant factor rather than the somewhat superfluous Sugar Plum Fairy who existed solely in the original version for a *pas de deux* with variations.

There is also a threatening element in much of the music, particularly in the dream sequence of the battle of the mice and soldiers. To underline this I have invented a new character, a prospective suitor for Louise, Herman von Rattenstein, a distasteful character, who becomes distorted in her dream to a nightmare King Rat.

The problematic second act, which is merely a series of *divertissements*, I have sought to relate to the happenings of the party scene, happenings which are distorted in the visions of the dreaming sisters.

Peter Docherty and I have above all tried to keep Tchaikovsky's score as our guide, yet at the same time preserving the contrast of everyday reality with its related fantasy which gives Hoffmann's tale its warmth and peculiar fascination.

By turning back to Hoffmann and by listening to the score, Hynd has contributed to produce an action in which the old ballet acquires both a greater logic and a much more appealing mixture of fantasy and truth. The Stahlbaum household is shown to us as an ordinary bourgeois home in which all the elements of the dream sequence are given their 'real' antecedents, from the child Marie's obsession with a box of sweets to the disposal of a rat in the vast stove which heats the drawing room. Everywhere in the opening party sequence, where none of the social behaviour seems fantastic or improbable, the seeds of the later dream action can be discerned. At one moment Herman von Rattenstein puts on a turban in the fancy-dress games, and he returns in Act II in the 'Danse Arabe', while the children at the party acquire hats and fans which will explain much of the last act *divertissement*. Clues are slight, but effective; eventually all the disparate incidents are neatly explained. Ronald Hynd's staging was first presented by London Festival Ballet in November 1976.

For the Scottish Ballet, Peter Darrell also devised a new and attractive production, first given in 1973. Like his *Giselle* and *Swan Lake* stagings for his company, it takes a fresh and theatrically vivid look at a traditional classic. The ballet is also in many repertories in Canada and Australasia.

Swan Lake
Ballet in four acts. Music: Tchaikovsky. Choreography: Julius Reisinger. Libretto: V. P. Begichev and V. I. Geltser. First performed Imperial Theatre, Moscow, 4 March 1877. Act II, Choreography: Lev Ivanov. First performed

*Maryinsky Theatre, St Petersburg, 29 February 1894; the whole ballet –
Act I and Act III, Petipa; Act II and Act IV, Ivanov, 15 January 1895.
Pierina Legnani: Odette-Odile.*

ACT I: It is Prince Siegfried's birthday and in the garden of his palace he
is celebrating with his friends, with Benno, his attendant, and with
Wolfgang, his tutor. Peasant boys and girls are also present, and two girls
and a boy who dance a *pas de trois*. Siegfried's mother enters with her
attendants; she chides her son for revelling, and announces that at a ball the
next day a group of young and eligible girls will be presented; from among
them he must choose a bride. Despite Siegfried's protestation, his mother is
firm. She leaves, and wine flows again. Wolfgang becomes drunk and tries
to dance with a peasant girl, and the assembled peasants start a general
dance. Siegfried is oppressed by his mother's news and, as dusk falls and
the guests leave, he seems lost in thought. Suddenly Benno sees a flight of
swans, and he urges the Prince to come hunting by night with his companions. Eagerly Siefgried agrees; Wolfgang is left alone and the hunting
party departs.

ACT II: Beside a lake. As the hunters enter they decide to watch for the
swans here. Siegfried orders them to leave him so that he may watch alone,
and suddenly he is amazed to see a swan landing on the lake and immediately change into a beautiful girl wearing a crown. Siegfried approaches
her; terrified she tries to flee, but he reassures her that he means no harm
and he already seems attracted to her beauty. She tells him that she is
Princess Odette, Queen of the swan-maidens whom the enchanter,
von Rothbart, has bewitched. The lake is made of her mother's tears. She
can never be released from the enchantment that turns her into a swan
during the daylight hours unless a man falls in love with her and swears
eternal fidelity. Siegfried, now obsessed with her beauty, promises to love
her, but at this moment von Rothbart appears. Odette pleads with the
magician, while Siegfried reaches for his crossbow and attempts to shoot.
him; Odette rushes towards Siegfried and prevents him from shooting.
They leave the lakeside as the swan-maidens appear and dance. Suddenly
Benno returns. He is dazzled by the sight of these white figures whom he
takes for swans; he calls to his companions who enter, but just as they are
about to shoot, Siegfried runs in, ordering them to put down their bows,
while Odette flutters protectively in front of her maidens. As the swan-
maidens dance, and Odette moves away, Siegfried turns to search for her;
he fears she may have flown away, but she appears and they dance an
intense and lyric duet which tells of their ever-growing love. As they leave,

four cygnets enter to perform a celebrated quartet, and then Odette enters to dance a solo. There follows a general dance, and as day breaks the maidens must return to their swan form again. Odette takes an impassioned farewell of Siegfried who is left staring in wonderment at the sky where the swans have disappeared.

ACT III: The ballroom of Siegfried's castle. The guests are assembling to celebrate the coming betrothal of the Prince. The Queen Mother arrives with Siegfried, and six eligible girls are presented to him. He dances with each, but his mind is filled with thoughts of Odette, so that at the end of the dance he refuses to choose a bride. The Queen Mother's angry remonstrances are interrupted by the sound of trumpets which announce the belated arrival of an unexpected guest. The orchestra sounds the swan theme in ominous tones, and suddenly von Rothbart appears, disguised as a nobleman, bringing with him his daughter Odile, who has assumed the face and form of Odette. (Although originally the roles of Odette and Odile were danced by two ballerine, Legnani instituted the continuing tradition of a single ballerina interpreting both roles.) The enraptured Siegfried rushes to her and leads her away, while a *divertissement* of national dances – Spanish, Neapolitan, Hungarian and Polish – entertain the guests. As these dances end, Odile and Siegfried enter to dance the great *pas de deux* in which the enchantress dazzles and tricks the young Prince who is exultant with happiness. The duet is filled with virtuosity – in its coda, Legnani introduced her favourite trick of multiple *fouettés*, thirty-two in all, which she performed with incredible ease and these have since been retained by almost all subsequent interpreters – but it is also a scene of high drama. As the entrée proceeds, the sorrowing figure of Odette appears outside the castle windows, seeking to warn Siegfried, but von Rothbart casts a spell over the assembled guests so that they shall not notice this, and Odile mockingly echoes the swan movements of Odette which further bemuse and delight Siegfried. At the conclusion of the duet Siegfried asks for the hand of Odile: von Rothbart demands that he swear eternal fidelity to Odile, which Siegfried does. At once von Rothbart and Odile reveal their true nature. With peals of mocking laughter they jeer at the Prince and exit amid clouds of sulphurous smoke, while Siegfried rushes to his mother, realizing that he has broken his vow, and then hastens to the lakeside in an endeavour to find Odette.

ACT IV: The lakeside, later that night. The swan-maidens are mourning their queen's departure. A moment later she returns, heartbroken at what seems the stupidity of Siegfried and his lack of faith. Von Rothbart summons up a storm to try to prevent Siegfried reaching the swans, but he appears in the forest, seeking desperately for his love. He discovers Odette amid her swans, and begs forgiveness. In a last elegiac *pas de deux* they reaffirm their love and Odette states that the only possible means of escaping from her enchantment is to kill herself in the lake. Despite Siegfried's pleas she makes as if to throw herself into the waters. He restrains her, then agrees to join her in death – thus their love shall be consummated and they will be united. Von Rothbart enters, struggling with Siegfried for possession of the Swan Queen, but the strength and determination of the two lovers defeat him. As they plunge into the lake to their death, von Rothbart's power fades and he dies, while the swan-maidens, now restored to their human form, watch an apotheosis in which Siegfried and Odette are reunited in a kingdom of eternal happiness beneath the waves.

The history of *Swan Lake* is the history of the most popular ballet in the world – a popularity sustained partly by the magnificence of Tchaikovsky's score, with its irresistible melancholy and melodic riches, and partly by the splendour of the work of Ivanov and Petipa. Yet its initial production might have seemed to have doomed it to oblivion. Tchaikovsky's score was originally written for the Bolshoy Theatre, Moscow, where it was choreographed by an entirely inadequate ballet master, Julius Reisinger, for the benefit performance of an undistinguished ballerina, Pelagia Karpakova. The score was found to be too 'difficult' and alterations and interpolations by both ballerina and conductor guaranteed that the ballet as performed must have been singularly unlike what Tchaikovsky intended. In 1880, and again in 1882, a rather more able choreographer, Joseph Hansen, staged versions of the ballet, but it still failed to keep any permanent place in the repertory.

It was not until 1893 that St Petersburg and the Maryinsky Theatre enter the story. In 1890, *The Sleeping Beauty* had been staged and had won an enthusiastic audience after an initial coolness; in 1892 *Casse Noisette* had had a mixed reception, but Tchaikovsky's death in 1893 had occasioned an upsurge of interest in his theatre works, and in 1894 an evening devoted to the memory of the composer was given at the Maryinsky. It included the second (lakeside) act of *Swan Lake* in a choreography by Lev Ivanov. The role of Odette was taken by the visiting Italian virtuoso ballerina Pierina Legnani, and the performance was a great success. Inspired by this, Marius Petipa decided to stage the entire ballet; he asked Riccardo Drigo, conductor at the Maryinsky, to clean up the score, restoring numbers that had been excised in Moscow, but also concocting a couple of variations from some *salon* pieces by Tchaikovsky, and on 15 January 1895, the full length ballet was given at the Maryinsky with Legnani in the double role, and Paul Gerdt as Siegfried. The ballet was a huge success and started on its career – that seemingly interminable series of incarnations which have, alas, brought it to nearly every ballet company in the world, whether or not they have forces sufficient to dance it. Inevitably, it has been restaged, rethought, rechoreographed, punched, pulled, twisted and generally mangled in the years since the Maryinsky première.

In Russia, the most significant stagings were by Alexander Gorsky, who even during the life of Petipa (when the old master was in retirement) had started the vulgarizing and humanizing of Petipa's classically perfect creations. Gorsky made no less than five productions in Russia. Later Agrippina Vaganova (the great teacher and founder of the Soviet ballet school) also produced a version in 1935. A significant and influential staging was later made for the Stanislavsky Theatre in Moscow by Vladimir Bourmeister in 1953, in which he sought to return to the ballet as originally conceived by Tchaikovsky. This production, later given at the Paris Opéra and revised when partially staged for Festival Ballet, had many innovations: among them a prologue showed Odette's abduction and the national *divertisssement* of Act III was given as if the dancers were in the magical train of von Rothbart. In another staging for Festival Ballet, reproduced from an earlier version he made for the Teatro Colon, Buenos Aires, Jack Carter returned even more wholeheartedly to Tchaikovsky; replacing musical numbers that had been given in different sequence, and using two ballerinas for the roles of Odette and Odile – very necessary since in his staging they meet at the Act III ball – and also introducing the whole of the *grand pas des fiancées* from the score.

But the most rewarding and most 'authentic' version remains that staged by Nicolai Sergueyev for the Sadler's Wells Ballet at Sadler's Wells Theatre on 29 November 1934. When Sergueyev fled Russia after the Revolution he brought with him a collection of notebooks, in which were written down all the current Maryinsky repertory. From these notebooks stem all the classical staging of the old Imperial Russian repertory in the West. His *Swan Lake* for the Sadler's Well Ballet was, and largely remains in the version preserved by the Royal Ballet at Covent Garden, the most pleasing production in the West because original intentions (those of Petipa, who knew his craft far better than the lesser talents who have tinkered with his ballets) are respected. Of the 'correctness' of the text there can be many doubts – the eroding effects of time and the doubtful memories of dancers, as well as their tendency to iron out nuances of style, have all taken an inevitable toll – but the ballet has the correct 'feel' of a nineteenth-century classic. Attempts to 'improve' and to substitute are unnecessary and serve merely to weaken the impact of what was, and can still seem in sensitive and respectful stagings, a masterpiece.

In December 1979 the Royal Ballet's production was overhauled, and the choreography for the fourth act, which Sir Frederick Ashton had provided for a radically different staging in 1964, was restored. Elsewhere in the world new productions of *Swan Lake* proliferate, variously different, variously innovative, variously adventurous in reassessing the old text, and variously awful.

But what is *Swan Lake*? Apart from being the most performed ballet in the world, it is also one of the most misunderstood and the most misinterpreted. The perennial attraction of Tchaikovsky's score lies in its melancholy as well as in the profusion of melody; the story looks back to the simpler romantic forms of the 1840s rather than following the complicated and usually quite idiotic stories that were needed to sustain the whole complicated paraphernalia of Petipa's spectacular creations. It is a story that offers the great romantic dilemma of impossible love finding its resolution only in death – and though we can say that *La Bayadère* or *Le Roi Candaule* also offer a similar debased romanticism, *Swan Lake* has the advantage of a grand simplicity that recalls *Giselle* or *La Sylphide*. It also provides our only serious view of a choreographer who has always been overshadowed by his master, Petipa – Lev Ivanov. Soviet scholarship has done much in recent years to try to rescue the reputation of this sad figure. Born in 1834, he became a pupil of Jean Petipa (Marius' father) and Christian Johannson, at the St Petersburg school, entered the company in 1850, and spent the remainder of his life as dancer, mime and teacher in the theatre. He possessed an extraordinary musical talent (he could reproduce music after hearing it once) and this was to stand him in good stead later on. But he lacked ambition and drive: he never tried to forward his career either as choreographer or as composer (he wrote interpolated solos for certain ballets). After his appointment as *régisseur*, in 1882, he restaged many of the old ballets, and three years later became second ballet master. He was responsible for the ballets in operas: he mounted the Polovtsian dances in *Prince Igor* (which were given – in Sergueyev's reconstruction from notation – by International Ballet just after the Second World War) and they are plainly the basis on which Fokine made his version. Ivanov's first long ballet was *The Haarlem Tulip* in 1887; the score was by the Baron

60

Firtingov-Schell, and it has been suggested that Ivanov's inspiration was entirely weighed down by the score. His first important work came with *Casse Noisette* (q.v.).

This experience contributed to his success with *Swan Lake*, in which we can see his genius completely at one with that of a composer of markedly similar temperament. It is interesting to consider how Petipa, who had all those qualities of experience and cut and dried matter-of-fact practicality, could work with the superabundant emotionalism, the personal neuroses, of Tchaikovsky. All the easier, then, to see what emotional sympathy Ivanov must have felt when faced with the melancholy of *Swan Lake*, Act II. The result is a thoroughly original conception of what the classical ballet should do. Ivanov offers the complete opposite from what was the standard procedure of Petipa's ballets. He was working quite freely – there were none of the detailed notes (see *The Sleeping Beauty*) that Petipa provided for his composer and with which he prepared every moment of the stage action before coming into the rehearsal room. The music spoke to Ivanov and he proceeded to find a marvellous realization of it. With Petipa by this time – though not earlier (see *La Bayadère*) – the formal structure of such an act was set hard and fast: the *pas de deux* would unfold against the rigid patterns of the *corps de ballet*. How different Ivanov's conception: his *pas de deux* remains central, but there is constant participation in its emotional structure by the *corps de ballet*. It is entirely dependent in its shape on the shape of the music; technical proficiency of course is called for, but instead of virtuosity there is emotion; instead of the tight, bright fireworks of the French master, there is the broadly spaced, very Russian flowing of arabesques, characteristic poses of head and arms that remind us constantly of Odette's swan nature by day. It is a masterly conception, not least in the way the *corps de ballet* are called on to enhance the central duet – in a marked advance on the originality of *La Bayadère*, or on *Giselle* Act II, both of which contain similar structural devices.

The staging of Act II was a success, and Vsevolozhsky (or possibly Petipa) decided on the staging of the whole ballet. Petipa's notes here are far less full than for *Beauty* or *Casse*; they state quite simply 'that the second scene has already been done', and we are assured that the fourth act is also by Ivanov. The rest of the task (Acts I and III) may have been shared between the two, as certain Soviet authorities state; certainly their form bespeaks the usual Petipa formula of general dances, brilliant solos and *divertissements*.

Whatever the division of labour, though, the ballet as staged at the

Maryinsky was still a typical formal display such as Petipa had been creating for nearly forty years: its score was superior to most, its drama more clean-cut than many others, but it was still no novelty. It was, however, a beautifully and soundly constructed piece, and (as we know it from the Sergueyev staging) totally effective in the theatre. This is exactly what none of the later recensions, alterations, rethinkings and general assaults on the work, has ever been, in our experience. Those versions that have sought to show us 'the ballet that Tchaikovsky intended' have been markedly less successful. We are forced to the inescapable conclusion that the genius and long experience of Petipa were infinitely more sure in theatre matters than the romantic visions Tchaikovsky had hoped to see.

Raymonda

Ballet in three acts and four scenes. Choreography: M. Petipa. Music: Glazunov. Décor: Allegri, Lambini, Ivanov. First performed Maryinsky Theatre, St Petersburg, 19 January 1898. Legnani: Raymonda.

ACT I, *Scene 1*: The libretto, largely invented by Lydia Pashkova – a society authoress – has always been the downfall of *Raymonda*; it is a farrago whose complications and inadequacies are barely comprehensible. The scene is medieval Provence at the chateau de Doris where we meet the Comtesse Sybille, and her niece Raymonda. On Raymonda's birthday the Comtesse chides various girls for their idleness, and tells them about the statue of a former Comtesse, who appears as a ghostly White Lady to warn the family when there is any danger. A messenger appears with a letter from Raymonda's fiancé, Jean de Brienne, announcing his imminent return from the crusades, and Raymonda makes her first entrance to read the letter. Jean will be back tomorrow, and everyone hastens to prepare a worthy reception. Raymonda plays the lute, but is overcome by a mysterious sleep; the ghost of the White Lady appears to her and leads her on to the terrace.

Scene 2: Through mists, a vision of Jean de Brienne appears; Raymonda rushes to him and they dance a grand *adage*. There follows a *divertissement* for Jean's attendants and assorted sprites, but the White Lady shows Raymonda another figure, that of the Saracen Chief Abdérâme, who declares his love for her, which she rejects in horror. Elves and goblins appear and dance and Raymonda faints; as dawn breaks her attendants find her and take her into the castle.

ACT II: In the courtyard everything has been prepared to welcome Jean. Guests arrive from neighbouring castles, and trumpets announce the arrival of Abdérâme and his Saracen knights. Raymonda shudders with horror as she recognizes the figure of her vision: Sybille calms Raymonda, but Abdérâme now speaks of his love and becomes more and more pressing in his declarations (*grand pas d'action*). Abdérâme presents his suite of Arabs, Saracens and Spaniards who dance for Raymonda and pour out quantities of wine for the guests; while the entire assembly is thus occupied, Abdérâme prepares to abduct Raymonda, but Jean de Brienne appears, together with King Andrew II of Hungary. Jean immediately rescues Raymonda and a general mêlée ensues. King Andrew orders Jean and Abdérâme to settle their dispute in single combat. Raymonda gives her scarf to Jean and, furious at this, Abdérâme attacks Jean fiercely, but the White Lady appears and protects Jean, who kills Abdérâme. The Saracen is carried away by his attendants, while King Andrew joins the hands of Jean and Raymonda amid general rejoicing.

ACT III: King Andrew and the now happily married couple watch a grand Hungarian *divertissement* given in their honour; after numerous dances it ends with a final *galop* and an apotheosis showing a brilliant tourney.

Idiotic though this scenario is, the ballet as we know it is a glorious work. It boasts a magical score by Glazunov, filled with melody, colour and grand effects which inspired the eighty-year-old Petipa to produce his last masterpiece. If there seems something autumnally golden about the beauties of Glazunov's score – and the ballet was the last great work produced by the Maryinsky Theatre before the Revolution – Petipa's choreography, as we know it from Rudolf Nureyev's versions for the Royal Ballet and Australian Ballet, is dazzling. The ballet has been maintained in the repertories of both the Kirov and Bolshoy companies, though neither, alas, has yet brought it to London. The Royal Ballet Touring Company presented a three-act version by Rudolf Nureyev, after Petipa, at the Spoleto Festival in July 1964. This was the version, slightly amended, which he staged for the Australian Ballet and which was seen in London in December 1965 with Fonteyn, Fifield and Doreen Wells as Raymonda, and Nureyev and Garth Welch as Jean. The Royal Ballet Touring Section (and later the larger company) present only an amplified version of Nureyev's third act.

FOUR

Diaghilev's Ballets Russes

MIKHAIL FOKINE (1880–1942)

Trained at the Imperial Ballet School of the Maryinsky Theatre, St Petersburg, Fokine graduated in 1898 and achieved the rare distinction of entering the Imperial Ballet directly as a soloist. He began teaching in 1902, became a first soloist in 1904, and staged his first ballets the following year, *Acis and Galatea* for a pupil's performance and *Le Cygne* for Anna Pavlova. His first ballet for the Imperial Theatre was *Le Pavillon d'Armide* in 1907.

Had he not been a choreographer, Fokine would have lived in history as an outstanding dancer. His achievements in the one art have tended to overshadow his greatness in the other. And reasonably enough. As a choreographer he is the most influential figure of the first half of the twentieth century, matching Noverre in the importance of his reforms and providing a reference point for all his successors. The company he entered at the age of eighteen was fossilized in the precepts which Petipa had evolved through his long reign. This was the year of *Raymonda*, illustrating in the confusion of its story (q.v.) and the quality of its dances the formula against which Fokine rebelled. Not the meaning of a ballet but its prima ballerina was what mattered in this formula; not the story, but the set dances predetermined in their order and designed to show off the ballerina's virtuosity. Whatever the subject matter of a ballet the dances would be always *à pointe* with the *danseuses* clad always in variations of the conventional ballet tutu. The music, composed to the dictates of the choreographer, would probably be a pastiche prepared to its own formula, with numbers interpolated or changed at the ballerina's whim. And in the same way the set designer would have worked independently without reference to costume designer or choreographer.

Deeply influenced by the lofty qualities of romantic ballet, with its emphasis on expression, and by a personal passion for art which carried him into museums and galleries to study the noblest works of the past, Fokine formulated his ideas even before creating his first ballets. 'Dancing should be expressive', he wrote in a note submitted to the management of the imperial theatres with the scenario of *Acis and Galatea*:

It should not degenerate into mere gymnastics. It should reflect the feelings of the character portrayed. Above all, it should be right for the place and period indicated by the subject. The dance pantomime and gestures should not be of the conventional style . . . but should be of a kind that best fits the style of the period. The costumes also should not be established ballet style, but be consistent with the plot . . .

The ballet must be uninterrupted – a complete artistic creation and not a series of separate numbers. In the interests of retaining the scenic illusion the action must not be interrupted with applause and its acknowledgement by the artists.

The music should . . . express the story of the ballet and, primarily, its emotional content . . . Instead of the traditional dualism, music-dancing, complete and harmonious artistic unity of the three elements, music, painting and movement . . .

Such were the principles of the choreographic revolution he effected in the next ten years, principles evolved before meeting Diaghilev and before the visit of Isadora Duncan to St Petersburg in 1904, supposed by many to have had a decisive influence on Fokine's thinking.

This thinking in search of change was paralleled by a similar movement in the artistic world of St Petersburg, centring on the magazine *Mir Iskusstva (The World of Art)* edited by Sergey Diaghilev, and by the exhibitions of paintings which he had masterminded in Petersburg from 1895 onwards. In both these enterprises he had been much helped, and influenced, by two artists, Alexandre Benois and Leon Bakst, as also by the example of the Moscow industrialist Savva Mamontov, whose encouragement of Russian artists, and whose private stagings of otherwise neglected Russian operas with fine design by the artists he patronized, was to be markedly important on Diaghilev's thinking. The two movements of artistic reform, typified by Fokine's choreographic aspirations and Diaghilev's quest for broader horizons for Russian art, came together during the creation of Fokine's ballet *Le Pavillon d'Armide*, first performed at the Maryinsky Theatre, St Petersburg, 25 November 1907, for which Benois provided the designs and wrote the libretto. Benois introduced Fokine into the artistic circle surrounding Diaghilev, who made of the two movements a single force: the Ballets Russes.

The Ballets Russes made its first appearance in Paris in May 1909, as a group of dancers on annual leave from the imperial theatres in St Petersburg and Moscow. Their repertory was by Mikhail Fokine, designs were by Benois and Bakst, and the sensation created by Pavlova, Karsavina, Nijinsky, Bolm, and the whole ensemble was sufficient to waken ballet which had been sinking into a catatonic trance of inadequacy and vulgarity in Western Europe. By 1911 the Ballets Russes had become a permanent troupe directed by Diaghilev, whose constant quest for the new was to inspire the artistic aims of the company until 1929, when Diaghilev died, and the Ballets Russes ceased instantly to exist.

Fokine's first ballets for the Diaghilev enterprise – *Firebird, Schéhérazade* (both 1910), *Le Spectre de la Rose, Petrushka* (both 1911) – brought immense success to the company, and to Fokine. Other works were less successful, and Diaghilev could afford to dispense with Fokine by 1912, at which time his hopes were pinned upon Nijinsky as a creator. Nijinsky's marriage and departure from the Ballets Russes brought back Fokine for a brief period, but the outbreak of the war in 1914 ended his association with Diaghilev, and he returned to St Petersburg and continued working for the Maryinsky Theatre, for whom he made thirteen ballets as well as dance scenes in operas. He quit Russia in 1918 for Scandinavia, and thence travelled to the USA. The remaining twenty years of his life – he died in New York in 1942 – were spent in restaging his former triumphs and creating some new works, few of which achieved any comparable success, though his ballets made for the Monte Carlo Ballets Russes in the 1930s – *L'Epreuve d'Amour* (1936); *Don Juan* (1936); *Paganini* (1939) – were much admired.

Les Sylphides (Chopiniana)

Ballet in one act. Choreography: Fokine. Music: Chopin; orchestration, Glazounov and Keller. Scenery and costumes: Benois. First performed at an examination performance, Maryinsky Theatre, St Petersburg, 20 March, 1908; then in the theatre proper, 4 March 1909. First performed Western Europe: Ballets Russes, Théâtre du Châtelet, Paris, 2 June 1909.

The Dances

Prelude, Op. 28, No. 7		*Overture*
Nocturne, Op. 32, No. 2	*ensemble*	*The company*
Valse, Op. 70, No. 1	*solo*	*première danseuse*
Mazurka, Op. 33, No. 2	*solo*	*danseuse étoile*
Mazurka, Op. 67, No. 3	*solo*	*premier danseur*
Prelude, Op. 28, No. 7	*solo*	*première danseuse*
Valse, Op. 64, No. 2	*pas de deux*	*danseuse étoile and premier danseur*
Valse, Op. 18	*ensemble*	*The company*

The ballet was titled *Chopiniana* for its first Maryinsky performance and remains so titled still in Russia. It was renamed *Les Sylphides* for its first performance in Paris by the Ballets Russes.

Scene: A forest glade. On one side the grey ruins of a monastery, on the other leafless trees with, in the background, the faint outline of a tomb. It is night. The moon throws patches of silvery light.

When the curtain rises, the *corps de ballet* and four principals (one *danseuse étoile*, one *premier danseur*, and two *premières danseuses*) are grouped in a semi-circle against the forest background. The *danseuses* wear the traditional white ballet skirts of the Taglioni period. When they move the effect is of mist dissolving and reforming. *Les Sylphides* is composed in the manner of the pure romantic ballet as a series of four *variations* and a *pas de deux* framed in two ensembles. The mood is spiritual, tinged with sadness, except for the more animated concluding ensemble. The total effect is poetry for whose proper performance purity of style is essential without any form of excess of exaggeration.

Although descended from storyless *divertissements* like the shades scene in *La Bayadère*, *Les Sylphides* introduced what was essentially a new genre, the ballet of mood with no narrative structure whatever and no clearly defined characters. Its inspiration was the romantic ballet and the title by which it is known in Western Europe was suggested by Benois from the original *La Sylphide*. Thus it expresses in the purest form the essence of that neo-romantic revolution (or renaissance of romanticism – as you wish) which lies at the heart of the reforms initiated by Fokine.

Fourteen years after *Swan Lake*, *Les Sylphides* carried further the search for a more expressive movement which Ivanov had initiated in his lakeside scene. The dance style of *Les Sylphides* is quite different from that of a Petipa ballet. In technique, no virtuoso double turns and pirouettes, in partnering, a genuine equality between man and woman based on music; in the patterns and lines of the choreography, a more rounded lyrical quality than the classical lines of Petipa's time, and seeming to flow out of the music. The great achievement of *Les Sylphides*, in fact, is its musicality. Fokine wanted it to be 'the personification of a poetic vision'. This is what his original cast led by Pavlova, Karsavina, Baldina and Nijinsky sought to interpret.

Polovtsian Dances from 'Prince Igor'
Ballet in one act. Choreography: Fokine. Music: Alexander Borodin. Scenery and costumes: Nikolay Roehrich. First performed Ballets Russes, Théâtre du Châtelet, Paris, 18 May 1909.

Scene: A Polovtsian camp at dawn. The outline of tents with, in the distance, hills in the smoke of dying camp fires. The whole lit by the glow of embers.

The second act of Borodin's *Prince Igor* is set in the camp of the Polovtsi, a Tartar tribe occupying the plains of the Don, where Prince Igor and his son, Vladimir, have been taken prisoner. Instead of treating the two princes as captives, Khan Kontchak of the Polovtsi seeks to dispel Igor's depression by giving a banquet in their honour, followed by dances in which the warriors, their womenfolk and slaves take part.

When the opera was first given at the Maryinsky Theatre on 4 November 1890 these dances were arranged by Lev Ivanov, but when Diaghilev decided to include extracts from the second act in his first Paris season with Chaliapine as Prince Igor, he asked Fokine to stage a new version of the dances. The result was one of the ostanding successes of the season and a work rightly acclaimed as a masterpiece. Nothing could be more different from the traditions of Petipa, nor more indicative of Fokine's genius as a choreographer.

Fokine himself considered the Polovtsian dances one of the most important of all his works, illustrating much more than *Les Sylphides* the expressive power of group dance and therefore the importance of the *corps de ballet*. Marvellous as was the architecture of Petipa's use of the *corps de ballet*, it rarely *danced* in the sense that principals and soloists danced. Fokine, on the other hand, disposed his *corps* as a collective whole, or as groups of individuals – in both uses demanding great dance ability. The Polovtsian dances are a supreme example of this choreographic revolution in the use and standing of the *corps de ballet*. No one thereafter could ever argue that the *corps'* main value was only to provide a background or framework for the principal dancers. Here the importance of the work lies in the ensemble; the *corps* are the ballet, putting into practice also Fokine's theories of appropriate steps and gestures to depict period and place. It is a character ballet in which the movements of oriental slaves are contrasted with a wide range of primitive and barbaric movements for the warriors and their chief. In the role of the chief on that historic opening night, Adolphe Bolm achieved a success greater than Nijinsky's in *Les Sylphides*. If anyone can claim the right to have restored by his dancing the position of the male dancer in the West, it is Bolm.

Le Carnaval

Ballet-pantomime in one act. Libretto and choreography: Fokine. Music:

Schumann; orchestration, Rimsky-Korsakov. Scenery and costumes: Léon Bakst. First performed Pavlov Hall, St Petersburg, 1910; first performed Western Europe: Ballets Russes, Theater des Westens, Berlin, 20 May 1910.

Characters

Columbine	Papillon	Eusebius
Chiarina	Harlequin	Pantalon
Estrella	Pierrot	Florestan

Waltzers, Philistines

Scene: The ante-chamber of a ballroom, its only furniture two small striped settees. Columbine, Harlequin, Pantalon, the wistful Pierrot, and other characters from *commedia dell'arte*, intrigue, frolic and suffer with the characters of Schumann's youthful imagination in a succession of dances and situations linked by the antics of Harlequin.

No great success with the Parisian public who saw it a month after Berlin in 1910, *Le Carnaval* became beloved elsewhere and is recognized as one of Fokine's more important works. It is another exercise in his romantic revival, another restoration of the male dancer through the roles of Harlequin, Pierrot and Pantalon, first danced respectively by Nijinsky, Bolm and Cecchetti (with Karsavina as Columbine), another ballet of contrasting moods evoked through dances which extend the range and forms of the *pas de deux, pas de trois* and *pas seul* which it uses. The elusive combination of gaiety, sadness and precise timing required for the total effect is extremely difficult to achieve and a reason why satisfactory performances of this ballet have very rarely been seen since the end of the Diaghilev Ballet.

L'Oiseau de Feu (The Firebird)

Ballet in one act and two scenes. Libretto and choreography: Fokine. Music: Stravinsky. Scenery and costumes: Golovine, with the original Firebird costume by Bakst. First performed by Ballets Russes, Paris Opéra, 25 June 1910. Revived with new designs by Natalia Gontcharova, Lyceum Theatre, London, 1926.

In a dark garden a tree glows, its branches laden with golden fruit. As the scene lightens, a bird, gleaming with orange radiance, flashes across the background of foliage and is gone. Dimly one sees Ivan Tsarevitch in hunting dress climb a high wall to the right and drop into the garden. The bird appears again. Ivan aims with his crossbow and misses. The third time

69

she appears, attracted by the gleaming fruit of the tree, he catches her in his arms. She struggles until exhausted then offers him a golden feather for ransom, provided he allows her to go free. She promises that if he is in trouble and waves the feather she will come to his aid. She flies off and Ivan is about to leave when twelve girls appear through the gates of the garden. Ivan watches from the shadows as the girls are joined by another, more richly dressed. They shake down the golden apples from the tree, throwing them from one to the other until Ivan is discovered. The Princess warns him to leave at once since he is trespassing on the land of the magician, Köstchei, who will turn him to stone. But Ivan already loves the Princess and wishes to stay.

Suddenly a discordant trumpet sounds, the maidens run through the gate, which closes after them, and Ivan is left in darkness unable to find his way out. He runs to the gates and shakes them. They fly open and disappear; the forest blazes with light, and a motley horde of demons and goblins seize the Prince to await the coming of Köstchei. The maidens appear, then more guards, finally the magician, who tries to cast a spell on Ivan. But Ivan remembers the golden feather and waves it aloft. The Firebird appears, scatters the demons and compels everyone to dance until, exhausted, she puts them to sleep. She bids Ivan search in the roots of a hollow tree. He draws out a casket containing an enormous egg. Köstchei trembles, for it contains his soul. Ivan Tsarevitch dashes the egg to the ground where it breaks. There is a dreadful crash and darkness falls.

When the stage lightens Köstchei, his court and the Firebird have vanished. The Princess appears with nobles and ladies freed from Köstchei's enchantment. Then follows a procession of knights, priests and pages who invest Ivan with sceptre, crown and ermine robe to proclaim him their deliverer and sovereign lord.

When Diaghilev returned from the success of his first Paris season in 1909, it was already agreed to present another season the following year with new ballets. One of these would certainly be *L'Oiseau de Feu*, since the ballet was already in hand and only delayed by the dilatoriness of Liadov, Diaghilev's first choice as composer. The commission was transferred to Stravinsky, then aged twenty-eight, who set to work at once with Fokine.

The libretto had been prepared by Fokine and Grigoriev, Diaghilev's *régisseur*, collating several Russian fairy tales. The result of this first and closest collaboration between Fokine and Stravinsky became one of the seminal works of modern ballet, changing ballet music for ever and anticipating in style their finest work, *Petrushka*.

70

The Firebird is chiefly important because it revealed so clearly the nature of the revolution represented by the Ballets Russes. Not just a choreographic revolution, nor a revolution in scenic design, but a profound change in the whole direction of ballet. It rested upon a new conception of music for choreography and a new partnership between composer, choreographer and designer. 'Becoming free,' said Fokine, 'the music grew richer and enriched the dance itself.' Beyond this the ballet again illustrates the gradual fulfilment of the principles Fokine had already put forward before joining Diaghilev: scenery and costumes to realize and recreate exactly the mood and characters of a story; choreography pursuing the same purpose. Hence the Firebird's special role and powers are illustrated in her dancing, the only role created *à pointe*. The Princesses are given dances of elegant style on *demi-pointe* to emphasize their captive state as well as their gentleness. The demons and monsters have heavy character steps. Above all, an atmosphere of mysterious and threatening enchantment is produced by the perfect fusion of music, décor and choreography.

Schéhérazade

Choreographic drama in one act. Libretto: Alexandre Benois. Choreography: Fokine. Music: Rimsky-Korsakov. Scenery and costumes: Léon Bakst. First performed by Ballets Russes, Paris Opéra, 4 June 1910.

Shahryar, King of India and China, is seated in his harem with his favourite wife Zobeida on his left hand and his brother Shah Zeman on his right. Shahryar is in an angry mood because his brother has hinted that his wives are unfaithful. To test the harem, Shahryar departs on a hunting expedition.

As soon as he is gone the wives adorn themselves with jewels and bribe the Chief Eunuch to open two of three blue doors at the back of the room where the male slaves live. The Chief Eunuch is about to depart when Zobeida demands that the third door, too, shall be opened. Deaf to his warning and entreaties she insists and bribes him. There is a flash of gold and a Negro leaps from the open door to Zobeida's side. Together they fall upon the divan.

Immediately young men, musicians and servants bring in food, wine and music. They dance, led by the Golden Slave, joined by Zobeida. Into the midst of this orgy Shahryar returns. The slaves and women seek blindly to escape only to be cut down by Shahryar's soldiers. The Chief Eunuch is strangled; Shahryar himself destroys the gold-clad Negro. There remains Zobeida. Proudly, she confronts the Shah, then, preferring death to public dishonour, snatches a dagger and takes her own life.

71

Schéhérazade is based on the first tale in the book of *The Thousand and One Nights*. Although creating a tremendous impression through the performance of its principal artists with Ida Rubinstein as Zobeida, Cecchetti as the Chief Eunuch and, above all, Nijinsky as the Golden Slave, the honours must go chiefly to Bakst's décor. Its skilful juxtaposition of violent, glowing colour with cunning use of perspective created exactly the atmosphere of sensuality and passion which the theme required. What *L'Oiseau de Feu* did for music, *Schéhérazade* did for décor, demonstrating the essential contribution of a painter's imagination to the creation of ballet. So successful were Bakst's designs that they influenced Parisian fashions at once and continued to influence interior decoration for many years thereafter.

Fokine's choreography, based on a study of Persian miniatures, was economical and dramatic, realizing in movement every feeling and thought of the characters. Even so, the ballet requires artists of the quality of its original performers to interpret the subtleties of Fokine's style, and achieve a proper suspension of disbelief. Consequently, it is a work by which to remember the Russian Ballet rather than to revive today. No revival has managed to achieve more than a bogus orientalism, crude, feeble and very far from the power of the original.

Petrushka

Burlesque ballet in one act and four tableaux. Libretto: Stravinsky and Benois. Choreography: Fokine. Music: Stravinsky. Scenery and costumes: Benois. First performed by Ballets Russes, Théâtre du Châtelet, Paris, 13 June 1911.

Scene 1: Admiralty Square, St Petersburg, in 1830. The Butterweek Fair. Hawkers, gypsies, dancing girls, showmen of all kinds and their customers fill the square. One showman dressed as a magician calls attention to his curtained booth by a drum roll. He displays to the crowd three puppets; the pretty, doll-like Ballerina, the sad-faced insignificant Petrushka and the splendid, but foolish, Moor. At a touch of his wand he seems to bring them to life. They dance, then chase each other round the square.

Scene 2: Petrushka's cell inside the booth. Petrushka bemoans his fate, his hopeless love for the Ballerina, his subservience to his master the Showman, his suffering inside his puppet's body. The Ballerina visits him but in his agitation he frightens her away.

Scene 3: The Moor's cell. The Moor plays idly with a coconut. Stupid and coarse he thinks only of his material needs. The Ballerina visits him and exerts her charms to rouse his interest. Finally, she succeeds but in the midst of their duet Petrushka forces his way into the cell. The Moor attacks him, stamps on him and kicks him out.

Scene 4: The fair. The fair is at its height. Suddenly the crowd becomes aware of tumult behind the curtains of the showman's booth. Out runs Petrushka, pursued by the Moor and the Ballerina. Cut down by the Moor's scimitar, Petrushka dies in the snow. The crowd, horrified by the tragedy, angrily summon the Showman, but he picks up the body and reveals it as only a puppet of cloth and sawdust. The crowd drifts away and the Showman turns for home, dragging the puppet behind him. Suddenly he hears a cry. Above the booth appears the ghost of Petrushka, defying him for the last time. Terrified, the Showman runs from the scene as the figure of Petrushka falls inanimate once more over the edge of the booth.

Of all the masterworks created by the Diaghilev Ballet, *Petrushka* is generally considered the greatest because it is the supreme example of a perfect collaboration. Alexandre Benois recreated the Butterweek Fair from childhood memories of St Petersburg, stimulated by Stravinsky's short piece, *Petrushka's Cry*, which had first roused Diaghilev's interest in the theme.

The scenario achieves an exceptional continuity through the device of a plot within a plot. To match it, Stravinsky composed music within music: first, national dances and traditional dances for the people at the fair, marvellously enriched with background accompaniment; second, music for the principal characters describing not only their external characteristics but also their inner feelings. Thus the music contributed incident, character, psychological interpretation, atmosphere and narrative continuity through a variety of rhythm and sound colour which startled dancers and musicians when first they heard it.

Petrushka also shows very vividly the motivating principle of Fokine's revolution. He sought to make ballet a powerful art in its own right, not just spectacular entertainment. To do this he used images and symbols like poetry: Petrushka, the downtrodden; the Ballerina, symbol of empty womanhood; the Moor personifying all smug, self-satisfied people. Hence the strength of this ballet is also the strength of Diaghilev's own work as an impresario/artistic director, a perfect fusion of music, design and dancing to communicate meaning.

The process can be shown through Petrushka himself. Benois creates his outer form in the costume and grotesque make-up of the puppet. The torment of his inner personality is revealed in Stravinsky's music. His relations and conflict with the outside world are portrayed in the choreography.

Fokine uses a turned-out second position, for instance, to depict the extrovert Moor; a turned-in position to depict poor, introvert Petrushka, in love with the Ballerina, knowing always he is despised. Against these main streams of movement, Fokine allows every individual in his *corps de ballet* to create the seething life of the fair. Nothing in the dancing is virtuoso, everything is expressive, the principles of romanticism translated into character ballet.

Le Spectre de la Rose

Choreographic tableau in one act. Libretto: Jean-Louis Vaudoyer, after Théophile Gautier. Choreography: Fokine. Music: Weber (The Invitation to the Waltz; *orchestration, Berlioz). Scenery and costumes: Léon Bakst. First performed by Ballets Russes, Théâtre de Monte Carlo, 19 April* 1911.

Scene: A young girl's bedroom, painted white, its windows open to the summer night. She returns from a ball, holding to her lips a rose, breathing its scent. Dreamily, she removes her cloak, sinks into a chair and falls asleep. Suddenly a spirit, half-youth, half-rose, floats into the room through the open window. Like a petal blown by the wind he dances, seeming hardly to touch the ground. As he dances he bends over the sleeper and draws her into the dance. But the dream cannot last. He leads her back to her chair, brushes her lightly with his lips and is gone. Her eyes open, and she stoops to retrieve the rose whose scent recalls her dream.

This composition in the style of the romantic ballet illustrates exactly Fokine's contention that the technique of the classical ballet should be used only where it is appropriate. *Le Spectre de la Rose* is a classical *pas de deux* with Nijinsky's wonderful elevation and dancing used in leaps and bounds to evoke an ethereal being, the spirit of the rose, rather than to display an extraordinary technique. 'In no circumstances,' observed Fokine, 'is he a "cavalier", a ballerina's partner. The arm positions in this ballet are the opposite of the "correct" arm positions of the old ballet. The arms live, speak, sing and do not "execute positions".'

Thus the basis of the choreography is purely classical for the legs. To this Fokine added movements in a contrasting romantic idiom for the shoulders, head and arms, to establish a dance style which suggested the product of a young girl's romantic imagination. What made the role of the Rose one of supreme virtuosity was the contrast of Nijinsky's great elevation with these ethereal qualities, just as the young girl's dreamy dance, eyes closed, was not only a contrast with the spirit but required the exceptional acting ability which was one of Karsavina's greatest attributes. Hence this work of atmosphere, simplicity and great poetic integrity became so linked with the two artists who gave it life that it should – like Pavlova's *Le Cygne* – be left with them, uncopied by others, a memory.

VASLAV NIJINSKY (1890–1950)

Born in Kiev, of Polish parentage, Nijinsky was the child of travelling dancers. It was natural he should be entered for the Imperial Ballet School in St Petersburg at the age of ten, in 1900. From the first he displayed rare gifts for dancing and mime. Studying under Legat, Gerdt, Oboukhov and Cecchetti, he was first noticed in 1905, when he danced a faun in a student performance of Fokine's *Acis and Galatea*. He then created a great impression at his official debut three years later in Mozart's *Don Giovanni* – after having already created the part of the slave in Fokine's *Le Pavillon d'Armide*.

Since it was through *Le Pavillon d'Armide* that Benois brought together Fokine and Diaghilev, it could not be long before Nijinsky made the acquaintance of Diaghilev. Thus that personal and professional partnership was launched which made their names inseparable in the history of the theatre. No other dancer, except Taglioni and Pavlova, has become so legendary during and after his lifetime; no other male dancer of his generation could match him in the range of his powers though some, like Bolm, might make more impression in a particular direction. His astonishing *ballon*, elevation, beats, and quality of movement were unsurpassed, providing Fokine with the matchless material from which he fashioned the Golden Slave, Harlequin, the poet of *Les Sylphides*, Petrushka and the Spectre of the Rose. Most especially, Nijinsky had the gift of merging himself completely in all his roles. 'The fact that Nijinsky's metamorphosis was predominantly subconscious,' wrote Benois of this phenomenon, 'is, in my opinion, the very proof of his genius.'

This was the being whom Diaghilev sought to make into a choreographer – and not just for reasons of personal affection. Changes, only possible through a new choreographer, were necessary in the Ballets Russes. Through ballets like *Les Sylphides*, *The Firebird*, *Petrushka* and *Le Carnaval*, created for Diaghilev over four seasons in Paris and London, Fokine had carried choreography into the twentieth century and reestablished the male dancer and ballet as an art in Western Europe. All choreography since then looks back to him.

But Fokine's reforms had been carried out entirely within the context of a wholly Russian company drawing its resources from the Maryinsky Theatre in St Petersburg. By 1912, not only were these reforms complete, it was clear the company must draw upon additional resources to retain its leadership in the arts. It could not continue to offer the work of only one choreographer, however great. Yet when Diaghilev presented Nijinsky's *L'Après-midi d'un Faune* it produced inevitably a break with Fokine. And *Faune* was itself preliminary to other things – *Le Sacre du Printemps* and *Jeux*, and then a more profound break with Russia, when war and Russian revolution accelerated a trend already apparent. From 1914 onwards, the history of the Diaghilev Ballet merges more and more with the culture of Western Europe, especially France, so that it becomes no longer Russian, but Franco-Russian. *L'Après-midi d'un Faune* was the first step in this direction.

L'Après-midi d'un Faune

Choreographic tableau in one act. Libretto and choreography: Nijinsky. Music: Claude Debussy. Scenery and costumes: Bakst. First performed by Ballets Russes, Théâtre du Châtelet, Paris, 29 May 1912.

From a hillside one summer afternoon, a faun sees seven nymphs in the valley below. Filled with curiosity he descends from his hill, but they run away. Soon, they return and the faun tries to woo them. Again they run away – except one who is half frightened, half attracted to him. They touch, then fear overcomes her too, and she escapes, leaving behind her scarf. For a moment she hesitates, hoping to retrieve the scarf, but caution prevails and she follows her companions. Filled with sadness, the faun takes the scarf in his arms and returns to his hillside. He kisses it, places it upon the ground and lies upon it.

Nijinsky sought to represent in this ballet the solitary passion of a faun for a nymph in the pastoral setting of ancient Greece, using movements inspired by ancient Greek friezes. He and his designer, Léon Bakst, tried to keep the two-dimensional quality of a frieze through a special style of movement, bodies facing the audience, heads and limbs in profile. Further to preserve the impression of a two-dimensional surface, the dancers moved only in straight lines, from side to side of the stage at different speeds and sometimes on different planes, the faces expressionless, the arms angular.

It was not easy for classically trained dancers, accustomed always to the turnout of the legs, to achieve the naturalistic, turned-in movements Nijinsky wanted. Moreover Debussy's luminous music, though exactly right for the ballet, was employed simply as an accompaniment, for atmosphere, rather than to give the kind of guidance and support dancers usually expect from music. Therefore this brief, twelve-minute ballet needed 120 rehearsals before it was finished, not to speak of a visit to Greece and intense research in museums. The result was something which seemed to break with all the classical traditions of the Ballets Russes – yet the choreographer needed very good classically trained dancers in order to succeed.

Thus the new ideas and new lines of Nijinsky's *Faune* signalled the begining of a new period for the Ballets Russes. The 'new ballet' of Fokine, and the classical vocabulary itself, became a base for further exploration. Fokine, of course, remained in the wings – and returned briefly as choreographer in 1914 – so that the new period did not begin seriously until the appointment of Massine as choreographer in 1915. But the sound of the flute, with which *Faune* begins, did indeed announce a new era. Diaghilev had discovered for himself Dalcroze and eurhythmics some time around 1910. Interested in these ideas, he took Nijinsky to see Dalcroze at Hellerau near Dresden, when the libretto of *Faune* was already sketched out. The ideas appealed to a young man, aged twenty, who sought to react against academic constraints and was feeling his way towards a new kind of choreographic expression and perhaps a new kind of dance language. Especially, it seems, he wished to prove that movement, any movement however apparently heavy and ugly, could become beautiful if it was placed to express some idea or emotion.

Fokine, of course, had sought the same ends and also used the profile position in his creation of the Venusberg scene from the opera *Tannhäuser* at the Maryinsky the previous year, but this does not diminish Nijinsky's further exploration of what Fokine began. He continued it with less success in *Jeux* at the Théâtre des Champs-Elysées on 15 May the following year, and then two weeks later in *Le Sacre du Printemps. Jeux* is only notable now because it introduced the first contemporary theme of modern times and was the first time dancers had appeared on stage in contemporary dress. *Sacre*, on the other hand, with its complicated score by Stravinsky and its vision of pagan Russia, was exactly suited to the *terre à terre* ideas of Jacques-Dalcroze. Hence Dalcroze was asked to delegate an adviser to Nijinsky. He sent Marie Rambert. Partly from Dalcroze arose the turned-in feet, earthbound, heavy movements and groups of massed dancers which characterized Nijinsky's rites – and shocked his Parisian audience.

It is difficult today to recapture the curiously exotic atmosphere of the

Ballets Russes with its almost desperate search for the new and *avant-garde*. *Sacre* was one result; *Faune* another, indeed the only remaining example, since it alone continues to be performed. The design and costuming by Bakst established an atmosphere of sun-warmed Hellenism, as potent as that in the earlier and more ambitious *Schéhérazade*. The result was a work whose direction was followed by no one else, as Nijinsky, too, had no successor. His career lasted a brief ten years in all; that of the Ballets Russes, only twenty. Both remain an influence throughout this century. For a most intriguing commentary upon Nijinsky's *Faune*, and a sensitive updating of its theme, we refer the reader to Jerome Robbins' *Afternoon of a Faun*.

LEONID MASSINE (1894–1978)

Born in Moscow, Leonid Massine studied at the Imperial Ballet School there, and joined the Bolshoy Company in 1912. His interest was in acting as well as dancing and he had even considered giving up dancing in favour of acting when, in 1913, Diaghilev came to Moscow in search of a dancer to take the leading role in the projected *Légende de Joseph*, which was to have starred (and been choreographed by) Nijinsky. But Diaghilev had broken with Nijinsky, following his marriage, so the young Massine was promptly offered the role of Joseph, and set to work with Maestro Cecchetti, then ballet master to the Diaghilev company. *La Légende de Joseph* had its first performance in May 1914, but the declaration of war later that summer brought an end to the first great Russian period of the Diaghilev Ballet. Massine stayed with the nucleus of artists that surrounded Diaghilev in Switzerland, being educated in the usual Diaghilev manner by visits to galleries and close contact with creative artists and musicians, as well as working with Cecchetti; inevitably Diaghilev was grooming him for choreography and in 1915 he staged his first ballet, *Soleil de Nuit*. It was a success and initiated the long sequence of ballets that extend to recent times, a total output of ballets and dances numbering more than a hundred. As a dancer he demonstrated throughout his life a tremendous skill in character roles and many of his ballets reflect this same quality – though he also had a sensational success in the 1930s creating symphonic ballets. His first, *Les Presages*, in 1933 used Tchaikovsky's Fifth Symphony; there followed *Choreartium* (1933) to Brahms' Fourth Symphony and *La Symphonie Fantastique* to Berlioz' work of the same name. In 1938 he used Beethoven's Seventh Symphony for *Septième Symphonie* and he made another essay – *Rouge et Noir* – in 1939 to Shostakovich's First Symphony. He is best known today, though, for the early ballets that did so much to enhance post-war Diaghilev seasons: *The Good-Humoured Ladies* (1917), *La Boutique Fantasque* (1919), *Le Tricorne* (1919), together with *Le Beau Danube* (1933) and *Mam'zelle Angot* (1943). A man of very considerable intellectual gifts, Massine experimented with a notably adventurous spirit in ballet, as with his symphonic works. His *Parade* (1917) was a Cubist manifesto, and in America in the 1940s he collaborated with Salvador Dali in producing a series of surrealist-inspired ballets: *Mad Tristan* (1944), *Labyrinth* (to Schubert's great C Major Symphony) (1941) and *Bacchanal* (1939), which had a *succès de scandale* but little other reported merit. (*Mad Tristan* turned up in the De Cuevas repertory in London after the war, and was hugely enjoyable for all the wrong reasons.) But those ballets of Massine's that now seem most likely to survive are the early masterpieces of the Diaghilev era. Here he introduced to the Ballets Russes the dramatic tradition of the Moscow company from which he came, basing himself not on the classical canon direct, but rather on that canon as modified by Fokine. Building on what Fokine began, he developed enormously the character ballet and character dancing through a personal language which drew particularly on national sources, and extended the use of the *corps de ballet* through his orchestration of mass movement on stage. He devoted the later years of his long life to reviving his ballets for companies all over the world and to his theoretical study of the essentials of choreography. Some of this study was tested and worked out on students of the Royal Ballet School where he became a guest teacher in 1969, thus contributing to the creation of the school's present choreographic department.

Parade

Realistic ballet in one act. Libretto: Cocteau. Choreography: Massine. Music: Satie. Décor. Picasso. First performed by Diaghilev's Ballets Russes, Théâtre du Châtelet, Paris, 18 May 1917.

The atmosphere is that of a parade, that is, the parade of artists which circuses and small touring theatre companies often offer the public before a performance to advertise their presence and attract an audience. A drop curtain, revealed during the overture, depicts the interior of a booth and a miscellaneous group of performers awaiting their call. When this curtain rises the scene shows the exterior of the booth. In front of it, pacing to and fro, is the French manager. One by one there appears during the ballet a Chinese conjurer, an American girl dancer and two acrobats. They are

79

joined in their appeals to the public by a manager from New York and a pantomime horse. The trouble is they try far too hard. At the end of the parade the public cannot believe there is anything more to see which is worth paying for. The drop curtain slowly falls to hide this tragedy of misunderstanding.

As Cyril Beaumont points out in his *Complete Book of Ballets*, *Parade* is not only a satire on well-known music-hall types of the period but also 'a tragi-comedy in miniature'. Its significance as a ballet is its early place in the Massine canon – only his third work after *Soleil de Nuit* and *Les Femmes de Bonne Humeur*; its collaborators, drawing together some of the most talented young artists of the time; and the cubist costumes of the managers which became one of the most discussed examples of cubist art in the theatre. It was revived only once by Diaghilev – in 1920 – but it has been revived more recently by Béjart's Ballet of the Twentieth Century (1964), City Centre Joffrey Ballet (1973) and London Festival Ballet (1974).

La Boutique Fantasque

Ballet in one act. Choreography: Massine. Music: Rossini, arranged Respighi. Décor: Derain. First performed by Ballets Russes, Alhambra Theatre, London, 5 May 1919. Massine and Lopokova: the cancan dancers.

Curtain-rise reveals a toy shop, through whose windows we can glimpse a Mediterranean harbour. The shopkeeper and his assistant enter; a street urchin dashes in and tries to steal something but is speedily ejected, and now the customers start to arrive. First are two English old maids, then an American husband and wife with their son and daughter, and next a Russian family wilting in the heat, with father carrying one daughter, three more girls in tow, plus mother and son. All these visitors are delighted with the variety of toys that are displayed: two dolls on a stand, a pair of Taran-tella dancers, a quartet of court cards, a snob, a melon seller, a Cossack chief, his five soldiers and a Cossack girl, two dancing poodles and finally a pair of cancan dancers. These last win everyone's hearts, the Russian father is pestered to buy the girl; the American father must then buy the man for his children. The two dolls are packed up, the customers pay and leave, with a promise that the dolls shall be delivered in the morning. The shop is closed for the night, and as in every well-regulated fantastic toy shop, the dolls promptly come to life. They are filled with sadness that the two cancan dancers are to be separated; this must not be! The two cancan lovers decide to flee, and take a fond farewell of their companions, who aid their flight. In the morning the shopkeeper and his assistant open the shop;

80

soon their customers of the previous day arrive demanding to know why the two dolls have not been delivered as promised. The shopkeeper re-assures them and shows them the two parcels ready; but on examining them, the dolls are found to have flown. The irate customers turn on the shopkeeper, but before they can do much damage all the dolls return to life and chase the terrified customers and the shopkeeper out into the street.

The ever-popular idea of dolls coming to life (source of a number of ballets from *Coppélia* onwards) is given an irresistible charm in *Boutique*, not least because of the skill with which Ottorino Respighi orchestrated a series of unpublished piano works by Rossini with merry titles, like *Four Hors d'Oeuvre, Castor Oil, Asthmatic Study, Ugh! Peas,* and *Abortive Polka.* Equally attractive are the designs by André Derain, still appealing even after fifty years . . . but then so is the ballet. Unlike many works of this period, *Boutique* can still (with loving, careful performance) retain some-thing of that first rapture it must once have had so abundantly. The choreography is witty, strongly made, even more strongly characterized (with what economy Massine captures the Snob) and the action combines drama with *divertissement* elements in marvellous balance. And, of course, the roles were excellently created.

Massine and Lopokova were the original cancan dancers. When, in 1947, Massine came as guest artist to the Royal Ballet at Covent Garden, and mounted *Boutique* for them, he danced the male cancan dancer again. In the following year Alexandra Danilova also came to Covent Garden as a guest and we had the joy of seeing her performance as the cancan girl in partnership with Massine. Danilova's beautiful legs, her wit, the sheer bubbling champagne of her presence on stage set a standard that no later Royal Ballet performer has yet approached.

Le Tricorne (The Three Cornered Hat)

Ballet in one act. Choreography: Massine. Music: de Falla. Décor: Picasso. First performed by Ballets Russes, Alhambra Theatre, London, 22 July 1919. Massine: the Miller Karsavina: his Wife.

The Three Cornered Hat is unique because of the mastery with which Massine adapted the techniques of Spanish dancing to the theatre; the steps are all authentic. However, their organization and arrangements are the fruit of classical choreography. The story tells of a miller and his beautiful wife, who is the recipient of numerous attentions. A dandy crosses a bridge, flying a kite, and blows her a kiss. He is soon to be followed by the Corregidor (the provincial governor – the wearer of the tricorne) who

81

passes by with his wife and a retinue, and takes a fancy to the Miller's wife. Their procession leaves, but soon the governor returns, and as the Miller is away, he indulges in a flirtation with the Miller's wife. But as they dance, he falls exhausted to the ground, and the Miller returning, joins his wife in mocking the old man. He exits and the Miller, his wife and their neighbours perform a general dance, which features a dazzling *farucca* from the Miller. Suddenly the Alguazils (the governor's guards) return bearing a warrant for the Miller's arrest, and desolated, the wife watches them lead her husband away. With the Miller out of the way, the Corregidor returns yet again to complete his supposed conquest of the Miller's lovely wife, but as he dodders after her on to the bridge, dropping his cloak, she pushes him into the river. As he struggles out, the Miller's wife threatens him with a musket and then leaves, while the Corregidor, old, cold and suffering, wraps himself into the Miller's huge hooded coat and takes refuge in the Miller's bed to try to warm himself. The Miller enters, escaped from the Alguazils, discovers the Corregidor, and mocks him by rudely caricaturing him on the wall of the house. The Alguazils now enter in search of the Miller, but they find instead the dripping figure of the Corregidor in the Miller's coat; they do not recognize him at first, and after maltreating him, drag him away; the villagers celebrate the departure of this petty tyrant with a final *jota* in which they toss him in effigy in a blanket.

During the first world war the relics of the Diaghilev Ballet found refuge in Spain (King Alfonso had for some time been a devotee and important supporter of the Ballets Russes); there Diaghilev heard the incidental music that de Falla had made for a version of Alarcòn's story, and he decided that it should be amplified to make a ballet score. Massine was already fascinated by Spanish dancing and took every opportunity to increase his knowledge, notably by employing a young Spanish gipsy boy, Felix, to teach him. The tragedy surrounding Felix's name is open to interpretation, but what we know for a fact is that he believed he was to create the role of the Miller. When in London he discovered that Massine was himself dancing the role, his mind, already unstable, became deranged; he was found dancing before the altar of a church in London in May 1919, was admitted to a mental home, and died there some twenty-two years later.

Tricorne was a triumph from the very first; the glorious de Falla score, which, like the choreography, takes folk art and makes it viable for the theatre (rarest of feats), is a masterpiece – as, too, the dazzling Picasso set; while Massine's choreography is thrillingly exact in its ability to evoke Spain and sustain the dramatic intrigue and reveal character. It remains a unique work. Despite countless attempts to make other 'Spanish' ballets, to reuse the music, even to cast Spanish dancers in it, Massine's *Tricorne* has never been rivalled – nor even approached in its genre.

Gaîté Parisienne

Ballet in one act. Book: Comte Etienne de Beaumont. Choreography: Massine. Music: Offenbach-Rosenthal. Scenery and costumes: Comte Etienne de Beaumont. First performed by Ballets Russes de Monte Carlo, Théâtre de Monte Carlo, 5 April 1938.

The ballet takes some of the characters from Offenbach's *La Vie Parisienne* – a rich Peruvian, a glove-seller, a flower-girl, and an officer among others – and shows their flirtations, quarrels and misunderstandings on the terrace of Tortoni's restaurant, Paris, a fashionable resort during the Second Empire. The curtain rises on waiters and girl attendants setting out tables and chairs for the nightly ball while a glove-seller and flower-girl set out their wares. Thereafter the ballet centres on a rich Peruvian (originally danced by Massine) who immediately pays attention to both girls. An Austrian baron falls in love with the Glove-seller thus upsetting the Flower-girl. There is a celebrity, a duke, soldiers, an officer and Tortoni himself. The final *divertissement* includes a cancan, a Venetian dance, and a *farandole*, before the curtain falls as the Baron moves away with the Glove-seller and the Peruvian departs to his next adventure.

Although filmed by Warner Brothers in 1941 and revived by American Ballet Theater in 1970 and London Festival Ballet in 1973 this is not really vintage Massine. The structure of the ballet follows his well-established method of bringing together a number of stock characters in a series of situations, encounters and conflicts, all resolved in a long, vigorous *divertissement*. The ballet seems to have survived mainly because of Offenbach's music and one or two highlights in the choreography such as the waiters' dance and the *pas de deux* between the Glove-seller and the Baron. The rest of the choreography is of indifferent quality. Hence the ballet only find its place here because it is one of the few remaining Massine ballets still in occasional performance on British stages.

Mam'zelle Angot

Ballet in one act. Choreography: Massine. Music: Lecocq; orchestration, Gordon Jacob. Décor: Doboujinski. First performed by Ballet Theater, New York Metropolitan Opera House, 10 October 1943.

The plot of Lecocq's operetta, *La Fille de Madame Angot,* is complicated enough as a romp at the time of the Directoire; shortened to make a ballet and without even the dubious help of words, its intrigue and incessant activity can still fox even the most hardened ballet-goer, who after a couple of dozen viewings is often unable to explain coherently what it is all about. In essence it is the story of Mam'zelle (a vile Americanism) Angot, a market girl betrothed to a barber.

Scene 1: A market. Mlle Angot falls in love with a political caricaturist, who seemingly returns her love (much to the barber's dismay); but the caricaturist whilst drawing a cartoon of a government official falls for the latter's mistress, an aristocrat, and forgets Mlle Angot. The cartoon offends the official who orders the caricaturist to be taken to prison, and Mlle Angot, in an attempt to escape from marrying the barber, insults the aristocrat and is also carted off to jail.

Scene 2: At the government official's house a reception is in progress and the aristocrat is dancing, when the caricaturist enters, fleeing from soldiers. He declares his love for the aristocrat, but suddenly the soldiers are announced and though he hides, posing as a statue, the soldiers find him. Mlle Angot, who has come to explain her behaviour to the aristocrat, enters; their meeting reveals that they are old school friends, and anger dissolves into happy reunion. The barber enters in search of Mlle Angot.

Scene 3: The carnival. Mlle Angot has plotted a meeting between the caricaturist and the aristocrat at a carnival, and she exposes their intrigue to the government official. They all mock him, and Mlle Angot decides that she is really in love with the barber. General rejoicing!

If, after you have read this scenario, you are confused, there is no need to feel alarm; the ballet is incomprehensible in its later development. Ballerina after ballerina, as Angot, has industriously mimed, torn up letters, and cut a dozen merry capers without elucidating this operative tangle. And it doesn't really matter; what does matter are Lecocq's charming tunes, the pretty Derain sets, and the opportunities given the principal dancers. Massine restaged the ballet for the Royal Ballet in November 1947 (when it gained its designs by Derain) and its busy joviality has kept it in the repertory regularly ever since.

BRONISLAVA NIJINSKA (1891–1972)

Sister of Vaslav Nijinsky, Bronislava Nijinksa was a pupil at the Imperial School in St Petersburg and graduated into the Maryinsky Company, whence she joined Diaghilev for his first season, dancing subsequently with

(*above*) *Symphonic Variations*: Brian Shaw and Pamela May; Michael Soames and Margot Fonteyn; Henry Danton and Moira Shearer, 1946. (*below*) London Festival Ballet in *Études*

(*above*) Marion Tait and the Sadler's Wells Royal Ballet in *Les Rendezvous*.
(*below*) Lynn Seymour as Juliet in Act I of *Romeo and Juliet*

him for several years. She spent the war years in Russia, but came to the West in 1921 to participate in staging *The Sleeping Beauty* for Diaghilev. Her gifts suggested to Diaghilev that here was a choreographer able to replace Massine, who had left the company for the first time in 1921. (He was to return later.) After the failure of *The Sleeping Beauty* in London, Nijinska made her first ballet for Diaghilev, *Le Renard*, which was a success, and she followed it with *Les Noces* (1923), *Les Biches* (1924), *Les Fâcheux* (1924), *Les Tentations de la Bergère* (1924). She then left Diaghilev, returning in 1926 to stage *Romeo and Juliet*, and thereafter worked in Buenos Aires, and with the Ida Rubinstein Ballet in Paris. Here Frederick Ashton became a member of the company and eagerly watched her rehearsals as well as appearing in many of her ballets. She worked later for De Basil and then settled in the USA, afterwards staging ballets for the De Cuevas Company. In 1963, on assuming directorship of the Royal Ballet, Ashton decided to pay a tribute to Nijinska and acknowledge her influence by staging two of her greatest works: *Les Noces* and *Les Biches*.

Les Noces

Ballet in one act. Choreography: Nijinska. Words and music: Stravinsky. Décor: Natalia Goncharova. First performed by Ballets Russes, Paris, 14 June 1923.

Les Noces has four scenes: *Scene 1*: The blessing of the bride. *Scene 2*: The blessing of the groom. *Scene 3*: The bride's departure from her parents' home. *Scene 4*: The wedding feast.

Stravinsky originally conceived the idea of a *divertissement* based on the traditional ceremonies of Russian peasant weddings in 1914, and he made an abstraction of those elements of liturgy and folk-experience that are their basis. He saw the work as a masquerade ('Very reluctantly', as he notes in his memoirs, he 'agreed to Diaghilev's staging which did not correspond to my original plan') with singers, musicians and dancers mingled on stage. But Nijinska sought to lay bare the ritualistic elements underlying peasant ceremonies, and aided by the stark simplicity of Goncharova's final setting and costumes (earthy browns and black and white) she made a ballet that reached the very essence of peasant life. The Bride and Groom are two central icon-figures at the heart of the dancing; in the first scene the Bride is blessed by her parents as her friends dress her long plaits; the dancing is solemn, apparently simple, and there is a use of point work that stresses the abstract quality of the whole concept. There follows a tremendous contrast with the second scene, The Blessing of the Groom, who is surrounded by a stamping whirlwind of his friends while he stands still. After he has been blessed by his parents, we return to the Bride's house; her plaits are wound round her, the groom's friends come to escort her to church and as she leaves, her mother mourns her departure. In the final scene, the bridal party are seen on a raised inner stage while below them there are the joyous festivities of the guests: the women are meekly lyrical, the men stamp and pound the earth with huge energy, and two soloists (a man and a girl) are called upon to sum up certain moments of the work in what are, in effect, variations. The Bride and Groom move into a bedroom that can just be seen at the side of the inner stage, the door is closed, a curtain is pulled to hide the whole of the inner stage while down below the guests form a final pyramid shape (an architectural theme in the choreography throughout the work) as the bells ring out in the score.

Small wonder that Diaghilev wept when he first heard the score; this is a deeply nostalgic work, a glance back at the world that died with the Revolution, the Diaghilev Ballet's last look at Holy Russia. The fruit of exile by war and social change, *Les Noces* is the most authentically nationalist of Diaghilev's post-Fokine ballets, and after its creation he was never to look East again, save for the late, unsuccessful flirtation with Soviet ideas in *Le Pas d'Acier*.

In the Royal Ballet's scrupulous staging (first performed at Covent Garden, 23 March 1966), *Les Noces* compels attention and admiration by the skill of the conception, and by the continued novelty of Nijinska's choreographic inspiration. It is, in the best sense, an abstract ballet. Depersonalized, yet warm with humanity, it catches a whole social attitude, transmutes it into theatrical form, and never loses touch with its roots in human experience. The actual dance language is amazing; everything looks simple, inevitable, but the underlying structure is rhythmically very complicated. Nijinska uses the dancers as blocks of movement, great shapes of corporate activity that contrast the soft, yielding femininity of the women with a thick muscular style for the men. The work has an extraordinary momentum which builds up through a gradual crescendo until the final scene.

Les Biches

Ballet in one act. Choreography: Nijinska. Music: Poulenc. Décor: Marie Laurencin. First performed by Ballets Russes, Monte Carlo, 6 January 1924.

Les Biches is an untranslatable title: literally it means 'Does' (portrayed on the drop curtain) and cocottes have been known to address each other as

86

'*ma biche*' – but none of this quite conveys the idea of a young girl ready for adventure. An English staging – by the Markova-Dolin Ballet in 1937 – was called *The House Party*, which at least suggested the setting. Marie Laurencin's décor reveals a pale, airy drawing room, presumably in the south of France and it is here that the action takes place. In writing about the ballet, Poulenc noted:

> *Les Biches* has no real plot, for the good reason that if it had it might well have caused a scandal. In this ballet, as in certain of Watteau's pictures, there is an atmosphere of wantonness which you sense if you are corrupted, but which an innocent-minded girl would not be conscious of . . . This is a ballet in which you may see nothing at all or into which you may read the worst.

The eight numbers of the score each contains a dramatic idea: first the twelve young girls in the party, pink-clad, partly innocent, partly wanton; then three heroes of the beach, all muscles and bathing suits, who tread a wary and deliberate path among the girls. They show little interest in the ladies at first, but the entry of an ambiguous figure in a blue velvet jerkin, white tights and white gloves, moving self-absorbedly across the stage awakens the interest of one man in particular. (The figure, since it is danced by a girl, is always called 'The Girl in Blue', a piece of nice-mindedness that cannot disguise the fact that the character is, in fact, a pageboy, and the proclivities of at least one of the bathers are in no doubt at all.) The girls flirt and play with the athletes, and then the bather and the blue-clad girl enter and dance, while the others peer inquisitively over the sofa. Now the Hostess enters, a lady, in Poulenc's words, 'no longer young, but wealthy and elegant', flaunting beads and cigarette holder, who flirts with the two remaining athletes during a rag mazurka. When they leave, the athlete and the pageboy return to dance the lovely andantino. Next two girls in grey arrive – two dear friends, like girls from a *Claudine* novel, exchanging a timorous kiss expressive of their *amitié particulière*, before they exit in different directions. The ballet ends with all the characters on stage in a brisk finale.

Les Biches is a delicious piece the *Les Sylphides* of the twenties in its romanticism – as light and airy in style as the décor and music, and yet exhaling a delicate, pungent air of sensuality. It is an understated *fête galante* where things are certainly not as pretty as they seem; mocking, witty, its slightly *faisandé* air is marvellously sustained. It is a triumph of choreographic stylishness; a shimmering soap-bubble that might so easily be burst, but which Nijinska's skill sustains from first to last. How lightly she treats of the passions, how sweetly they are masked under the air of almost febrile gaiety of the party; but how surely the choreography is made. The cunningly different *ports de bras*, the freshness of use of the classic dance, the clarity of texture in the movement all make it a delight. Without this soundness of the choreography it would never have lasted, and still won its audiences as it does today.

FIVE

British Classical Choreograhy

By August 1929, when Diaghilev died in Venice – almost exactly twenty years after he first brought his Russian dancers to Paris – the art of ballet in Western Europe had been enlarged and changed, through three achievements. He had inspired some of the most perfect works of theatre art then seen; he had blazed the trail of the new and the *avant-garde*; and he had inspired, and largely schooled, those who were about to create the national ballets which arose after his death: Balanchine in America; Lifar in France; Ninette de Valois and Marie Rambert in Britain.

De Valois and Rambert were both in different ways members of Diaghilev's company and both had begun to gather dancers around them in Britain some years before Diaghilev died. So they were ready for the scattering of his company and the tremendous reinforcement of their work which this provided in teachers and dancers after 1929.

Rambert's contribution to the Diaghilev Ballet was as an expert in eurhythmics helping Russian dancers to disentangle the complex rhythms of Stravinsky's *Sacre* (see page 77). Attached to his company, she studied under Cecchetti, then opened her own school in London in 1920, six years before de Valois opened the Academy of Choreographic Art which has become today the Royal Ballet School. By 1926 Rambert was giving successful recitals with her pupils (among them Frederick Ashton) and appeared herself in *A Tragedy of Fashion*, Ashton's first choreography and his first collaboration with Sophie Fedorovitch who designed some of his later ballets. Rambert's contribution to her company as a dancer was never significant, but her contribution as a teacher of dancers and as the moulder of interpretative artists was profoundly important for the character and quality of early British ballet. Especially, she employed her gifts in moulding choreographers and combining their talents with those of suitable musicians and designers. From this came not only the first ballets of Ashton, but of Antony Tudor, Andrée Howard, Walter Gore and, latterly, Norman Morrice. From the same source, too, have come distinguished principal dancers like John Gilpin and dancers who have become directors like Peggy van Praagh of the Sadler's Wells Theatre and Australian Ballets.

89

Soundly trained by Edouard Espinosa and Cecchetti, de Valois' contribution to the Ballets Russes was directly as a dancer. She was accepted into the company in 1923, rose to soloist by 1925, and in those two years learned much also about the organization and administration of a great company. When she left, it was with the stated intention to train dancers and choreographers for a British repertory ballet.

Her ambition was not so remote from British capacity as many people then thought, and she had expert support. 'After the Russians,' said Diaghilev, 'the English have by far the greatest aptitude; some day in the future they will form their own school.' The English have always had this aptitude, although it was long concealed by historical circumstance. After the famous Elizabethan 'dancing English', the court ballet of Elizabeth's successor James I became the most famous in Europe, its masques by Ben Jonson and Inigo Jones influencing the development of ballet at the French courts of Henry IV and Louis XIII. Even after civil war and puritan repression the interest remained strong enough to sustain a brilliant group of dancing masters and dancers in the reigns of Anne and George I. These not only produced Europe's first *ballet d'action*, *The Loves of Mars and Venus*, but supported Marie Sallé in experiments she could not pursue in France. Only during the eighteenth century, in fact, did native English dancers cease to appear regularly in leading roles and the taste arise for foreign dancers which made London famous in Europe for its generosity to visiting artists. The climax of this trend came in the 1840s when London, rather than Paris, was the creative centre of romantic ballet under Lumley and Perrot.

This is the background of English ballet today. It has not sprung up suddenly, like a plant in a desert, but derives from contact with the three great European schools of ballet, all of which happen to be included in de Valois' professional education. The French tradition descends to us through teachers like Espinosa and the Danish ballerina, Adeline Genée. Trained by the successors of Vestris in Copenhagen, Genée was not only the most important dancer in London preceding Diaghilev, but became with Espinosa, a founder of Britain's Royal Academy of Dancing. The Italian tradition descends through Enrico Cecchetti and the Cecchetti Society, transmitting experience from the Academy at Milan which trained almost all the ballerinas who dominated European stages at the end of the nineteenth century. Lastly, the Russian tradition descends through the Ballets Russes and the Russian teachers and dancers who settled in England after the Russian Revolution.

Out of this background it is fair to acknowledge that the dominant technical influence on English performers has been Italian–Russian, almost all leading British dancers being trained by Cecchetti or his pupils, or by Russian teachers. The dominant influence over choreography, however, is Franco-Russian. Rambert's taste was decisively influenced as much by living in Paris as by her attachment to Diaghilev; both de Valois and Ashton acknowledge the creative influence of Massine and Nijinska, the two principal choreographers of Diaghilev's most Franco-Russian period. To these influences, of course, each choreographer brought personal experience to evolve a personal style.

The development of British classical choreography during the last fifty years should be clear from the descriptions and commentaries in the pages which follow. The last ten years, however, have confirmed some positions, changed others and seen new trends emerge which need to be noted. Principal among them are: a clearer view of the significance of Frederick Ashton and Ninette de Valois in the creation of a British school of classical ballet; the cost of developing new classical choreographic talent; a consequential need for greater efforts to find finance for choreographic talent; the growing interrelationship of modern dance with classical choreography; and the growing opportunity for experiment and for the dissemination of choreography through the development of regional classical companies.

The last ten years have seen the confirmation of Frederick Ashton as one of the greatest (some say the greatest) master choreographers of the second half of the twentieth century on the international dance stage. The others are George Balanchine, Jerome Robbins and Martha Graham. We assess the nature of his choreographic achievement later, through the ballets we describe, so we emphasize here the significance of his world position because of its significance for British classical choreography in the international context. His qualities and taste, transmitted through his dancer-interpreters in the company – especially Margot Fonteyn – have largely fashioned the Royal Ballet's style and established the qualities of the British school. This was clear already in 1970. Since 1970, however, we have been able to review the canon of Ashton's work. However many important new ballets he will create in future, those which have been created thus far, seen as a whole, clearly have acquired now the distinction of being the major part of the life's work of a great artist. They have become the summation of a period, a starting point and foundation of all future classical choreography in Britain. Already, for example, their influence can be seen in the work of Kenneth MacMillan and in the repertories of the Canadian and Australian national companies. Moreover this fundamental influence of Ashton on classical choreography is spreading with his ballets across the world, wherever classical choreography is performed. This is the significance of his world position for the British school.

Likewise the place of Ninette de Valois has been confirmed as the founder-teacher of the British school. It is interesting to reflect on the strategic decisions she had to make, now coming to light. The conscious translation of the European classical heritage on to British physique and temperaments. The development from Diaghilev of the concept of total theatre in relation to classical ballet. Her understanding of the necessity of alliance with the British repertory movement in the 1920s and 1930s rather than with the commercial theatre, which would have been easier at the time. Her insistence on the need to develop tradition. 'A tradition is there for you to revive,' she told David Dimbleby on television in 1979. 'If you've not started anything, there's nothing to revive. I'd like my life's work to be a real root in the English theatre. It's there for others to develop something else.' She could not have done this without Ashton, nor he without her.

The need to find and encourage young choreographic talent in British classical ballet is thus a real worry. No one of importance has emerged in the Royal Ballet since Kenneth MacMillan, although there have been hopes along the way and there are hopes today, as we show at the end of this book. Hence the value of a choreographic department at the Royal Ballet School now established with the help of the Gulbenkian Foundation. This not only ensures that talent can be spotted and encouraged earlier than the traditional method of letting it emerge during a professional dancing career; it also links the Royal Ballet School's work in this field with similar work conducted by the London School of Contemporary Dance and the National Choreographic Summer School, both also launched under Gulbenkian auspices.

Such development is all the more urgent in light of the establishment of the Scottish Ballet and the Northern Ballet Theatre. Classical ballet has taken root outside London during the last decade. It will need the nurturing of new choreographic talent which cannot all be done locally.

This talent will certainly be influenced by the spread of modern dance styles, especially the styles of Graham and Cunningham from the United States. The dramatic translation of Ballet Rambert in 1966 from being a company with a repertory of classical works, to a company consciously seeking to blend modern and classical styles is an example of one possible

92

direction for classical choreography. Other directions, no doubt, will place greater emphasis on classical lines; others on the lyrical tradition established by Ashton. What is certain is that the launching of British classical choreography on firm principles has been confirmed during the 1970s so that it has every chance to grow in many directions provided it is confined neither by too much regard for tradition nor too much disregard of the individual qualities of dancers. 'I'm all for people breaking away from something, as well as staying with it,' said de Valois to David Dimbleby in the interview we have quoted, 'but the standard is so high now that the individual tends to be overshadowed. It will have to tone itself down and let the individual have a chance.'

NINETTE DE VALOIS (b. 1898)

De Valois was not only well grounded academically by Espinosa and Cecchetti, but, at the age of twenty-five, brought to the Diaghilev company considerable performing experience in pantomime, revues and opera-ballets. After she left Diaghilev in 1925, she deepened this experience, and the contacts of her dancers, through choreography for the Abbey Theatre, Dublin, the Festival Theatre, Cambridge, and the Old Vic, as well as giving class in stage movement to drama students. The influence of this experience, as well as her classical training, appears in the early ballets of the young Vic-Wells Ballet, almost all of which she had to create herself.

Job

Masque for dancing in eight scenes. Libretto: Geoffrey Keynes. Choreography: de Valois. Music: Ralph Vaughan Williams. Scenery and costumes: Gwendolen Raverat. First performed by Camargo Society, Cambridge Theatre, London, 5 July 1931. Entered repertory of Vic-Wells Ballet, 22 September 1931. Revived at the Royal Opera House, Covent Garden, with new décor by John Piper, 20 May 1948.

Scene 1: Job in the sunrise of prosperity. The Godhead (Job's spiritual self) consents that his moral nature be tested by Satan in the furnace of temptation.

Scene 2: Satan, after a triumphal dance, usurps the throne of the Godhead.

Scene 3: Job's sons and daughters are feasting when Satan appears and destroys them.

93

Scene 4: Job's peaceful sleep is disturbed by Satan with terrifying visions of War, Pestilence and Famine.

Scene 5: Messengers come to Job with tidings of the destruction of all his possessions and the deaths of his sons and daughters. Troubled by the three Comforters, Job invokes the Godhead only to find Satan upon the throne.

Scene 6: There enters Elihu who is young and beautiful. 'Ye are old and I am very young.' Job perceives his sin. The heavens again open to reveal Job's spiritual self restored to the throne.

Scene 7: Satan appeals to Job's Godhead, but is cast out.

Scene 8: Job, an humbled man, sits in the sunrise of restored prosperity, surrounded by his family upon whom he bestows his blessing.

Nowadays, *Job* has a certain emotional appeal for the regular ballet-goer as the oldest British ballet still extant. Inspired by Blake's drawings, it is nobly conceived, perfectly synthesizes theme and music, dancing and design, is perfectly English and perfectly individual in the work of its composer and choreographer.

It had been hoped originally that *Job* might have been produced by the Ballets Russes, but the subject did not appeal to Diaghilev. It was, he said, 'too English'! So it was natural its possibilities should have appealed to the Camargo Society, formed after Diaghilev's death to continue the production of ballet in England. It is, indeed, English. Its inspiration, through Geoffrey Keynes, comes from the drawings of William Blake; its music is not only the work of the finest English composer of his day, but itself draws on English folk sources; its conception as a masque is in the direct tradition of a theatrical form the English have made very much their own. The fact that it assumed this form partly because Vaughan Williams stipulated no 'toe dancing', which he detested, and therefore insisted it should not be described as a ballet, does not detract from its place in the English tradition.

It was also very appropriate to its moment in the development of an English company. It provided Constant Lambert – later to be the first musical director of Sadler's Wells Ballet and one of the company's architects – with his first big success as a conductor, and in the role of Satan it gave to Anton Dolin, the first important British male dancer, the first, and still one of the greatest, male roles in the English ballet repertory. Particularly, however, *Job* is an ensemble ballet, exactly reflecting the state of English classical dancing in 1931. Except in the one dominant role of Satan (for the one really good male dancer then available) it makes no great technical demands, but chooses rather to challenge its performers on the level of dramatic movement. Thus *Job* revealed the possibilities for serious English ballet and the creative force of de Valois as a choreographer. Although Ashton's *A Tragedy of Fashion* in 1926 had taken the first step towards the possibility of English choreography, with *Job*, in 1931, this choreography, and the English ballet, stepped firmly on stage for the first time.

The Rake's Progress

Ballet in six scenes after William Hogarth. Libretto and music: Gavin Gordon. Choreography: de Valois. Scenery and Costumes: Rex Whistler after Hogarth. First performed by Vic-Wells Ballet, Sadler's Wells Theatre, 20 May 1935.

Scene 1: The reception. Having inherited a fortune, the Rake, in his new house, is surrounded by people anxious to enter his service. He takes lessons in dancing, parts freely with money – and rejects the girl he has betrayed under promise of marriage.

Scene 2: The orgy. In gay, disreputable company, the Rake tastes the joys of wine, women and song.

Scene 3: A street. The Rake, having squandered his patrimony, is about to be arrested for debt when the betrayed girl pays his creditors with her savings.

Scene 4: A gaming house. The Rake attempts to retrieve his position at the gaming-table, only to lose all.

Scene 5: Near the prison gates. The Rake is commited to a debtors' prison, but the girl waits patiently for his release.

Scene 6: The madhouse. The Rake, ruined in body and mind, dies in a madhouse.

In its blend of dance and mime *The Rake's Progress* continues, in a sense, where *Job* left off. Like *Job* it is a superb piece of theatre craft, strongly native in inspiration, owing nothing to the style of the Russian Ballet. Like *Job* it is intensely English in every element. For his libretto, Gavin Gordon has drawn on one of the finest achievements of the founder of the British school of painting; in his music he has drawn on eighteenth-century English street ballads. Similarly, Rex Whistler, one of the most gifted English theatre designers of the day, has drawn on Hogarth for designs which capture the sober elegance of eighteenth-century London. De Valois' choreography reflects again the developing technical resources of her company and her decision once more to challenge their dramatic ability. The ballet offers a wide range of characterization and moods as well as two technically demanding male roles in the Dancing Master and the Rake, created originally by Harold Turner and Walter Gore. It also shows de Valois' mastery of choreographic construction and her narrative ability. Through movements combining acting and classical dance steps, the minor characters are etched within the manners of their calling and period. The girl's solos, first danced by Alicia Markova, are never solos of technical display in the Petipa manner, but continue the story and develop her character. Being the only innocent and honest person in the ballet she is distinguished from her sordid surroundings by being the only woman to dance on *pointe*. The Rake, too, is depicted choreographically with great economy. In the early scenes as a young *nouveau riche*, the basis of his choreography is classical, with legs turned out. *Port de bras* is exaggerated to show his gaucheness, the palms of the hands turned down and the elbows lifted to establish the eighteenth-century period. As his character deteriorates from brothel to gambling den to madhouse so he loses his classical style and stance. In the madhouse, no academic basis remains at all. The movements become wild, uncontrolled, like an animal.

The three collaborators achieved a magnificent unity of style and their reward has been a work which is now a classic of British choreography and de Valois' masterpiece, constantly in the repertory.

Checkmate

Ballet in one scene with a prologue. Libretto and music: Arthur Bliss. Choreography: de Valois. Scenery and costumes: E. McKnight Kauffer. First performed by Vic-Wells Ballet, Théâtre des Champs-Elysées, Paris, 15 June 1937. First performed at Sadler's Wells Theatre, London, 5 October 1937. Revived, and redesigned by McKnight Kauffer, Royal Opera House, Covent Garden, 18 November 1947.

A brief prologue before a drop curtain shows Love and Death at a chessboard. Love backs the Red Knight to win; Death the Black Queen. The curtain rises on a chessboard setting with an angry-coloured backcloth on which the red pieces are assembling. First the Pawns, light-hearted pages; then the two Red Knights, fierce and powerful fighters. Two enemy Black Knights enter on a reconnoitring visit of chivalry. They are followed by the entrance of the Black Queen, the most powerful piece on the board. Before her departure she wins the love of the Red Knight, who dances a joyous mazurka. The two Red Bishops enter, their dignified ceremony interrupted by two Red Castles, inhuman and menacing. Finally the Red King and Queen approach. The King, old and feeble, is the weakest piece on the board. The parade of the red pieces is complete.

The game begins. The enemy black pieces attack and 'check' the undefended Red King. His Bishops and his Queen try to defend him, but are defeated. The Red Knight jumps into the arena as champion to fight the Black Queen. He is torn between love and loyalty, hesitates to kill her, then is tricked and killed by her.

The Black Queen is now in possession of the board. The black pieces force the Red King back to his throne until, at the point of death, he faces his assailants. The Black Queen stabs him; he falls lifeless; it is 'checkmate'.

The figures play out their game as a strong human drama rather than an authentic game of chess, so that the ballet is very much in the dramatic genre of *Job* and *The Rake's Progress*, worthy to rank beside them. Bliss's scenario lacks the tightness of their scenarios; and his music, though vigorous and exciting in itself, tends to extend crucial scenes beyond the limits of the dancer's physical endurance, thus weakening the dramatic effects. Even so, the ballet makes a powerful piece of theatre, very much reflecting the 1930s in the expressionist influences behind McKnight Kauffer's designs and in the growing assurance of the dancing. Heavy technical demands are made now upon the *corps* and a major role is created for a female dancer, unlike the situation in earlier de Valois ballets. Especially it shows once more the craft of its choreographer, with the dual basis of classical technique and national dance on which de Valois' idiom rests. The clean, stabbing *pointe* movements of the red pawns in the opening sequence derive from classical technique. The movements of the black pawns reflect national dance. The *pas de basque* is used again and again; there are traces of Morris and sword dances in the black pawns' staves, and de Valois herself says that some of these movements were inspired also by a Japanese troupe then appearing in London.

FREDERICK ASHTON (b. 1904)

Born in Ecuador, where his father was then in business, Ashton saw Anna Pavlova in Lima in 1917, and the revelation of her dancing set the course for his whole life. He came to school in England and at the age of eighteen entered a business firm in the City of London. But the lure of dancing was too great; he started lessons with Massine (who had opened a school in London), and then went to work with Marie Rambert. While still a student he made his first choreography: *A Tragedy of Fashion or The Scarlet Scissors*, a short ballet in Nigel Playfair's revue *Riverside Nights* at the Lyric, Hammersmith, in 1926. He then joined the Ida Rubinstein Company in Paris, where he appeared in several ballets by Bronislava Nijinska,

Rubinstein's choreographer, during which time he was able to learn invaluable lessons in the art of making ballets. After a year he returned to Rambert as a dancer and also as a choreographer for the Ballet Club performances, organized by Rambert, which were the cradle of so many English choreographers. He was also to make ballets for the Camargo Society in the early 1930s, including the delectable *Façade* (1931), and for the young Vic-Wells Ballet – for whom he created his first major ballet, *Les Rendezvous* in 1933. In 1935 Ninette de Valois asked him to join the Vic-Wells Ballet permanently as dancer and choreographer, and there began the association which continues to this day.

In the years leading up to the outbreak of war, Ashton composed a series of ballets which were to be of inestimable value in establishing the Vic-Wells (Sadler's Wells) reputation: *Le Baiser de la Fée* (1935); *Apparitions* (1936); *Nocturne* (1936); *Les Patineurs* (1936); *A Wedding Bouquet* (1937); *Horoscope* (1938); as well as three slighter pieces: *Judgement of Paris* (1938); *Harlequin in the Street* (1938); and *Cupid and Psyche* (1939). In 1940 he made *Dante Sonata* and *The Wise Virgins*, but service in the Royal Air Force interrupted his career, and he was only able to make one ballet – *The Quest* (1943) – during a brief leave from his military duties. With peace, and the Sadler's Wells Ballet's move to Covent Garden in 1946, Ashton's creativity was given a fresh stimulus with the need to produce full-length ballets. He had already made his Covent Garden début with *Symphonic Variations* in 1946; he made two more short ballets – *Les Sirènes* (1946) and *Scènes de Ballet* (1948) (plus a work for the Sadler's Wells Theatre Ballet in 1947 – *Valses Nobles et Sentimentales*), and then in 1948 he created *Don Juan*, following it with his first long work: *Cinderella*. In 1949 he made *Le Rêve de Léonor* for Roland Petit, and the following year his first ballet for the New York City Ballet, *Les Illuminations*. Two works followed in 1951 for the Royal Ballet, *Tiresias* and *Daphnis and Chloe*, plus a staging of the Snow Flakes and Kingdom of Sweets scenes from *Nutcracker* for the Sadler's Wells Theatre Ballet. He made a second ballet – *Picnic at Tintagel* – in 1952 for the New York City Ballet, and the brief *Vision of Marguerite* for the Festival Ballet in the same year, which also included his second three-act work – a version of Delibes' *Sylvia* for the Royal Ballet. The festivities of Coronation Night, 1953, included Ashton's *Homage to the Queen*, and his next major creations were *Variations on a Theme of Purcell* and *Rinaldo and Armida* given jointly in January 1955. Four months later he created *Madame Chrysanthème* at Covent Garden, and then staged his next full-length work, *Romeo and Juliet*, for the Royal

Danish Ballet in May of that year. *La Péri* and *Birthday Offering* (for the twenty-fifth anniversary of the Royal Ballet) followed in 1956; and two years later he staged *La Valse* for La Scala, Milan, which entered the Covent Garden repertory in the following year. In 1958 he composed the three-act *Ondine* for Covent Garden, and in January 1960, made the first of his two-act ballets, *La Fille Mal Gardée,* which was followed the next year by *Les Deux Pigeons.* In 1961 he staged the Stravinsky/Gide *mélodrame, Persephone,* and in 1963 *Marguerite and Armand* as a vehicle for Fonteyn and Nureyev. For the Shakespeare quartercentenary celebrations in 1964, he made *The Dream* and at the Royal Ballet Benevolent Fund Gala in 1965, he staged the brief, lovely *Monotones I,* to which he added the second *Monotones* the following year. In 1967 came another ballet for the Royal Ballet's Touring Section, *Sinfonietta.* In 1968 he created two works for the Royal Ballet at Covent Garden: the light-hearted *Jazz Calendar* and the sensitive *Enigma Variations.* These were followed by three works in 1970, when he had just relinquished the directorship of the Royal Ballet: *Lament of the Waves,* a duet for Carl Myers and Marilyn Trounson at Covent Garden; *The Creatures of Prometheus* first given in Bonn by the Royal Ballet Touring Section, and the choreography for the film *The Tales of Beatrix Potter.* Thereafter Ashton produced little of any importance until 1976, when he created *A Month in the Country* for the Royal Ballet, although his *Five Brahms Waltzes in the Manner of Isadora Duncan* provided Lynn Seymour with a superb opportunity to evoke the presence of the great dancer.

To write about Sir Frederick Ashton is to write about the history of the Royal Ballet; in Ashton's ballets lie a portrait of the company; their range reflects the range of its dancers, their demands have enriched and ennobled its dancers' style and abilities. As Ashton's genius has developed, so has the Royal Ballet; the mutual stimulus existing between a choreographer and his company, between creator and instrument – and notably with Ashton, between him and Margot Fonteyn (their association having lasted longer and more fruitfully than any other in the history of ballet) – has made for great ballets and a great company.

He is a classical choreographer. That is, the academic dance provides both the stimulus and the material for his creativity which stamps the dance with a clearly personal classicism. In his ballets we sense a temperament that has all the classical virtues of harmony, restraint, control of means, and yet his choreography is full of emotion, poetry, passion, but ordered and refined to maximum effect by his understanding of the academic dance – and, very importantly, by his sensitivity to music. His craftsmanship is admirable; his skill in constructing a ballet no less so; and his fluency of invention (particularly in *pas de deux*, of which he is an acknowledged master) is unfailing; his musicality has stimulated the musical understanding of our dancers. These gifts have been of inestimable importance in creating the Royal Ballet and the British school of dancing.

Façade

Ballet in one act. Choreography: Ashton. Music: Walton. Décor: John Armstrong. First performed by Camargo Society, Cambridge Theatre, London, 26 April 1931. First performed by Ballet Rambert, Mercury Theatre, London, 4 May 1931. First performed by Vic-Wells Ballet, 8 October 1935.

Façade was originally an entertainment created by Edith Sitwell, who had written a sequence of poems in which she devised a series of linguistic *tours de force* – dazzling variations in rhythm, sound and sense. An intensely musical writer, Dame Edith's poems were designed to be recited with a musical accompaniment which high-lighted, pointed, underlined, the metrical and rhythmic qualities of her verse, and the young composer, William Walton, succeeded in no uncertain terms in achieving just these effects. Sir Osbert Sitwell notes that the title came from a remark made by an indifferent painter who observed of Edith Sitwell: 'Very clever, no doubt . . . but what is she but a façade?' The Sitwells' delight with this judgement is immortalized in the name given to the entertainment, which was first performed in January 1922. Wittiest of choreographers (and of dancers, as his Ugly Sister in *Cinderella* still proves), Ashton evidently found much to delight him in Walton's parodies, and *Façade* has proved a lasting and endearing view of the dances of the twenties since its first performance in 1931.

It has undergone some slight additions and alterations – and was redesigned in 1940 – but currently it comprises eight numbers: a 'Scotch Rhapsody' for two girls and a boy; a 'Yodelling Song' for a milkmaid (originally Lydia Lopokova) and three admiring youths in *lederhosen*, which makes wonderfully ingenious use of a stool, and offers a very original mime of milking a cow; a 'Polka' (first danced by Markova) in which an elegant and be-boatered lady steps out of her skirt, stands revealed in very natty corsets and dances with delectable *sang-froid*; a 'Foxtrot' follows for two couples, the girls in twenties' frocks, the boys in blazers and alarmingly Oxford bags; then comes a waltz for four girls, to be succeeded by a 'Popular Song', danced with a dead-pan precision by two boys; a 'Tango

Nadia Nerina as Lise, and David Blair as Colas in Act I of *La Fille Mal Gardée*

Michael Coleman in *The Concert* as staged by the Royal Ballet

Pasadoble' introduces the most oiled and Latin of dagoes and the most inane of débutantes, an irresistibly funny combination of boredom and ineptitude (first danced by Ashton and Lopokova), and the whole company joins in a hectic final 'Tarantella'. At one time there were two additional numbers: a 'Nocturne Peruvienne' for the Dago alone, in which both Ashton and Helpmann, in the ultimate of pinstriping and diamond rings were inordinately Spanish and funny, and a 'Country Dance' for a squire, a yokel and a country girl, but these have regrettably been dropped.

Les Rendezvous

Ballet-divertissement in one act. Choreography: Ashton. Music: Daniel François Auber, arranged Constant Lambert (the ballet music from L'Enfant Prodigue). *Design: William Chappell. First performed by Vic-Wells Ballet, Sadler's Wells Theatre, 5 December 1933. With Alicia Markova and Stanislas Idzikovski as the leading couple.*

'Les Rendezvous,' said Ashton at the time of its creation, 'is simply a vehicle for the exquisite dancing of Idzikovski and Markova,' but this enchanting *divertissement* already shows how sure and elegant was Ashton's handling of the classic dance. Of course the ballet focused upon the ravishing presence of Alicia Markova, a young ballerina for whom Ashton had already made several works, notably *La Péri* (1931), *Foyer de Danse* (1932) and *Les Masques* (1933) – at the Rambert Ballet Club. It celebrated her effortless, brilliant virtuosity, and the delicacy and charm of her presence, as it showed off the buoyant bravura of Idzikovski: both these dancers had been favoured Diaghilev artists, and two solos and a *pas de deux* exploited their qualities admirably. But in the comings and goings of the young lovers, in the sweetness of the amorous intrigues so gently hinted, and in the tripping grace of the *pas de trois*, Ashton provided a most delightful sequence of dances, framed within the gates of a park where the dancers met, flirted, and then happily departed, which showed off the classic abilities of the very young Vic-Wells Ballet. A detailed analysis of the ballet is given as Appendix D in David Vaughan's excellent study *Ashton and his Ballets* (see Further Reading).

Les Patineurs

Ballet in one act. Choreography: Ashton. Music: Meyerbeer, arranged Lambert. Décor: W. Chappell. First performed by Vic-Wells Ballet, Sadler's Wells Theatre, 16 February 1937. Harold Turner: the Blue Skater.

A frozen pond; bare, snowy branches of trees beyond a white trellis hung with Japanese lanterns, and Ashton's charming evocation of skaters as the pretty tunes that Constant Lambert found in *L'Etoile du Nord* and *Le Prophète* ring out. On come the *corps de ballet* in blue and brown, sliding across the ice, to be followed by rather less expert girls; their inexperience is shamingly shown up when a boy in blue comes on and spins, turns and leaps with superb virtuosity. He is joined by two no less expert girls, who indulge in a multiplicity of spins and pirouettes, and we also see a couple in white who dance a lyrical and beautiful *adagio*. The fun becomes faster and more furious; there are what circus posters always call spills and thrills, and eventually snow starts to fall; the dancers glide away, leaving the blue boy spinning round and round as the curtain falls.

When he made this charming *divertissement* in 1937, Ashton cast Harold Turner, a dancer of splendid technique, as the Blue Skater, and no interpreter since has ever quite matched the panache and bravura that Turner showed in the role. The ballet is compact of delights, and it calls for a very real virtuosity from two girls who have to dash off multitudinous pirouettes and *fouettés* in a celebrated showpiece. The ballet has lasted well in spite of being something of a period piece evoking the Sadler's Wells Ballet of the thirties. It is in both Australian and Canadian repertories.

A Wedding Bouquet

Ballet in one act. Choreography: Ashton. Music and décor: Lord Berners. Words: Gertrude Stein. First performed by Sadler's Wells Ballet, Sadler's Wells Theatre, 27 April 1937.

The original idea of *A Wedding Bouquet* seems to have come from Lord Berners (1883–1950) a man who stylishly combined the gifts of composer, writer and designer. He was a friend of both Gertrude Stein and Frederick Ashton, and when he came across a play by Miss Stein, *They Must be Wedded to Their Wife*, he realized that it contained the germs of a very amusing ballet. Ashton set to work. Only the beginning of the play was used to provide a dramatic basis for the ballet, and it was Constant Lambert who conceived the idea of giving Miss Stein's description of the play's characters in the ballet's programme. An addition to the cast was Pepé, Miss Stein's Mexican dog, and it was also decided that certain phrases from the play should be spoken from the stage by a narrator, seated at a table, to accompany the action; they do not explain it in any sense, but provide an atmospheric and often amusing commentary on the characters. The ballet is set in provincial (very provincial) France at the turn of the century. We see the maid Webster (' a name was that was spoken') supervising the

102

preparations for the wedding, and then the guests start to arive: Josephine, Ernest, Violet, Paul, John, Thérese, and also poor dotty Julia ('is known as forlorn') and her Mexican terrier, Pepé ('little dogs resemble little girls'). Meanwhile Violet ('oh, will you ask him to marry you?') has made determined advances on Ernest, but is repulsed in no uncertain terms. Josephine is remarkably devoted to Julia ('not in any other language could this be written differently') and tries to console her, and Pepé also manages to repulse the attentions of an unwelcome suitor to his mistress – who, as we all realize, has been 'ruined' by the Bridegroom and driven into a Giselle-like madness. Now the bridal party appear; the Bride ('charming, charming, charming') is the ultimate in hen-witted vapidity, while the Groom ('they all speak as if they expected him not to be charming') has the shifty air of a man realizing that he is about to be confronted with past indiscretions: it seems that most of the ladies present fall into this category. A wedding photograph is taken, and the Groom's evident unease is fully justified when Julia throws herself at him and refuses to be dislodged. Meanwhile Josephine, overcome by it all, has been sipping and sipping, and is suddenly taken drunk ('Josephine may not attend a wedding,' observes the narrator sagely) and has to be asked to leave. Alone at last, the Bride (who has put on a little tutu) and Groom dance a brief *pas de deux*, which is followed – when the Bride has left the stage – by a Tango in which the Groom partners a group of his former mistresses. The Bride returns, faints – we hope with delight – and as night falls, the guests leave ('Thank you. Thank you'), and the happy couple exit, leaving the disconsolate Julia alone on stage save for the comforting presence of Pepé.

A Wedding Bouquet is a unique ballet which has always aroused the most passionate admiration among its devotees. The combination of neat and funny dances, the inconsequential relevance of the words, the splendid characterizations (Helpmann unforgettably brilliant as the original Groom) and the delicacy and lightness with which Ashton has put together this ballet *bouffe* makes it a connoisseur's piece, particularly since it is far too infrequently performed.

Symphonic Variations

Ballet in one act. Choreography: Ashton. Music: César Franck (Variations Symphoniques *for piano and orchestra*). *Décor: Sophie Fedorovich. First performed by Sadler's Wells Ballet, Covent Garden, 24 April* 1946.

Symphonic Variations presents an essence of Ashton's classic genius; it is perfectly attuned to the music – he is totally responsive to a score – and it is, throughout, warmed by a 'drama of the emotions' that flavours the dancing with a strong character that never bursts through the classical surface though it is readily perceptible; it reflects with uncanny skill the dramatic shifts and emphasis of the score itself.

In February 1946, the Royal Ballet took up residence at the Royal Opera House, and in a world sated with six years of war's tragedies, still constrained by shortages and rationing, the opulent revival of *The Sleeping Beauty* reaffirmed the traditional order and splendour of the classic dance. Three months later the first performance of Ashton's *Symphonic Variations* was as significant an event for ballet in this country as *Beauty's* triumph. On his return from military service Ashton found that 'there seemed to be a clutter of ballets with heavy stories, and I felt that the whole idiom needed purifying. So I made *Symphonic Variations*, and it was a kind of testament.' A testament, as we now see, not only for Ashton, but for the Royal Ballet and its audiences about the supremacy of classicism as the most fruitful means of future development.

The ballet had originally been intended – and how rightly – as the first creation by the company at Covent Garden, but an injury to Michael Somes, who was to dance the central male role, necessitated a month's postponement, and Helpmann's *Adam Zero* had the honour of baptizing the stage, on 10 April. A fortnight later, on 24 April 1946, *Symphonic Variations* had its première, with Margot Fonteyn, Pamela May, Moira Shearer, Michael Somes, Henry Danton and Brian Shaw as its cast, and with designs by Sophie Fedorovich who, twenty years before, had decorated Ashton's very first ballet, *A Tragedy of Fashion*.

The ballet was recognized as a masterpiece from the start; Ashton's 'testament' was a declaration of faith and intention whose importance has been enhanced with each succeeding year. It was, significantly, his first major 'plotless' ballet, but in a conversation with Richard Buckle, recorded in the magazine *Ballet* in November 1947, Ashton commented on the various themes that had occupied his thoughts in the period immediately prior to the ballet's creation. It is important to stress that *Symphonic Variations* is a plotless ballet, free of any direct literary or dramatic incident, but the strength of its formal structure (which follows the scheme: a, b, a, b,) is best explained by reference to the themes that sparked off Ashton's creativity. The work owes something to Ashton's seeing a reflection of the Seasons in human relationships; in brief, the opening *poco allegro* was 'the woman, winter, the period of waiting', the *allegretto* saw 'the arrival of the men, the sun's rays, the summer . . . Life, Love'; the *molto piu lento* was

104

'the search, the wound of love, and rapture caused by the spark of love; the dance of union; fertility'; while the final *allegro non troppo* became 'the festival, the summer, the marriage, the heart's joy in union'. But Ashton insisted:

> All these things were only 'put in' the ballet, if they *were* 'put in', to be eventually refined and eliminated. I did not want to load the work with literary ideas; and I was quite willing for people to read whatever they liked into it.

Scènes de Ballet
Ballet in one act. Choreography: Ashton. Music: Stravinsky. Décor: André Beaurepaire. First performed by Sadler's Wells Ballet, Covent Garden, 11 February 1948.

Ashton's *Scènes de Ballet* is a classic ballet about classic ballet. Stravinsky had originally written the score for a revue staged by the American impresario Billy Rose, in which it was choreographed by Anton Dolin; he intended it as a recreation of the forms of the classic dance in which, to use his own words, 'the parts follow each other as in a sonata or in a symphony in contrasts or similarities'.

Ashton has made the ballet what Stravinsky intended: a study in the formulae of the classic dance. In a broadcast he stated:

> When I was doing this ballet I immersed myself in geometry and Euclid ... and the fact that you could make the front anywhere, not necessarily, as it were, where the public sit and see. So that *Scènes de Ballet*, if you were to sit in the wings, would still have the same effect as it has from being viewed from the auditorium. You would get a different, but logical, pattern, and this was a fascinating problem for me. I used to place the dancers in theorems and then make them move along geometric lines and then at the end I would say: 'Well, QED,' when it worked out. Sometimes we got into the most terrible muddles, but it was a very interesting problem for me to unravel them.

Ashton wrote the work for a ballerina and her cavalier, four male soloists and a *corps de ballet* of twelve girls. With these forces he has made a ballet which offers, in an amazingly succint way, a fascinating and revealing study of the emotional and technical attitudes of the classic dance of Petipa. Here are variations, ensembles, *pas de deux* – even an apotheosis; the ballerina seems at times the heroine of any great Maryinsky spectacle; the male soloists and the *corps de ballet* of girls evoke memories of the most

105

brilliant passages in the classic repertory; and yet Ashton's language –
though entirely classical – has a freshness and a novelty of outline that are
constantly exciting. It is a work whose ingenuities (and it is most deft and
allusive in structure) never weigh down the actual quality of the invention,
which shows Ashton at his most masterly.

Cinderella

*Ballet in three acts. Choreography: Ashton. Music: Prokofiev. Décor: Jean
Denis Malclès. First performed by Sadler's Wells Ballet, Covent Garden,
23 December 1948. Moira Shearer: Cinderella. Michael Somes: the Prince.
Frederick Ashton and Robert Helpmann: the Ugly Sisters. Pamela May: the
Fairy Godmother. (Redesigned by Henry Bardon [sets] and David Walker
[costumes], 23 December 1965.)*

ACT I: A room in the house of Cinderella's father. At curtain rise
Cinderella sits quietly by the fire while her two Ugly Stepsisters are busily
sewing a scarf, in anticipation of the ball to which they are going that
evening. They bicker – do they ever do anything else? – about the scarf,
which is finally torn in half, and they exit to start their preparations, leaving
Cinderella alone. She too dreams of going to the party; she dances with her
broom, but suddenly becomes sad, and going to the fireplace she lights a
candle before the picture of her dead mother. Her father, browbeaten
within an inch of his life, enters and is seized with remorse at this sight,
but the two termagants return, nagging him for indulging the girl and
chiding Cinderella for not working. A shimmering, magical tune announces
the arrival of an old beggarwoman; the Sisters jeer at her, but Cinderella
offers her a crust of bread, and just as the old woman leaves she strikes
the bossier of the two sisters dumb for one agonizing and glorious moment.
Now the cohorts of attendants needed to prepare the two Sisters for the
ball arrive, bringing clothes, wigs, hats, jewels, maquillage, plus a handsome dancing master over whose charms the two old girls squabble as they
squabble about everything. In a final flurry of powder and malevolence
they leave for the ball, with their stepfather in depressed attendance,
leaving Cinderella alone. She dances again with the broom, but suddenly
the old beggarwoman returns to reveal herself as Cinderella's Fairy God-
mother. The walls of the room melt away to show the four Fairies of the
seasons who each in turn dance a variation, with a culminating dance for a
group of stars during which time the pumpkin is transformed into a coach
which bears the now gorgeously dressed Cinderella away to the ball – but
not before the Fairy Godmother has issued the traditional warning that at
midnight everything will be turned back to rags.

ACT II: The ballroom. The guests are already moving through the formal patterns of a court dance, while a Jester leaps and curvettes among them. The Ugly Sisters make a devastating entrance, followed by an even more devastating dance from each one as they are introduced to their partners. The Prince's four friends herald the arrival of the Prince himself, which is followed soon by the magic appearance of Cinderella, revealed as the loveliest of young women. The Prince, of course, falls in love with her, and their *pas de deux* and variations make the glowing romantic heart of the act. The Prince presents Cinderella with an orange, and then also makes a gift of an orange each to the two Ugly Sisters (which occasions yet another display of temper), and the ball progresses, with Cinderella lost in delight, until suddenly the ominous ticking of a clock is heard. Desperately she tries to flee, but she is hindered by the guests and by the Prince. As she rushes away, midnight sounds and her clothes are turned again into the rags she wore in the kitchen – save for a shoe left on the stair. The Prince picks it up and swears that he will find and marry the owner.

ACT III: The kitchen. A front cloth scene shows the Ugly Sisters returning homeward with the other guests; soon they are back in the kitchen. Cinderella is asleep; as she wakes she asks herself if she has been dreaming of the ball and the Prince, but suddenly she discovers a dazzlingly beautiful shoe in the pocket of her apron: her delight is interrupted by the return of the Ugly Sisters, reliving with customary bickering the splendours of the ball. A fanfare announces the arrival of the Prince who has come in search of the girl who owns the slipper. The Ugly Sisters eagerly protest that it is their shoe; but despite their agonized attempts they cannot fit the slipper on their bunioned feet. Cinderella moves forward, and as she does so, the other slipper falls from her apron. The Prince realizes that she is the girl he had met and loved; the sisters are aghast when the Prince declares that he will marry Cinderella, but they realize that she is the rightful bride and hobble away to their beds.

The scene is transformed into a magic garden where the Fairies and stars dance once again; Cinderella and the Prince enter, grandly attired, and they leave for a life of ideal happiness as the curtain falls.

In *Cinderella*, Ashton took up the challenge of the full length ballets of the Maryinsky repertory which had featured so significantly in the development of the Royal Ballet. It was the first important long classic ballet created in England. In a sense Ashton had been preparing himself for this task for years – his mastery of the classical vocabulary was complete, and by choosing a tale that had been hallowed in the British theatre through years of pantomime, he was making a very apt and clever choice of subject. He further strengthened the link with a native tradition by having the roles of the Ugly Sisters played by men, first – and subsequently – performed with superlative comedy and finesse by Helpmann and Ashton himself. Helpmann, looking like a roguish horse, was the bossy one; Ashton, paddling about the stage like the ugliest of ducklings was the sadly put-upon nervous Sister. The two interpretations complement each other perfectly: Helpmann rampages shamelessly with eyes in a permanent ogle; Ashton gets into frightful neurotic muddles, and can suddenly be seen overcome with a dreadful attack of the Sylphides – and contrives to be so endearing that one often longs for the shoe to fit.

The writing for Cinderella (a role intended for Fonteyn, though first danced by Moira Shearer because of Fonteyn's illness) is effortlessly lovely, from the skittish and charming dance with the broom in Act I, to the ecstatic walk down the ballroom which Fonteyn gave with a superb sense for the dreaming enchantment the girl feels, and the wonderful *pas de deux* and variations with the Prince. The soloist roles for the Fairy God-mother and the Season Fairies are equally fine – there have been slight changes over the years, none of which detract from the delight of the ballet. The only complaint which can be levelled at the work is that structurally it is weak; the first act is something too long; the second act is ideal in size and shape, but the third act tails away to nothing, lacking even a final grand *pas de deux* for the happy pair. The fault here lies in the score: Prokofiev provided a lengthy travel *divertissement* in which the Prince journeyed round the world in search of Cinderella, but the music is hardly of the quality of the rest of the piece, and Ashton suppressed it in his version. In Soviet versions, this *divertissement* is used, as also is the character of the stepmother, but both of these are rejected in the Ashton staging.

Daphnis and Chloe

Ballet in three scenes. Choreography: Ashton. Music: Maurice Ravel. Décor: John Craxton. First performed by Sadler's Wells Ballet, Covent Garden, 5 April 1951. Margot Fonteyn: Chloe. Michael Somes: Daphnis. Violetta Elvin: Lykanion. John Field: Dorkon. Alexander Grant: Bryaxis.

Scene 1: A sacred grove before the cave of Pan. A group of young shepherds and shepherdesses are bringing gifts to the god Pan, and dancing in his honour; among them are Daphnis and the girl he loves, Chloe. Another shepherd, Dorkon, has also fallen in love with Chloe, and after he has paid rough and lusty attentions, which she rejects, there is a dance contest arranged between the two men in which Dorkon's coarse dancing is easily outshone by the grace of Daphnis. After Chloe has given Daphnis a kiss as the victor, she leaves with her friends, and Daphnis remains alone dreaming of his beloved. Lykanion, a beautiful girl, appears and makes determined advances to him; he is excited by her, but quickly dismisses her. Suddenly the scene is invaded by pirates who pursue the village girls and capture Chloe; Daphnis, held by Dorkon, cannot rescue her, and he sinks despairingly to the ground. The nymphs of Pan appear, waken Daphnis, reveal the god Pan to him, and Daphnis prays that the god will help him recover Chloe.

Scene 2: The pirate camp. The pirates are celebrating their raid with dances. Chloe is brought in with hands bound, by the pirate chief Bryaxis, who is determined to keep her for himself. She pleads with him, but Bryaxis is adamant. Just as he is about to attack her, the god Pan appears; Chloe's bonds mysteriously fall off, the pirates cower in terror, and the god leads Chloe away.

Scene 3: By the sea shore. Daphnis is lying in despair as dawn breaks. His friends come to console him, and he learns that Chloe has been restored to him. She appears, and they are reunited amid general rejoicing.

In 1909 Maurice Ravel was commissioned by Diaghilev to write the score for *Daphnis and Chloe*, with choreography by Fokine. The ballet was first given three years later with Karsavina and Nijinsky as the two lovers, and with a beautiful classic setting by Léon Bakst. In his version Ashton rejects the idea of an 'antique' appearance, and his choice of a designer for the work fell on John Craxton, a painter who knew and loved Greece; the result was a staging that happily caught the timeless quality of Longus' great love story despite modern dress; it is remarkable how the trousers of the shepherds, the girls' dresses and the intervention of Pan are made to work harmoniously together.

The choreography contains some of Ashton's loveliest writing; he has avoided any 'archaisms' in the general dances of the first act which recapture the feeling of ritual and homage to the god (as he does also in *Persephone*) in beautifully simple and convincing terms; they catch, without aping, the innocence of folk dances.

The contrasted dances for Daphnis and Dorkon, the fierce passion of Lykanion, are all dramatically exciting, and the pirates' dances of the second scene are excellently crafted. But it is in the final scene (in which Ashton has rejected the interpolated mimeplay about Pan and Syrinx called for in the original libretto: it is his only real departure from it) that the ecstasy of the two reunited lovers and the joyous gaiety of their friends are so wonderfully expressed.

The ballet was misunderstood by the majority of the critics after its première, but continued acquaintance soon revealed that it is one of Ashton's most moving and rewarding short ballets.

Ondine

Ballet in three acts. Choreography: Ashton. Music: Hans Werner Henze. Décor: Lila de Nobili. First performed by Royal Ballet, Covent Garden, 27 October 1958. Margot Fonteyn: Ondine. Michael Somes: Palemon. Julia Farron: Berta. Alexander Grant: Tirrenio.

ACT I, *Scene 1*: Outside Berta's castle. Berta has returned from hunting, and Palemon courts her by offering her an amulet, which she rejects. He is left alone in the courtyard, when a mysterious creature, Ondine, appears from a waterfall in the garden. From a hiding place Palemon watches Ondine as she dances in the moonlight, frolicking delightedly with her shadow. Attracted to her, he shows her the amulet which she takes from him. Suddenly she feels his heart beating; she flees into the forest, and Palemon, by now in love with her, rushes after her. Berta's friends witness this, and organize a hunt to pursue Palemon.

Scene 2: The forest. Tirrenio, Lord of the Mediterranean, and his water-sprites lie in wait for the lovers. Tirrenio tries to separate them, but when this fails he warns Palemon that if he should be unfaithful to Ondine he will die. Ondine defies Tirrenio, and together with Palemon finds a hermit who marries them. As they leave, Berta and the hunt enter only to be driven in terror from the forest by Tirrenio and his creatures.

ACT II: On board a ship. Palemon and Ondine decide to take passage in a ship; Berta, who has followed them but does not know of Palemon's marriage, also comes on board unobserved. When they have set sail, she is made jealous by seeing Palemon offer the amulet again to Ondine, who accepts it. Berta now accuses Palemon of faithlessness; Ondine promptly gives her the jewel, but Tirrenio, rising from the sea, snatches it from Berta. Ondine seeks to compensate Berta for this loss by pulling a magical necklace from the sea, but Berta rejects this witchcraft and tosses it back at her. The sailors are by now thoroughly alarmed at the presence of Ondine on board, and threaten her. Tirrenio arises in fury from the sea again, creates a great storm in which the ship is endangered. He carries Ondine away to the bottom of the sea, and Palemon and Berta escape shipwreck by climbing on to a rock.

ACT III: Palemon's castle. Palemon and Berta, saved from the storm, have just been married, and Berta shows Palemon her wedding gift to him, a portrait of herself. She leaves him alone while she goes to welcome their

110

guests, and Palemon has a vision of Ondine mourning him below the waves. His reverie is interrupted by the arrival of the guests who join in a series of brilliant dances, suddenly disturbed by the appearance of Tirrenio with a host of sea-sprites. They drive the guests away, Berta is led out, and Tirrenio causes Ondine to appear. Palemon realizes that he loves her still, and though Ondine tells him that if he kisses her it will mean his death, he cannot resist her beauty and his love for her; they kiss, and he falls dead in her arms. A final scene shows Ondine back at the sea-bed, cradling her dead lover in her arms.

Friedrich de la Motte Fouqué's tale of *Ondine* appeared first in 1811, and was soon to prove a happy hunting ground for romantic choreographers: Paul Taglioni, Jules Perrot (in the celebrated ballet for Cerrito which contained the *pas de l'ombre*) and a second version by Paul Taglioni, all used the tale within thirty years of its publication. In making his version, Ashton has in some part been influenced by this romantic tradition – even to the extent of providing a *pas de l'ombre* for his Ondine, too. The interest in this, his fourth full-length ballet, though, lies in the fact that Ashton was completely in control of all its elements; he devised his own libretto, and worked for the first time with a commissioned score, rather than with one already written. The result is a ballet imbued with a splendid mystery. Throughout its length one is conscious of the sea; the movement is largely inspired by it, the mysterious forest of the second scene is plainly near water, the second act takes place at sea, and the castle of the last act looks out on to the sea, and indeed is invaded by the waters with magical effect. It is also a ballet which depends, more than any other of Ashton's large works, on one great central role, that of Ondine, which Ashton made as a superlative statement about Fonteyn's gifts. It is part of the ballet's quality that so much of the background seems misty and strange; the characters other than Ondine are given little detail, they exist as subordinate figures to the central portrait of the water-sprite. In it, too, Ashton has rejected the formal devices that he adapted from Petipa for his other big ballets: the work's structure is freer. Like water itself, it flows along, with none of the set-pieces that one might expect, its central act, in fact, being almost entirely devoted to the scenic possibilities of the presentation of a ship in full sail and its wrecking. In this there is a return to the older traditions of the romantic ballet (as *Le Corsaire*, for example, contains a celebrated wreck), but we must under no circumstances suggest that Ashton has been niggardly with the dancing. The ballet is filled with superb movement, much of it, of course, given to Ondine, but there is also a magnificent, though over-long, *divertissement* in the last act, which was first intended to be given by Tirrenio's creatures in disguise. At its close they were to throw off their costumes and drive the guests into the sea. Alas, this thrilling idea did not prove possible. What is most remarkable about the ballet, though, is its atmospheric quality; partly due to a marvellous design by Lila de Nobili, more particularly because Ashton has devised a style that manages to evoke the mysterious quality of a doomed and impossible love set against the constant surge of water.

La Fille Mal Gardée

Ballet in two acts. Choreography: Ashton. Music: Hérold (arranged Lanchbery). Décor: Osbert Lancaster. First performed by Royal Ballet, Covent Garden, 28 January 1960. Nadia Nerina: Lise. David Blair: Colas. Stanley Holden: Widow Simone. Alexander Grant: Alain. Leslie Edwards: Thomas.

ACT I, *Scene 1*: The farmyard. Lise, the only daughter of Widow Simone, a prosperous farmer, is in love with Colas, a young farmer. Unfortunately her mother plans a far more advantageous marriage for her. At dawn the farm labourers go off to work, and a cockerel and hens wake up to the new day. Lise starts her work but her thoughts are on Colas: she leaves a ribbon as a token of her love and when Colas enters he finds it. The lovers' meeting is interrupted by Simone who chases Colas away, and sets her daughter churning butter. The lovers contrive to meet and express their devotion, but soon the farm girls come in and Lise dances with them. Simone dispatches her workers off to the field, and Lise tries to escape with them. Just as her mother is chastising her, Thomas, prosperous owner of a vineyard, enters with his simpleton son, Alain, who is destined to be Lise's husband. Lise is far from impressed by Alain's antics, but she and her mother accompany Thomas and Alain to the harvest field.

Scene 2: The cornfield. The harvesters have finished their labours and Colas leads them in a joyful dance. When Lise arrives with Alain and their parents, she manages to escape with Colas, while the harvesters make fun of Alain. Lise and Colas express their love in a *pas de deux*. When Simone discovers this she is angry, but is persuaded to show off her prowess in a clog dance. However, a storm interrupts the merrymakers, and they scatter to shelter.

ACT II: Inside Simone's farmhouse. Mother and daughter return soaked to the skin. They sit down to work, but Simone nods off to sleep, and Lise contrives to dance with Colas across the locked door of the kitchen. The farm workers bring sheaves from the field, after which Simone leaves to

112

arrange the signing of the marriage contract. Left alone, Lise talks to herself about the delights of marriage and motherhood. Suddenly Colas springs from his hiding place under the piled-up sheaves. They declare their love yet again, until Simone suddenly returns. In desperation, Lise sends Colas to hide in her bedroom. Simone bustles in, suddenly suspicious: she is sure that Lise has been meeting Colas, but cannot prove anything. She hustles Lise up to her bedroom, locks her in, telling her to get ready for the signing of the marriage contract with Alain. Thomas and Alain now arrive with the village notary and the marriage contract is signed. Alain, given the key to Lise's bedroom, is told to go and claim his prize. As he unlocks the door, Lise and Colas are revealed in each other's arms. Thomas is furious, but the young couple plead with Simone. Thomas storms out, tearing up the contract, and dragging his hapless son with him; Simone relents, blesses the happy pair, and the ballet ends in a dance of general rejoicing.

Ashton's *La Fille Mal Gardée* is an entirely new version of one of the most famous and most significant ballets of the eighteenth century. In 1789, in Bordeaux, Dauberval staged the original, which made a complete break with the formal classical/heroic ballets of his time; in *Fille* (whose staging in the very year of the French Revolution is symbolic) Dauberval was following the precepts of his great master Noverre, in providing truthful observation, a *ballet d'action* rather than the stultified display pieces so prevalent at this time. Here were real peasants, as opposed to the artifices of the French court playing at shepherds and shepherdesses. Here was observation based in life, and a true and urgent dramatic intrigue that goes back to the good sense of Molière's greatest comedies. The ballet went through a variety of stagings, including the acquisition of an entirely new score; and in 1885, Virginia Zucchi, the dramatic ballerina, scored an immense success in the work in St Petersburg. As a touching link with this great past, the mime scene for Lise in Act II was revived by Tamara Karsavina for the Ashton staging.

From the moment that the curtain went up on the first night Ashton's *Fille* was a triumph. The wonderful eccentric dance for the cockerel and hens caught the audience, and when Nerina spun prettily through her first variation; when Blair bounded through his, and Stanley Holden poked Simone's outrageous old face out of the window and started hurling artichokes and almost (but not quite) a flower pot at Colas, the success was absolute. The ballet seemed to convey everything that was happy, sunlit and pastorally delightful; its construction was masterly – dances and mime flowed one into another; its action was purposeful, and told with a gorgeous sense of fun – and at moments, of seriousness; its dances seemed to pile delight on delight. Ashton was writing the ballet for two fine virtuoso dancers, and he responded to all the needs to show off their prowess in dazzling inventions. Nerina's superbly easeful technique – with a lovely jump and *à terre* clarity; Blair's dashing skill, and his dramatic strength; Holden's comic talent, and the immense eccentric resource of Alexander Grant, inspired Ashton to make a masterpiece of comedy without peer, and yet the dramatic development is never lost. We feel for Lise and Colas – as we feel for the lovers in a Molière comedy – and we rejoice in their tricking of authority so that their love may win in the end. For all the artificiality of its means, *Fille* is still a work of truth; its dancing is inspired by real characters, real and touching situations, all shown with a radiant sense of joy and a feeling for the countryside that is a particular quality of Ashton's poetic genius. Above all, the ballet celebrates the quality and achievement of the new English school. It enjoys equal success in Australian and Canadian national company productions.

The Two Pigeons

Allegory in two acts. Choreography: Ashton. Music: Messager. Décor: Jacques Dupont. First performed by Royal Ballet Touring Section, Covent Garden, 14 February 1961. Lynn Seymour: the Girl. Christopher Gable: the Painter. Elizabeth Anderton: the Gipsy Girl. Richard Farley: her Lover.

ACT I: A studio in Paris. A young painter is trying to make a portrait of his girl friend, but her inability to keep still infuriates him. The painter, too, is restless; he feels bored, not only with his life, but even with the charms of his lady-love. His mother enters with a group of young girls, friends of his model, but they cannot distract him from his disconsolate mood, and the young girl is upset that all her charms and her sense of fun cannot affect the painter's feelings. The sound of a troupe of gipsies is heard in the street below; quickly they are invited up, and the arrival of these dashing creatures – and particularly a beautiful girl, mistress of the chief of the gipsies – brings the painter to life in no uncertain manner. Despite the wiles and entreaties of his beloved, he manifests the greatest interest in the gipsy girl. When the gipsies leave, he follows them, abandoning his lady-love.

ACT II, *Scene 1*: The gipsy camp. The gipsies are dancing, and mingling with the passers-by who have come to see bohemian life (and lose their valuables). The painter enters in pursuit of the gipsy girl, who at first greets him with pleasure; gradually the gipsy leader manifests his anger at this interloper, they essay a trial of strength and the young man is set upon, bound and mocked by the gipsies, including the lovely girl whom he has followed. He staggers from their camp, and makes his way sadly home.

Scene 2: The painter's studio. The girl lies sorrowing and alone in the studio, faithfully awaiting her lover's return. As he comes down the staircase, she greets him with unbelieving joy, and their *pas de deux* expresses all the happiness of true love found again.

To say that a ballet has charm nowadays is often to dismiss it as unworthy of further comment; yet *The Two Pigeons* is a work of the greatest and most engaging charm, as it is also a masterpiece of poetic choreography. Together with its companion piece, *La Fille Mal Gardée*, which was created a year previously, *The Two Pigeons* shows Ashton's complete mastery of the two-act ballet. His previous full-length works, *Cinderella*, *Sylvia*, *Romeo and Juliet*, and *Ondine*, had demonstrated how he could develop the traditions of the Maryinsky grand ballets and suit them to the needs of the twentieth-century theatre. In the most clearly individual of them, *Ondine*, he made a strong personal statement on the form of the big ballet as he understood it, giving it an emotional force that it had rarely known before, but even so there remained problems of spacing the dramatic action significantly throughout the length of an evening. With a two-act ballet these problems are solved, without *divertissements* and interpolated dances to break into the flow of the drama, and in *La Fille Mal Gardée* Ashton showed a complete control of form, telling the story in dances that developed the action through buoyant, sparkling inventions. This is not to decry the achievements of his larger ballets, but in *Fille*, and *The Two Pigeons*, we are presented with long, lyric works as concentrated in their poetic imagination as his finest short creations. The sunlit extrovert *Fille* is a study in young love at its happiest; Lise and Colas are positive, yea-saying in their view of life; *Pigeons* is the reverse of the coin – softer, gentler and more searching in its emotional appeal. Ashton called it an 'allegory', and it probes and explores our experience in precisely the way that allegories should. The young painter's wanderlust, his search for sensation and the illusory delights of a 'different' passion, and his eventual realization of the truth of his first love are all aspects of human behaviour that must awake a response in an audience. By casting them in terms of young people seemingly just on the brink of life Ashton has also expressed a great deal about the dreams and aspirations of youth and their adjustment to life itself; the greater marvel is that we are shown all this in choreography of such beauty and freshness.

The Two Pigeons was first staged for the Royal Ballet's Touring Section, and, like every Ashton ballet, sums up a particular stage in the development of his company. Just as *Fille* is a comment on the virtuoso dancers who first created it, so *Pigeons* presents the lyric gifts of the second company's young stars in 1961. It had its origins in the discovery at Covent Garden of Messager's score, first performed at the Paris Opéra in 1886 – which he had staged in 1906 when he was musical director at the Opera House. Its enchanting melodies and tremendous 'dancing' qualities were inspiration enough for Ashton, but the scenario as originally written – set in eighteenth-century Thessaly and devised to give its first ballerina a double, Odette-Odile role as both innocent girl and gipsy seductress – was plainly unworkable. In transposing the action to a *vie de bohème* Paris, and separating the two female roles, Ashton gave the piece a far greater poetic sensitivity.

And how sensitive the dances are. By presenting the dramatics in deliberately free terms, with little specification as to the day-to-day reality of the characters, Ashton conveys – as allegorical style requires – the truth of certain emotions in a 'universal' form. The supporting dance action of the gipsies and the young girl's friends is treated as abstract *ballabili* against which, as in a plotless ballet, the principal characters are seen. This in itself is a brilliantly effective innovation for a dramatic work; we do not worry about the whys and wherefores of the drama, we accept the varied – and very exciting – dances for the *corps de ballet* as an accompaniment to Ashton's analysis of his main characters. The ballet can even be seen to be following, in this respect, concerto form, with the principals as the solo instrument set against the orchestration provided by the *corps de ballet*.

Ashton's dramatic works have always been distinguished by the clarity with which emotional states are captured and moods evoked. Ballets as diverse as *Nocturne* and *A Wedding Bouquet* are two examples that spring to mind. In *The Two Pigeons* he shows us sentiment without sentimentality, the tender feelings of youth without mawkishness, emotion communicated with a rare truth and understanding. This alone would make the ballet a fine achievement; but to have done so through dancing of such freshness, lyricism and wit has made *The Two Pigeons* a very special joy to watch.

The Dream

Ballet in one act, adapted from A Midsummer Night's Dream by *Shakespeare. Choreography: Ashton. Music: Mendelssohn (arranged Lanchbery). Décor: Henry Barden. Costumes: David Walker. First performed by Royal Ballet, Covent Garden, 2 April 1964. First performed by Royal Ballet Touring Section, décor and costumes: Peter Farmer, 3 May 1967.*

116

Oberon and Titania are quarrelling over the changeling Indian boy, so Oberon sends his sprite, Puck, to fetch a strange flower, whose juice, when dropped in the eyes during sleep, causes the sleeper to fall in love with the first living being seen on waking. He intends in this way to spite Titania by causing her to fall in love with some unsuitable creature. Enter two happy lovers, Lysander and Hermia, and two unhappy lovers, Helena and Demetrius. Oberon tells Puck to drop some of the magic essence into Demetrius' eyes so that the unhappy pair may be reconciled. Oberon, meantime, squeezes the magic flower over Titania's eyes and causes her to be awakened by the coarse rustic, Bottom (on whom Puck fixes an ass's head – which scares Bottom's companions, who flee into the forest). Titania wakes and falls in love with Bottom, but Puck has charmed the wrong human lover and Oberon, by endeavouring to redress this mistake, brings it about that both Lysander and Demetrius are in love with poor Helena, while Hermia is now unloved. To right this tangle, Oberon causes a mist to rise; the correctly paired lovers are guided to sleep, Oberon arranging that Lysander on waking shall first see Hermia and fall back in love with her. Titania is shown the ass-headed Bottom, is reconciled with Oberon and gives him the Indian boy; the lovers wake to happiness, and Bottom, with his human head restored, is left to puzzle out what seems to him a dream. 'I will get Peter Quince to write a ballet of this dream. It shall be called Bottom's Dream.'

For nearly two hundred years Shakespeare's plays have attracted choreographers who have hoped, usually in vain, to transpose both the action and the poetry into dance. With the play treated simply as a scenario, success has been possible – though what merit there lies in setting this dramatic skeleton dancing when the original offers poetic flesh as well is highly arguable. But to translate Shakespeare's poetry into dances, to devise movement able to capture or mirror its verbal splendour, demands a genius denied all but the greatest choreographers. The three Shakespeare works that the Royal Ballet offered as its contribution to the quatercentenary celebrations in 1964 were notable for the originality with which the adaptation to the lyric stage was achieved. Robert Helpmann's *Hamlet* showed the action in the fevered, Freudian imaginings of the dying Hamlet; Kenneth MacMillian's *Images of Love* presented studies in human passion developed and extended from a series of quotations; Ashton proved that the magical element in *A Midsummer Night's Dream* could with advantage be displayed within the conventions implied by Mendelssohn's ethereal, incidental music. With characteristic sensitivity he captured the essence

117

of this double inspiration and produced a piece that was true both to Shakespeare and to Mendelssohn. The sheer mastery of his craft (not the least important element in Ashton's genius) can be clearly judged in his treatment of the *scherzo*, where the imponderable scoring is perfectly matched in the layout of Oberon and Puck's choreography with its flashing entries and the brief intervention of Titania's attendants. Spinning, soaring, barely touching the ground, the dancers seem buoyed up on the feather-light music which in its turn has captured the essence of their dramatic and poetic qualities. Throughout the ballet this same sureness of touch fixes the essential midsummer magic of the play – even the antics of the mechanicals are touched with some special enchantment; the work does more than justice to Shakespeare – and Mendelssohn – and boasts a clear lyricism of its own that shows, once again, that Ashton is a great English poet. It is in the national repertories of Canada and Australia.

Monotones

MONOTONES I. *Ballet in one act. Choreography: Ashton. Music: Satie,* Trois Gnossiennes; *orchestration, Lanchbery. First performed by Royal Ballet, Covent Garden, 25 April 1966. Antoinette Sibley, Georgina Parkinson, Brian Shaw.*

MONOTONES II. *Ballet in one act. Choreography: Ashton. Music: Satie,* Trois Gymnopédies; *orchestration, Debussy and Roland-Manuel. Lighting: William Bundy. First performed by Royal Ballet, Covent Garden, 24 March 1965. Vyvyan Lorrayne, Anthony Dowell, Robert Mead.*

Monotones II was first given as a *pièce d'occasion* at the Royal Ballet Benevolent Fund Gala in March 1965. Despite the competition offered by the Royal Ballet's staging of the *Polovtsian Dances from Prince Igor*, and such gala fare as a *pas de six* from *Laurencia* with a stellar cast, *Monotones*, with three dancers in white leotards, no décor other than sensitive lighting, and just ten minutes of choreography, made the greatest and most lasting impression. Since Ashton is intensely musical, the key to the work lay in the pure, uncluttered lines of Satie's music – music stripped down to its essentials, marvellously calm, beautifully ordered. The dancers seemed like three athletes involved in some celestial game, Henry Vaughan's 'angels in some brighter dream', moving calmly, deliberately, unemotionally through their rites, borne along on the clean, spacious sonorities of the music, sharing its qualities of peace and measured beauty. The trio cluster together, separate into solos and duets, rejoin again, always with an unhurried grace, forming sculptural poses of great plastic beauty. Ashton concentrated on

118

exploiting his dancers' qualities of line, with movement followed through to its conclusion with superb logic, as if stating and proving some choreographic theorem with tranquil assurance.

Monotones I, which followed a year later, reversed the casting of No. II by offering two women and one man, and the stronger pulse of the *Gnossiennes* inspired Ashton to create movement that seems more sharply accented than in the earlier trio. There is the same insistence on beauty of line and control of extension, and the same essentially classic nobility, but the dancers are treated as separate entities in a pattern rather than as links in a chain of dynamics. There is a fascinating counterpoint of dancing, with shapes echoed and repeated, lines of movement interweaving and answering each other; the effect, as in the earlier trio, is of timeless beauty.

Enigma Variations

Ballet in one act. Choreography: Ashton. Music: Elgar. Décor: Julia Trevelyan Oman. First performed by Royal Ballet, Covent Garden, 25 October 1968.

In *Enigma Variations* Ashton created one of his most original and moving ballets. Superficially it may seem that he has provided a skilful realization of 'the friends pictured within' of Elgar's *Variations*. Curtain rise shows Elgar's house and the surrounding garden and countryside; the *Variations* have been written, Elgar holds the score and there are the friends whose inspiration he has acknowledged in the music. Mrs Elgar stands watchful on the stairs as Dorabella, an enchanting girl, dashes in and hugs the composer, and slowly the *tableau vivant* of the opening pose comes to life. First Stewart Powell enters on his bicycle, dances briefly, knocks out his pipe on his heel and, suddenly conscious that it is getting late, rushes off. Then Baxter Townshend arrives on his tricycle, surrounded by a group of children – readers of his 'Tenderfoot' books, who dance with him as he struggles with his ear-trumpet. Then Meath Baker bounds down the stairs, brandishing a list of arrangements for the day, in a boisterous character solo, which ends with a bang as he rushes back into the house. Now Isobel Fitton rises from the hammock where she has been lying, with Richard Arnold in attendance, and in two linked variations they express a lyrical affection, before returning to the hammock. Next Troyte Griffith bursts on in a dazzling classical variation and dashes off, and it is the turn of Winifred Norbury to rise from the table where she has been sitting with A. J. Jaeger, Elgar's close friend and publisher, to dance a graceful variation. Then Jaeger rises, and in the most celebrated section of the work

(Nimrod) he walks slowly across the stage, and is joined by Elgar in a danced conversation referring to the closeness of their friendship, in which they are joined by Mrs Elgar. (This trio emotionally, though not technically, brings memories of the *Monotones* trios to mind.) As they leave, Dorabella enters in a *scherzo* (which includes swift hesitant steps recalling the fact that she had a slight speech impediment), ending her variation by dancing with her adored friend Elgar. As they exit, G. R. Sinclair comes on with a troupe of children; the musical variation really refers to Sinclair's dog, Dan, who dashed with much barking into the River Wye, and Ashton shows Sinclair making pawing gestures during his solo. Now Basil Nevinson pulls forward a stool and sits playing the cello while Elgar and his wife dance a *pas de deux* expressing all her desire to comfort and sustain him, and his reliance upon her support in his whole life. The mysterious opening of Lady Mary Lygon's variation brings a vision of that lady (who was absent on a voyage at the time Elgar was writing) surrounded by curls of mist, as she drifts across the stage like some unattainable ideal. The martial strains of the final variations find all the friends returning to the stage; a telegraph boy brings on the telegram from Richter announcing he will conduct the first performance of the *Variations*, Elgar is summoned and receives the news with almost uncomprehending joy, as does his wife, and in a final pose the entire group of friends join together while Stewart Powell photographs them.

This is the surface of Ashton's ballet, the first layer of his creativity, and very fine it is, with its well-made variations, its contrasts, its humour, its unerring sense of style and effortless realization of the music. But the true concern of the ballet is with something more serious and more enduring; the artist's life, his loneliness, and those inner doubts of the creator that not even the love and affection of friends or wife can ultimately touch. This theme runs through the ballet, supporting and giving it shape, just as Elgar's theme does to the score. At the opening, when the musical theme is stated, and leads into Caroline Elgar's variation, we see how Dorabella's youth and joyful affection could delight the composer, and how his wife's 'romantic and delicate inspiration' could sustain him. Then Ashton's theme runs underground until Variation IX for Nimrod. Here it bursts out into the most deeply emotional section of the work, in which we sense the intense relationship of love and affection between Elgar, his wife and Jaeger, which helped the creative artist at his most self-doubting moments. With Dorabella's variations the theme runs underground again, but it reappears in the *pas de deux* for Elgar and his wife in Nevinson's cello passage, and it takes a different form in Lady Mary Lygon's solo, in which that lady becomes a vision of some imagined ideal. The resolution of this 'interior' action comes in the finale, where the recognition of an artist's creativity is seen as the true climax of the work.

A Month in the Country

Ballet in one act freely adapted from Ivan Turgenyev's play. Choreography: Ashton. Music: Chopin; arranged by John Lanchbery (Variations on Là ci darem *Op. 2;* Fantasy on Polish Airs, *Op. 13; Andante spianato and grande polonaise, Op. 22). Décor and costumes: Julia Trevelyan Oman. First performed by the Royal Ballet at Covent Garden, 12 February 1976. Lynn Seymour: Natalya Petrovna. Islayev, her husband: Alexander Grant. Kolya, their son: Wayne Sleep. Vera, Natalya's ward: Denise Nunn. Rakitin, Natalya's admirer: Derek Rancher. Belyayev, Kolya's tutor: Anthony Dowell. Katya, a maid: Marguerite Porter. Matvey, a footman: Anthony Conway.*

'All love, happy or unhappy, is a disaster when you give way to it.' Thus speaks Rakitin, the admiring friend of Natalya Petrovna in Turgenyev's *A Month in the Country*, and it is the theme of Ashton's skilled adaptation of the tragi-comedy to the dance stage. Ashton reduces the action to its essence: the disruptive influence of the young tutor Belyayev upon the Islayev household. At curtain rise we see the idle, charming Natalya reclining on a chaise-longue as her *cavaliere servante*, Rakitin, reads to her, and her ward Vera plays the piano. It is summer in the Islayev country house, and the serene atmosphere is first only disturbed by Islayev's frantic search for a set of lost keys, and by the buoyant dances of young Kolya. But when Belyayev appears, tensions are felt eddying through the drawing room. Vera plainly adores him, and avows her love, but Belyayev manages to stop short of kissing her. Natalya discovers them embracing, and warns Vera of the unsuitability of the intrigue, and when the girl persists in declaring her love, slaps her face, and then is seized with remorse. Vera runs away, and Natalya goes out into the garden with Rakitin to soothe her nerves. Belyayev returns, and flirts momentarily with the maid, but when Natalya returns she offers him a rose for his buttonhole: and this seems to unlock the feelings he has kept hidden from her, and his passion serves to make her admit her own attraction to him.

An impassioned duet is interrupted by the return of Vera, who calls the rest of the household to witness what has been going on. Natalya shrugs the matter off, and is led to her room by her husband, while Rakitin

121

indicates to Belyayev that it is the time for them both to leave the house. Natalya returns to the empty drawing room in her négligée, and stands lost in grief by a chair. Belyayev returns in silence, and unseen by her, kisses the ribbons on her wrap before tossing the rose she gave him at her feet. He leaves, and Natalya sees the rose, as the curtain falls.

Ashton's return to creating a major ballet after a relatively fallow period produced a work that immediately won its audience. Stimulated by his memories of a production of the play which he had seen forty years before, inspired by the dramatic power of Lynn Seymour and her expressive dance style, Ashton produced a work which presents its narrative with all his customary skill, and explored the passions of his characters in a series of magnificent *pas de deux*. It is a free adaptation of Turgenev, but pinned at its crucial moments firmly into the play, and in the Chopin score it finds an ideal musical accompaniment. In musical terms, the ballet offers contrasts between narrative recitative and danced aria, and at every moment, Ashton's musical sensitivity makes it seem that the score might have been expressly written for him: the chain of variations at the start which introduce Natalya, Vera, Kolya and Islayev are exactly matched to the *Là ci darem* variations, and in the writing to the *Fantasy on Polish Airs*, the folk elements of the music are echoed in dance steps which recall the attitudes of polonaise and mazurka. The *andante spianato* seems the perfect accompaniment for the love duet for Natalya and Belyayev. The performances of the original cast were superb. Ashton chose several artists with whom he had worked before. Anthony Dowell was ideal as Belyayev, and in Lynn Seymour he found an interpreter as perfect in womanly caprice as in beauty of dance style. Most attractive, too, the performance of the young newcomer, Denise Nunn, as Vera, giving a girlish charm and a liveliness of temperament to the difficult role of an *ingénue*. The ballet has been filmed, and it forms a most satisfying record of exceptional dancers in an exceptional ballet.

Five Brahms Waltzes in the Manner of Isadora Duncan

Choreography: Ashton. Music: Brahms; Waltzes, Op. 39, Nos. 1, 2, 8, 10, 13, 15: the first played as a prelude. Costume: David Dean.

Frederick Ashton saw Duncan dance during the early 1920s. Isadora was then no longer the radiant young woman of twenty years before who had enraptured and intoxicated the whole of Europe by the grace and extreme emotional power of her dancing. Yet even during the last sad years of the 1920s her genius was not dulled, and the impression she made on the young Ashton was considerable. Thus, in the summer of 1975, Ashton made a short dance – to the best known of the Brahms' waltzes, Op. 39, No. 15 – for Lynn Seymour to dance at a gala in Hamburg. It was not a recreation of Duncan's dance to this same music, but an evocation of her presence, a tribute to Isadora's continuing beauty in Ashton's memory and to the fact that, of all contemporary dancers, Seymour most aptly could suggest the freedom and Dionysiac impulse that informed Duncan's art. But the piece was brief, and for the gala performance staged at Sadler's Well Theatre on 15 June 1976 to celebrate the fiftieth anniversay of the Ballet Rambert – in which company Ashton had made his first steps as a choreographer, and whose founder had also been inspired many years before by Duncan's dancing in Warsaw – Ashton amplified the piece to include four other waltzes. The first dance had included one moment which Ashton remembered from Duncan's dance – an ecstatic walk forward in which a stream of rose-petals fell from her cupped hands. In the new dances, Ashton made use of poses associated with Isadora; reclining and playful, lyrical with a scarf, heroic in emotion and pulse of movement, but his concern was to suggest something of the genius that informed her dancing without referring to any of the 'reconstructions' of Duncan dances which her erstwhile students provide. In Seymour he found the ideal, the only, interpreter: her performance was an extraordinary act of identification with Duncan's spirit; between them, Ashton and Seymour showed us Duncan plain.

ANTONY TUDOR (b. 1909)

As in most things throughout his career Antony Tudor requires a different approach and treatment compared with other choreographers. For a major creative figure who has exerted decisive influence on both sides of the Atlantic, comparatively few of his ballets remain in performance and so qualify for inclusion in this book. But, after a long period of silence, he began a new phase of creativity in Sweden, Britain, Australia and the United States, producing ballets which confirmed his international reputation yet which make it difficult to assess precisely the direction in which he may again be moving.

Born in London, Tudor is one of the many people whose lives were changed by Pavlova's missionary travels. Having seen her dance, then visited the Diaghilev company, he was no longer satisfied at the age of nineteen to pursue the prospect of a shopkeeping career. He telephoned

Cyril Beaumont for advice; Beaumont, wise and sympathetic, recommended Margaret Craske or Marie Rambert as suitable teachers. The year was 1928.

So began the career of a choreographer in whom several critics, particularly in America, see the fire of genius. Rambert was attracted by his intelligence, impressed by his determination. Employed in Smithfield meat market, he started work each morning at five o'clock, was finished by the middle of the afternoon and came to the Rambert studios for lessons at four. Presently Rambert gave him a two-year contract to act as stage manager and secretary to the Ballet Club, the early form of what was to become the Rambert Company. Through this contract he had just enough money to live on and so could work all day at the career he had chosen.

For Rambert he worked in every capacity – as dancer as well as stage manager; as pianist; in due course, as teacher. In this way he learned his craft and became a professional. His late start drove him forward in passionate study to make up lost ground, yet inevitably it affected his acquisition of the classical vocabulary, limited him as a dancer and influenced his application of the vocabulary on stage. It explains to some extent, his leaning towards dance drama and avoidance of any kind of technical display.

His first work, *Cross Garter'd*, was brought to Rambert already carefully plotted and with a full synopsis. The inspiration was Shakespeare; the music by Fescobaldi, a contemporary of Shakespeare. Massine praised the result, first seen at the Mercury Theatre on 12 November 1931, although Rambert was more cautious. In March 1932, *Lysistrata*, to piano pieces by Prokofiev, established him firmly with the audiences of the Ballet Club and satisfied Rambert that her assessment of his potential ability was correct. *Adam and Eve* in December of the same year carried him into the larger and smarter world of the Camargo Society. Prokofiev had disliked *Lysistrata* because he thought the piano pieces Tudor had chosen neither funny enough nor witty enough for the subject. Nevertheless Tudor was well grounded musically, and his ballets have usually been distinguished as much for intelligent choice of music as for its use.

The Planets, in October 1934, illustrated these qualities and confirmed him as one of the two important new choreographers to have arisen in Britain, the other being Ashton. Yet Tudor in Britain enjoyed neither the popular acclaim nor success of Ashton.

The Planets was Tudor's first major ballet on a serious theme. He used three movements or 'episodes' – Venus, Mars and Neptune – from Holst's music, later adding Mercury as a fourth. The clear, poetic dance images,

124

especially in Neptune, and their choreographic relation to the music, heralded the line of other, greater ballets to come: *Jardin aux Lilas, Dark Elegies* and *Pillar of Fire*. With *Jardin*, in 1936, he can be said to have reached maturity as a choreographer; with *Dark Elegies*, in 1937, he made his most enduring, and finest, contribution to British choreography which is, in his own opinion, his best work; with *Pillar of Fire* for American Ballet Theater in 1942, he created a masterpiece of the quality of *Dark Elegies* which not only established him in New York, but opened a new line of development to Ballet Theater itself. *Pillar of Fire*, in fact, established the image of Ballet Theater for the next quarter century.

From very early days no one, least of all Tudor, seems to have doubted Tudor's destiny to play a major role in the development of twentieth-century ballet. With *Jardin aux Lilas* the nature of this role began to be clear. The grasp of grouping and ensemble work which he showed in *The Planets* was developed further in the interests of expression and penetration of character. The ballet was built on Chausson's *Poème* and retained the French quality of its music in the dramatic atmosphere it created. The theme and treatment are described below but here, in fact, was Fokine's genre of mood ballet updated to reveal passions and frustrations running beneath an apparently formal social occasion. The result resembled a short story by de Maupassant with the same economy, and the same sharp delineation of its four characters against the ebb and flow of a *corps de ballet* of guests. It was a ballet of touched hands, original lifts and lines which has become a classic in the international repertory. It was also the clearest manifestation of Tudor's own genre, the psychological ballet.

This approach to character and its revelation beneath the surface of things is repeated in *Dark Elegies*, but in a more condensed form. Sombre, having a quality of epic poetry, *Elegies* is the masterpiece which first earned Tudor the recognition of genius. Its use of music is exceptionally skilful, the visual imagery flowing out of the score, yet sometimes seeming to rest upon it, the one enhancing the other. The effect lies in groupings and ground patterns contrasted with solo dances or dances for two in which arm, hand and head movements are built on a simple but subtle use of classical technique. The intensity of expression thus evoked from movement makes Tudor, in a sense, a modern Perrot recalling the poetry as well as the emotion of Perrot's best work in *Giselle*.

Tudor, again like Perrot, is concerned essentially with human beings. Even a suite of dances, like *Soirée Musicale*, created in 1938, was given the atmosphere of an evening party for young people, the dancers seated at the side of the stage when not dancing and so linking the various dances in the atmosphere of a *soirée*. More directly, Tudor used his observation and gift of characterization to create in *Judgement of Paris* (1938) and *Gala Performance* later the same year, two satirical pieces which revealed, beneath the humour, the pathetic lives of sleazy showgirls in the first, and the idiocy of rivalry among ballerinas in the second. Both ballets have since lost much of their satirical quality in productions which have stressed humour to the point of farce, but essentially they spring from Tudor's own genre of psychological ballet, and illustrate again his craft and observation.

They, with *Jardin aux Lilas* (called *Lilac Garden* in America), and *Dark Elegies* formed Tudor's first productions for American Ballet Theater when he was invited to become that company's resident choreographer in 1939. They were the link from Britain, the prelude to his American career, and curtain raisers for *Pillar of Fire*.

Today the change in the character of Ballet Rambert to become a company mainly using contemporary dance techniques, has meant that Tudor's great early works are all but lost to the British repertory. *Jardin aux Lilas* has entered the repertory of the Royal Ballet, but its style seems as alien to those dancers as it is now to the new generation of dancers in Ballet Rambert. Yet Tudor's reputation increases with time, as sure and sustained, say, as the novelist E. M. Forster's, on a similarly small corpus of distinguished work. The quality of this work guarantees Tudor a premier place in choreographic history even if he were to remain silent for the rest of his life. His ballets, after all, provided the choreographic base of Ballet Rambert for thirty years, though this is not Tudor's principal significance. Unknown outside a relatively small circle, his importance lies in his originality and, above all, in his approach to ballet as a serious art. Diaghilev, the most advanced taste of his time, had brought to Britain a ballet which was exotic, astonishing, boundless in its artistic influence, yet of a sophistication which could not admit the more humdrum world and characters of everyday life. Ashton in the thirties generally continued this sophistication with de Valois providing the dramatic emphasis, both within the traditions of Diaghilev.

Tudor was the one who moved away from the main channel and whose choice of themes, as well as his treatment of them, was as serious as that of a major dramatist. If Ashton has become Britain's greatest choreographic poet, Tudor remains our greatest dramatic example. And he is still unique.

These qualities were translated to America in 1939. Behind him, in the charge of Peggy van Praagh, he left the London Ballet Company formed the previous year, complete with sets, costumes and the prospect of becoming resident company in a small theatre in the centre of London, the Arts Theatre. No one but he and the impresario concerned seems to have known of this prospect when he departed in October saying the war would soon be over and he would be back. Indeed, many people thought the war would soon be over. That thought and the temporary closure of London's theatres were reasons, perhaps, for Tudor to accept a contract with Ballet Theater as resident choreographer.

The germ of *Pillar of Fire* was already in Tudor's mind before he left England. After mounting *Lilac Garden, Dark Elegies, Judgement of Paris* and *Gala Performance* for Ballet Theater in New York, *Pillar of Fire* became, in 1942, the work which established his name and reputation in America, the one work of his to achieve instant critical acclaim. Its success must also have confirmed finally his decision to leave Britain. Did this decision ultimately also becalm his creative life? John Percival's check list of Tudor's works in *Dance Perspectives 17* and *18* – the most authoritative assessment of his career on both sides of the Atlantic up to 1963 – shows a long line of ballets, opera ballets and dances in plays or musicals after *Pillar of Fire*. They include *The Tragedy of Romeo and Juliet* and *Dim Lustre* in 1943, the former with a magnificent role for Alicia Markova as Juliet. Later came *Undertow* in 1945, *Nimbus* in 1950, *Lady of the Camelias* in 1951 and *La Gloire* in 1952.

By and large these works suggest a declining inspiration, at first slow, then more rapid. At the same time nearly all of them included memorable passages, especially *Romeo and Juliet*, *Dim Lustre* and *Undertow* which were significant works by any standard. *Undertow* remained in the repertory for six years but *Nimbus*, a small scale work and his last creation for Ballet Theater, disappeared almost within the season. *Lady of the Camelias* and *La Gloire*, both for New York City Ballet, provided roles for Diana Adams and Hugh Laing in the first, and Nora Kaye in the second when each joined the company from Ballet Theater; they achieved little greater significance. After *La Gloire* Tudor severed his connection with New York City Ballet and accepted more and more educational administrative involvement at the Metropolitan Opera and the Juilliard School of Music, New York.

Yet during the 1950s and 1960s his reputation and influence continued to expand. His works were produced, often by himself, in many countries outside America and Britain, particularly Canada, South America, Sweden, Norway and latterly Australia, always exerting a profound influence on artists and audiences. Why then, with such encouragement, should he seem to have had no more to say ? History knows examples of artists who wither when severed from their home roots. Was this the case with Tudor ? And does his new creativity, dating from *Ekon av Trumpeter* (*Echoes of Trumpets*) for the Royal Swedish Ballet in 1963, indicate it took twenty years to establish new roots in the country he had adopted ?

For this reason, in spite of his early success, the value of what America has given to Tudor must be in doubt. What he has given to America, on the other hand, is beyond question. *Pillar of Fire* was like nothing American ballet had seen before. The promise of what he had brought from Britain seemed fulfilled. The psychological ballet hit America and received immediate acclaim – much more than in Britain. But then Britain has always been slow to accept contemporary dance, and Tudor's approach to theme and character has more in common with contemporary choreographers than it has with the strictly classical.

Here, you might say, was a Freudian ballet whose success sprang from the truthful psychological treatment of what was then a sensational subject. A frustrated unmarried girl in a small American town takes the only sexual outlet open to her. Tudor, of course, is not the only choreographer today creating psychological dramas. But he was the first to do so at top level, with uncompromising honesty and attention to detail. 'Tudor,' remarked Alicia Markova, his original Juliet for American Ballet Theater, 'was the first to put people with complex psychological reactions into ballet. In ballet before him, emotional tension was hidden; Tudor brought it out into the open. His characters had real human problems. His contribution was tremendous.'

Pillar of Fire used Arnold Schönberg's *Verklärte Nacht* and had expressionist settings and Edwardian costumes by Jo Mielziner. The rightness of both immeasurably enhanced the work. Undoubtedly, too, its American setting helped win audience sympathy. But the principal theatrical impact came from Tudor's delineation of character and Nora Kaye's interpretation of Hagar, the central role. Overnight it made her a star. It also illustrates the nature of Tudor's contribution to twentieth-century choreography, the point Alicia Markova has defined. Since audiences can learn only from movements and gestures what kind of person a character is, the character must be neither too complex, nor too difficult to describe visually. For this reason nineteenth-century choreographers have drawn their characters boldly, as in *Giselle*, or merely outlined them like Aurora in *The Sleeping Beauty*. In any event they did not attempt to describe the complex of emotions within a character. Fokine's treatment of character remains much in the same tradition. Tudor, however, succeeds in revealing character almost in as much depth as does a playwright. By showing Hagar's jealousy of her successful younger sister and the scorn she feels for the life of her older spinster sister, Tudor conveys to the audience the reason for Hagar's neurosis. Hagar's little mannerism, passing her hand up her face, shows her inner turmoil and agitation. Each character, in fact, is given a key movement, a leitmotiv arising from their psyche: a toss of the head for the younger sister; for Hagar, pulling at her collar; for the elder sister, putting on her gloves, the formality of the New England spinster. Such key movements, described by Hugh Laing, recur in all Tudor's ballets. More than anything else they are the mark of his craft, and of his place in choreographic history.

In his most recent ballets, for the American Ballet Theater, of which he is a director. Tudor has produced two works to Dvořák music, *The Leaves are Fading* (first performed in 1975) and *The Tiller in the Fields* (1978) – in which emotional narrative and dance combine to create allusive and atmospheric theatre pieces.

Jardin aux Lilas

Ballet in one act. Libretto and choreography: Tudor. Music: Chausson. Scenery and costumes: Hugh Stevenson. First performed by Ballet Rambert, Mercury Theatre, London, 26 January 1936. Revived for American Ballet Theater, Center Theater, New York, 15 January 1940. For the Royal Ballet, Royal Opera House, Covent Garden, 12 November 1968.

Characters

Caroline, the Bride-to-be	The Man she must marry
Her Lover	The Woman in his Past

Scene: The lilac garden of Caroline's house. Tudor's way of naming his characters explains exactly the motivation of the ballet. The period is Edwardian, when marriage is 'sacrosanct'. Caroline's marriage is one of convenience, therefore she and her lover seek desperately for a moment together in the garden to take a last farewell. The husband equally insists that the woman in his past must end their former relationship. At the end Caroline must leave on the arm of her fiancé without having had an opportunity to take the last farewell of her lover, which was her principal

129

reason for giving the party. It is a ballet of meetings soon disturbed, hurried partings and imploring glances.

Very varied in theme and origin, Tudor's ballets are presented through a choreography which is more cerebral than Ashton's. Each work is the result of a search for some style of movement particularly applicable to the subject and the music. In this ballet he uses classical technique to indicate the aristocracy of his characters, modifying it with the gestures and images necessary to indicate their tension and frustration underlying perfect manners. Hence *Jardin aux Lilas* shows very well Tudor's development of the mood genre from the point where Fokine left it. The characters are carried along on an endless belt of movement which arises from their conflict, one with another. It is the application of the mood genre to psychology.

The ballet's creation is interesting, also, for the insight it gives into Tudor's way of working. He tends to choose one or two dancers – often in Rambert days one or other of the principals in this ballet, Maude Lloyd (Caroline), Peggy van Praagh (the Woman in his Past) or Hugh Laing (her Lover) – to find a dance style before transferring it to the rest of the cast. Often his whole ballet will be worked out first in this way. He has always depended very much on sympathetic collaboration, not only with his dancers, but his designer. Hugh Stevenson, for example, was the author of *The Planets*, Tudor's first lasting success for Rambert in 1934, and played an equally significant part in the birth of *Jardin aux Lilas*, ultimately suggesting its title.

Dark Elegies
Ballet in two scenes. Libretto and choreography: Tudor. Music: Gustav Mahler (Kindertotenlieder). *Scenery and costumes: Nadia Benois. First performed by Ballet Rambert, Duchess Theatre, London, 19 February 1937.*

The ballet is an intensely human portrayal of grief and bereavement in which young parents mourn the loss of their children after a disaster has struck their village. Nadia Benois' sombre backcloths and severe costumes give the tragedy a maritime setting. The first scene of bereavement is conveyed through five songs – first a solo for one woman; second a *pas de deux*; third, male solo and ensemble; fourth, female solo; fifth, ensemble. The second scene of resignation is for the ensemble.

Like Nijinsky's *Le Sacre du Printemps* and Nijinska's *Les Noces, Dark Elegies* represents a whole community, not just an individual. Such ballets distil the essence of a community, rising to epic heights as if impelled by

130

communal emotion. No other ballet in the English repertory has succeeded so well in the epic genre. Its principal stylistic influence is expressionist, reflecting the tensions of the thirties, although the choreography derives also from folk movement and classical technique. Classical turn-out and *pointes* are discarded for the *corps*, but retained for the three principal characters, providing a contrast which helps to emphasize choreographically the sense of grief and personal loss. Tudor's choice of music illustrates an aspect of his creative method. He prefers to use existing music, which he can study, rather than music specially composed. Generally, he is attracted to the high emotional content of the late romantics and moderns (Chausson, Strauss, Mahler, Schoenberg, Koechlin), finding in such music the response to the social and psychological themes which move him.

Ekon av Trumpeter (Echoes of Trumpets)

Ballet in one act. Libretto and choreography: Tudor. Music: Bohuslav Martinu (Fantaisies Symphoniques). *Scenery and costumes: Birger Bergling. First performed by Royal Swedish Ballet, Royal Theatre, Stockholm, 20 September 1963. Revived for London Festival Ballet at London Coliseum on 27 April 1973.*

A man returns to a ruined village to seek his beloved. He is captured and executed. The girl dances a lament with his dead body.

Such are the bones of the ballet. Its dramatic source is the total destruction of the village of Lidice in Czechoslovakia during the Second World War as a reprisal for the assassination of Heydrich, Nazi governor of the country. The programme note for the London Festival Ballet staging of this stark work said that the ballet was set 'at any place and at any time where civilization has left its imprint'. And for civilization read, ironically, 'war'. Against the dull setting of a ruined bridge whose flat realism works remarkably well with the ballet's manner, the horrifying incident of rape and murder and reprisal acquires a ritualistic significance.

Tudor's dance language here is classical in the main, with folk dance elements for the soldiery who have invaded and occupy the village where the action is set. It is a language sharply defined and controlled in its emotions, and the performance manner insists upon a similar understatement. It is this stylization of tragedy which gives the work its special merit. The key section of the piece is the passage in which the woman mourns, in piercing imagery, over the dead body of her beloved, revealing depths of suffering and an anger towards death.

Shadowplay

Ballet in one act. Libretto and choreography: Tudor. Music: Charles Koechlin (Les Bandar-Log *and* La Course de Printemps). *Scenery and costumes: Michael Annals. First performed by Royal Ballet, Royal Opera House, Covent Garden, 25 January* 1967. *Anthony Dowell: the Boy with Matted Hair.*

The scene is a forest; a great tree with hanging rope structures for the monkey folk (Arboreals) and, below it, the hero, the boy with matted hair, alone. To the boy come inhabitants of 'the penumbra', people who communicate experience, the world, its social attitudes. Among them the Arboreals, silly and annoying; then Aerials, seeming like Cambodian dancers, communicating perhaps more worthwhile values; then Terrestrial, a male dancer representing passion and experience; finally, the Celestials offering the boy choice and combat. At the end, after great struggle, he returns to his place below the tree, sitting as we found him.

This obscure but magnificent work appeared at a time when many people thought they had seen their last new Tudor ballet. Two more essays in the same genre had followed *Pillar of Fire* in 1942, *Dim Lustre* was staged in 1943; *Undertow* in 1945. Nothing of the same quality had appeared since. Tudor left Ballet Theater in 1950, worked briefly with New York City Ballet, and was associated for many years with the Metropolitan Opera as well as teaching for the dance department of the Juilliard School of Music. It seemed that creativity had passed. Then in 1963 he produced *Echoes of Trumpets* for the Royal Swedish Ballet, a major work which contained all his old dramatic strength, psychological perception and theatre sense. A second phase of choreographic creation had begun in which *Shadowplay* takes its place as an extension of the psychological drama in which he is a master. Using symbols suggested by Kipling's *The Jungle Book* which had inspired Koechlin's music, *Le Livre de la Jungle*, he burrows deep beneath the surface of society to show the forces which mould individuals, and the individual struggling for self-assertion against these forces. The point of departure is Koechlin's music. The composer sees the monkeys as symbols of anarchy and vulgarity in opposition to the order and mystery 'of things and beings', represented by the jungle and its 'noble' creatures, and of course, Mowgli himself. In Tudor's treatment Anthony Dowell danced the boy; Derek Rencher the Terrestrial and Merle Park the Celestial.

132

ANDRÉE HOWARD (1910–68)

Andrée Howard, trained in the forming ground of Rambert's Ballet Club, made her first attempt at choreography in 1933. *Our Lady's Juggler* showed at once an ability to sustain mood and create atmosphere with a remarkable economy of movement, which remained her strength.

In her early days she was influenced by the two senior choreographers of the Ballet Club, Ashton and Tudor, inclining towards Ashton. Her qualities as an artist resemble his in flow of movement, taste, sensitivity and a restraint which is very English in its understatement but which in her case, has led to her worth being much undervalued. For Ballet Rambert in 1947 she created in *The Sailor's Return* the first British two-act ballet; her *Death and the Maiden* remained a classic of the Rambert repertory for over twenty years after its first performance in 1937; while the enormous popularity of *La Fête Etrange*, which contained so many of her best qualities, indicates better than anything else the appeal of her work. It retains an honoured place in the repertories of both the Sadler's Wells Royal Ballet and the Scottish Ballet.

La Fête Etrange

Ballet in two scenes. Libretto: Ronald Crichton, based on an episode in Le Grand Meaulnes. *Choreography: Andrée Howard. Music: Gabriel Fauré. Scenery and costumes: Sophie Fedorovitch. First performed by London Festival Ballet (with Ballet Rambert), Arts Theatre, London, 23 May 1940.*

On the terrace of a young bride's castle, young guests in carnival costume celebrate by dancing and playing in the wintry sunlight. A country boy, wandering in the woods, stumbles upon this world he has never experienced before. The guests welcome him and his happiness mounts to ecstasy when the bride allows him to dance with her. The gaiety is stilled and the mood changes when the bridegroom arrives. He misunderstands his bride's kindness to the boy, and leaves her, in spite of the pleading of all the guests. The unhappy boy tries to console the bride, but she turns from him and goes into the castle. As evening falls the boy who so unwittingly caused the tragedy retraces his steps alone through the woods.

The London Ballet was one of the first small companies to raise the flag of ballet in the early days of the war after the theatre shutdown of 1939. Andrée Howard's tender choreography became a memorial of that event. It showed her preference for literary subjects – *Lady into Fox* and *The Sailor's Return* were likewise based on stories – as well as her mastery of the mood form. The choreography of *La Fête Etrange* evoked the adoles-

133

cent wonder of *Le Grand Meaulnes* with a quite extraordinary intensity, aided by Fedorovitch's wintry, pale backcloth and the sweet melancholy of Fauré's songs and piano music. Bride, bridegroom and country boy are linked in tragic conflict never directly expressed by any of them, but ending in solitary grief for all three, having been visible as a whole only to the audience.

WALTER GORE (1910–79)

One of the first male dancers to make a reputation at Marie Rambert's Ballet Club and one of the best British character dancers of his day (he created the Rake in de Valois' *The Rake's Progress*), Gore received an early training at the Italia Conti School plus some encouragement from Massine, but owed most of his training as dancer and as choreographer to Rambert. His ballets fall into three main categories: strongly dramatic works like *The Night and Silence*; light comedy ballets like *Street Games*; and ballets of mood. Although the development of his style suffered from working for too many companies for too short a time, Gore was a prolific and original choreographer, too little appreciated in the last decade of his life by British ballet. Some of his finest creations were made to celebrate and display the exceptional gifts of his wife, the dramatic ballerina, Paula Hinton. In such pieces as *Antonia* (1948), *Night and Silence* (1958), *Eaters of Darkness* (1958), *Sweet Dancer* (1964), Gore's vivid theatrical sense, and Hinton's expressive powers were to create works of sure impact. In his last ballets – *Embers of Glencoe* for the Scottish Ballet, *Dance Pictures* for London Festival Ballet – Gore's talents were still sharply present. It was British ballet's tragedy, quite as much as Gore's, that he should have been so little used at a time when his abilities were sorely needed.

Street Games

Ballet in one act. Libretto and choreography: Gore. Music: Jacques Ibert. Scenery and costumes: Ronald Wilson. First performed by New Ballet Company, Wimbledon Theatre, London, 11 November 1952.

Scene: A wharfside stretch of ground near Blackfriars Bridge, London. To the left a stylized house with a window; to the right a dark wall. The dancers, as children, prepare to play games. First comes hopscotch for the girls followed by rugger for the boys, skipping for the girls and *pas de deux* for screen-struck lovers who have just left a cinema. The boys search for a lost ball, which a girl hides. And so the games continue with statues,

134

dressing-up and mock battles linked by the progress of the lovers.

Although *Street Games* is at least one game too long it illustrates very well the twists of humour and wry observation which Gore habitually introduced to his comedy ballets, so that humour is sometimes never far from tears. He was above all an inventor of situations and a commentator on the human state. This ballet entered the repertory of Western Theatre Ballet, with designs by André François, soon after that company was formed and owes its place in the English repertory largely to their loving performances.

JACK CARTER (b. 1923)

Jack Carter's experience as dancer and choreographer has been gained outside Britain as much as with British companies. He danced with the Ballet Guild in 1946, then with Original Ballets Russes, Ballet Rambert (creating a number of excellent works for Ballet Workshop), and Festival Ballet, where he was resident choreographer. Much of his experience was gained in Holland where he worked from 1954–7 with the Ballet der Lage Landen, and also in Sweden. His ballets like *Past Recalled* (originally named *Ouverture*, to a Proustian theme), *Agrionia*, *The Witch Boy* and *Cage of God* are strong in atmosphere and tell their stories through well-drawn characters which indicate a marked narrative ability in their creator.

The Witch Boy

Ballet in one act and three scenes. Libretto and choreography: Jack Carter. Music: Leonard Salzedo. Scenery and costumes: Norman McDowell. First performed by Ballet der Lage Landen, Amsterdam, 24 May 1956. First performed by London's Festival Ballet, Opera House, Manchester, 27 November 1957.

A ballet on the American ballad of Barbara Allen.

Scene 1: The general store. Barbara Allen, repelled by the unwelcome advances of the Preacher, flees to the mountains.

Scene 2: On the mountain side. Barbara Allen meets the Witch Boy, child of the Conjurman. They fall in love.

Scene 3: Saturday night at the general store. Barbara Allen brings the Witch Boy back to the village where they join in the dancing. The Preacher turns the people against the Witch Boy. Accused of witchcraft he is beaten up, then lynched. As his body hangs from the rope the Conjurman appears, and the Witch Boy is reborn.

135

It is hard to judge Carter properly beside his English contemporaries because so much of his work is scattered through theatres in Europe and South America. This ballet illustrates his sense of theatre and place in the tradition of English dramatic choreography.

JOHN CRANKO (1927–73)

As a young dance student in South Africa, where he was born, John Cranko had started to make choreography. By the time he reached London in 1946, Cranko had produced a handful of apprentice works, and when he joined the Sadler's Wells Theatre Ballet in that year it was evident that his gifts were ideally suited to the needs of the newly-formed company which was to be a cradle and nursery for interpretative and creative talent. Within four years Cranko was named resident choreographer of the troupe, and he made some of his finest early ballets for the Wells dancers: *Beauty and the Beast* (1949); *Pineapple Poll* (1951) and *Harlequin in April* (1951).

In 1950, Cranko was asked to create a ballet for New York City Ballet, then visiting Covent Garden, and he produced *The Witch* to the Ravel G major piano concerto, and during the rest of the 1950s Cranko created works for both the Covent Garden and Sadler's Wells branches of the Royal Ballet: notably *Antigone* (1959), *Bonne Bouche* (1952) for Covent Garden and *The Lady and the Fool* (1954) for the Wells.

In 1957 he choreographed his first full-length ballet, *The Prince of the Pagodas* for Svetlana Beriosova and David Blair at Covent Garden, a work further distinguished by its score commissioned from Benjamin Britten. But Cranko's bubbling energies needed greater opportunities than those offered by the Royal Ballet organization. He produced two reviews, *Cranks* (1955) and *New Cranks* (1960), made two ballets for the Rambert company, *La Belle Hélène* for the Paris Opéra Ballet and the Prokofiev *Romeo and Juliet* for the Ballet of La Scala, Milan. He also directed the Britten opera, *A Midsummer Night's Dream*, at Aldeburgh in 1960, and in that same year went to Stuttgart to restage his *Prince of the Pagodas*. This was to prove the turning point in his career. Stuttgart asked Cranko to assume the directorship of its company in 1961, and from that moment on Cranko was to find the ideal outlet for his energies; moulding a company, a school and a repertory, that were to bring the Stuttgart Ballet vast international acclaim. His example was to serve as an inspiration to other Germany companies, as to the German public, who took the Stuttgart Ballet to its heart. With Marcia Haydée as his prima ballerina, with Ray Barra, and then Richard Cragun and Egon Madsen as his principal men,

136

with Birgit Keil as a young native-born ballerina, Cranko's company was loved wherever it played. For his company Cranko continued to produce the full-length ballets which revealed Haydée as a superlative dramatic/lyric artist – *Romeo and Juliet* (1963), *Onegin* (1965), *Carmen* (1970) and the hilarious *Taming of the Shrew* (1969), in which Haydée and Cragun were the ideal Kate and Petruchio. He also made staging of the classics, which he felt so necessary for the development of his company, remounting *Swan Lake* and *The Nutcracker*, and acquiring Peter Wright's version of *Giselle*. Among his shorter ballets of the Stuttgart years such pieces as *Opus 1* and *Brouillards* are fine examples, and his *Initials RBME* (the initials of *R*ichard Cragun, *B*irgit Keil, *M*arcia Haydée and *E*gon Madsen) seems central to Cranko's personality, a declaration of the love and affection he had for his dancers, which they so warmly and totally reciprocated.

Cranko died on an aeroplane bringing his company from a triumphant season in New York: but his great talent, his great humanity, his humour and the love he inspired in everyone who knew him, are part of the fabric of the Stuttgart Ballet still, and they continue to give the company a special lustre and appeal.

Beauty and the Beast

Ballet in one act. Choreography: Cranko. Music: Maurice Ravel (Ma Mère l'Oie). *Scenery and costumes: Margaret Kaye. First performed by the Sadler's Wells Theatre Ballet at Sadler's Wells Theatre with Patricia Miller and David Poole on 20 December 1949. Revived for Northern Ballet Theatre, with set by Michael Holt and costumes by Peter Farmer, in Manchester, May 1977.*

Beauty and the Beast is an extended *pas de deux* set to four of the five fairy-tale evocations which make up Ravel's *Mother Goose Suite* for piano duet. The scene is the enchanted forest which is the Beast's domain. Here we see him reclining, his face horrible, his body shaken by weeping. When a beautiful girl wanders into the forest, the Beast hides lest he frighten her, although he wishes to greet her. The girl wanders deeper into the forest and is lost; she dances to keep up her spirits, then becomes exhausted and sleeps. When she awakens, she decides to eat some fruit she sees on a tree, but it is the Beast holding it with upraised arm. She faints with horror and the Beast carries her to rest on a bank. When she regains her senses she is again terrified by him. She tries to flee but the trees bar her way. The Beast offers her a flower, which she rejects, and the Beast falls to the ground and weeps. The way is clear for the girl to escape, but now she is seized with compassion for the Beast. When she reaches down to touch his face, a transformation takes place. He is revealed as a handsome young man. Enraptured, the girl dances happily in his arms, and as the music ends the lovers are seen united.

This short, admirably crafted duet showed Cranko dealing, early in his career, with a favourite theme of his work: the nature of love and the deceptiveness of appearance. Historically, it confirmed also his arrival as a significant choreographer. Showing early promise with the University of Cape Town School of Ballet under the direction of Dulcie Howes – for whom he created his first ballet on Stravinsky's *A Soldier's Tale* in 1942 – Cranko was offered further opportunities in Britain in 1946–7 by the Royal Academy of Dancing's Production Club. Initiated by Ursula Moreton, this was the first post-war attempt to organize for aspirant choreographers the kind of regular provision described in Chapter Eight. For the Production Club, Cranko created *Children's Corner* (m. Debussy, déc. Eberstein) in November 1947, taken into the repertory of the Sadler's Wells Theatre Ballet five months later. With the Theatre Ballet under Peggy van Praagh, Cranko developed his craft. *Beauty and the Beast* illustrates four of his finest characteristics: his invention of original, evocative movements based on the classical technique, his strong sense of atmosphere and place, his ability to develop character out of the qualities of his dancers, and his sympathetic use of music.

Pineapple Poll

Ballet in three scenes. Plot freely adapted by John Cranko from 'The Bumboat Woman's Story' by W. S. Gilbert. Music from the operas of Arthur Sullivan, chosen and arranged by Charles Mackerras. Scenery and costumes: Osbert Lancaster. First performed by the Sadler's Wells Theatre Ballet at Sadler's Wells Theatre, 13 March 1951.

Scene 1: Portsmouth. Sailors, with their sweethearts and wives, are gathered outside an inn on the quayside. Poll, the 'bumboat woman' enters, with a basket of favours and trinkets which she sells to the tars and their womenfolk. Jasper, pot boy at the inn, expresses his love for her but she rejects him. Then appears Captain Belaye, commander of HMS *Hot Cross Bun,* of such devastating good looks and charm that every woman collapses on seeing him, not least Poll. He is waiting the arrival of his fiancée Blanche, chaperoned by her garrulous aunt Mrs Dimple.

Scene 2: The quayside. Poll enters, gazing with helpless passion at Captain Belaye's ship. She disguises herself as a midshipman and goes aboard; other members of the crew appear, faces hidden by straw hats,

138

walking with a certain deliberation. Jasper comes in search of Poll, but finds only her discarded clothes and mourns her, believing her drowned.

Scene 3: On board HMS *Hot Cross Bun*. The crew, a somewhat mimsy bunch, obey Belaye's orders as best they can, with Poll, moon-eyed with unrequited love, tending to faint at Belaye's feet. The firing of the ship's cannon reduces the crew to jelly but Belaye is awaiting the arrival of his beloved whom he is to marry that day. When Blanche and her aunt arrive, the crew tear off their disguises as jolly jack tars, and stand revealed as the sweethearts and wives of the first scene. Belaye is aghast, but at this moment the real crew angrily return with Jasper, and mutiny is in the air, until Blanche and Mrs Dimple persuade the men to forgive their womenfolk. Matters seem to take a turn for the worse when Belaye reappears in even more splendid rig as an admiral, but Poll's affections are diverted back to Jasper when he is given Belaye's discarded captain's uniform. The ballet ends in a joyous dance with the apotheosis of Mrs Dimple as Britannia.

Poll is a comic masterpiece. Cranko's unflagging gift for humorous writing in which the very best of his talent was engaged, never seemed fresher than in this irresistible ballet. The jokes are effortlessly part of the dance fabric – witness Mrs Dimple's inability to hold both a stole and a parasol at the same time, or Belaye's splendid solo based upon the sailor's hornpipe, or the antics of the supposed crew in the third scene – while the pace and timing of each incident are masterly. David Blair created a supremely debonair figure of Belaye, Elaine Fifield was an adorable Poll and David Poole made a most touching Jasper. After three decades *Poll* has lost none of its ebullience, or its charm. The ballet was staged by Cranko in Australia in 1954 for the Borovansky Ballet, entered the repertory of the National Ballet of Canada in 1959, and was restaged for the Australian Ballet in 1966.

The Lady and the Fool

Ballet in one act. Libretto by John Cranko. Music from the operas of Verdi, selected and arranged by Charles Mackerras. Scenery and costumes by Richard Beer. First performed by Sadler's Wells Theatre Ballet at the New Theatre, Oxford, 25 February 1954. Moondog: Kenneth MacMillan. Bootface: Johaar Mosaval. La Capricciosa: Patricia Miller.

PROLOGUE: A street. Two clowns, Moondog and Bootface, seek a night's rest on a bench outside a great house. Guests pass on their way to a ball, and one of them, the masked and beautiful La Capricciosa, is amused by the clowns' antics and asks them to come and entertain at the ball.

Scene: A ballroom overlooking Rome. The guests flirt as the host, Signor Midas, greets new arrivals – Capitano Adoncino and the Prince of Arragona. The two clowns entertain the assembly with a dance in which they quarrel over a rose, destroy it and then share the fallen petals. Then La Capricciosa dances with three suitors, who represent wealth, gallantry and rank; but as each seeks to remove the mask that hides her identity, another mask is found underneath. They leave, and alone, La Capricciosa takes off the final mask to reveal her solitary nature. Moondog has been watching her, and she now responds to the love which has suddenly overtaken them both. When the other guests discover this they first try to lead La Capricciosa away, then when she obstinately returns to Moondog, they reject her, and she leaves the ballroom with her beloved. Bootface, thinking himself forgotten, huddles in a corner, but the lovers return for him and all three leave the ballroom.

That *The Lady and the Fool* is novelettish is obvious; but in performance the emotional energy of the piece and Cranko's well-made dances have guaranteed the ballet a continuing theatrical life. Edited after its first performances with the Sadler's Wells Ballet, the piece was considerably tightened and the characterizations sharpened, and the theme of true love being preferable to power or riches or passing attraction – typified by the three partners in the *adagio* for La Capricciosa and her suitors – is universal enough to appeal to audiences wherever the ballet has been performed.

The Lady and the Fool can often teeter on the edge of sentimentality: it is a danger that interpreters have to guard against, but when they succeed the piece continues to hold the stage by its emotional drive and the easy flow of Cranko's dances. The first Australian Ballet performance was on 14 November 1962, at Her Majesty's Theatre, Sydney.

Card Game

Ballet in 'three deals' (one act). Choreography: Cranko. Libretto adapted by Cranko from the original synopsis by Igor Stravinsky and M. Malaieff. Music: Stravinsky. Scenery and costumes: Dorothea Zippel. First performed by Württemberg State Ballet, Stuttgart, 22 January 1965.

FIRST DEAL: The pack of cards is shuffled, dancers passing across the stage behind huge cards. The first hand is revealed as two tens, two sevens and an intrusive Queen of Hearts. They are uneasy, and the Queen totters and poses disconsolately. The Joker appears from beneath the huge hand which features on the backdrop. He is anarchy itself, and he dismisses the Queen, turning the hand into a full house.

SECOND DEAL: A straight flush of hearts, from two to six, take the stage. Each dances a variation, and the Joker is unable to infiltrate their secure formations. They drive him away, strong in their unity.

THIRD DEAL: The Ace, King, Jack and Ten of Spades are aghast to find that their fifth member is a miserable two of diamonds (a role for a female dancer) who is ruining their chance of winning. The Joker appears, crowned and wearing a tutu, as the necessary Queen. He leads the Royal Flush across the stage, and joins in a final mêlée, before the pack is shuffled, and he awaits the next deal.

Stravinsky produced the score to *Card Game* in 1935, in response to a commission from George Balanchine and Lincoln Kirstein who were planning a Stravinsky Festival for their American Ballet Company. Stravinsky, then living in Paris, was given complete freedom as to theme, and produced *Jeu de Cartes*, which was staged by the American Ballet at the Metropolitan Opera House, New York, in 1937. Cranko simplified the original libretto when he mounted the ballet in Stuttgart and produced what is, in essence, a comic ballet exploring the idea of a winning hand at poker. In the central movement, the straight flush in hearts is given to five male dancers, each having a demanding variation; the outer movements are rather more frenetic. Guiding the mayhem is the Joker, a role whose comic possibilities have been notably revealed by Niels Kehlet with the Royal Danish Ballet, Egon Madsen for the Stuttgart Ballet and Stephen Jefferies for the Sadler's Wells Royal Ballet.

Onegin

Ballet in three acts. Choreography: Cranko. Libretto: John Cranko after Pushkin. Music: Tchaikovsky; selected and arranged by Kurt-Heinz Stolze. Design: Jurgen Rose. First performed by the Wurttemberg State Ballet, Stuttgart, 13 April 1965. Marcia Haydée: Tatiana. Ray Barra: Onegin. Ana Cardus: Olga, Egon Madsen: Lensky.

ACT I, *Scene 1*: Mme Larina's garden. Mme Larina, Olga and the nurse are sewing dresses and gossiping about Tatiana's forthcoming birthday party. Mme Larina remembers her own lost youth and beauty. Girls arrive and play games, seeking to learn the future by gazing in a looking glass. Lensky, a young poet engaged to Olga, arrives with his friend, Onegin, who has left St Petersburg because of boredom. Tatiana, a highly romantic girl, falls in love with this handsome stranger; Onegin considers her only to be a coltish country girl who reads too many romantic novels.

Scene 2: Tatiana's bedroom. Tatiana writes a letter to Onegin telling

141

him of her love; in her imagination he appears to her and dances passionately with her.

ACT II, *Scene 1*: Tatiana's birthday party. Provincial society is enjoying the party, but Tatiana's eyes seek out Onegin. He gives her the torn pieces of her letter to him, and he is further irritated by her distress at this action. Prince Gremin, a distant relation of Tatiana's, who is in love with her, pays court to Tatiana, but she hardly notices him. Onegin, bored, starts to flirt with Olga, seeking to tease Lensky. But Lensky takes the action as an insult, and challenges Onegin to a duel.

Scene 2: The duel. Tatiana and Olga try to persuade Lensky to pardon Onegin, but Lensky has been deeply hurt by his friend's behaviour and by Olga's light-mindedness. He insists upon fighting, and is killed. Onegin is horrified, and for the first time his emotions are touched. Tatiana realizes that he is entirely self-centred.

ACT III, *Scene 1*: A ball in Prince Gremin's palace. Years later Onegin returns to Petersburg after having travelled the world in an attempt to escape from the futility he senses within himself. He arrives at a ball given by his friend Prince Gremin, and discovers that Gremin's wife is Tatiana, now an elegant and beautiful woman. He realizes the great loss he suffered in rejecting Tatiana's love years before, and determines to have an interview with her.

Scene 2: Tatiana's boudoir. Tatiana is reading a letter from Onegin in which he declares his love for her. Onegin arrives, and eagerly demands to know if she loves him. Tatiana rejects him and he leaves.

Cranko's *Onegin* is a tribute to the extreme emotional richness of Pushkin's poem, to Tchaikovsky's operatic version of it – albeit Cranko's score is arranged by Stolze from other Tchaikovsky music – and also to the superb lyric/dramatic gifts of his Muse, Marcia Haydée. In four full-length ballets – *Romeo and Juliet*, *Taming of the Shrew*, *Onegin* and *Carmen* – Cranko produced four different and highly theatrical roles for this magnificent ballerina, whose career was so intimately linked with the development of the Stuttgart Ballet and with Cranko's choreographic achievements. *Onegin* is a most skilled realization of the Pushkin drama, losing nothing in intensity for all that it features big danced set-pieces in each act. Cranko maintains an intimacy in dealing with Tatiana's girlish emotions which somehow preserves their youthful bloom; in the last act when Tatiana has become a beautiful and elegant women, the reversal of Onegin's earlier rejection of her, is still managed in a closely focused scene. The choreography, indeed, offers a vivid contrast of *pas de deux* – the final duet between Onegin and Tatiana is one of Cranko's finest creations – with larger set pieces which make excellent use of social dance ideas in the parties which feature in each act.

The Taming of the Shrew

Ballet in two acts, after Shakespeare. Libretto and choreography: Cranko. Music: Kurt-Heinz Stolze, after Scarlatti. Scenery and costumes: Elisabeth Dalton. First performed by Württemberg State Ballet, Stuttgart, 16 March 1969. First staged by the Royal Ballet at Covent Garden, 16 February 1977.

ACT I, *Scene 1*: Outside Baptista's house. Three suitors (the coxcomb Hortensio, the silly student Lucentio and the old roué Gremio) arrive to serenade Baptista's pretty, younger daughter Bianca. Her older sister Katherina interrupts the idyllic scene. Baptista declares that Bianca shall not marry until Kate is wed. The rumpus awakens a crowd of neighbours whom Kate sends packing.

Scene 2: A tavern. The three thwarted suitors nurse their battle scars from this affray. Petruchio, a gentleman of more generosity than means, arrives tipsy and is stripped of his last penny by two ladies of the streets. The others offer to introduce him to an heiress. To their delight, he accepts.

Scene 3: Baptista's house. Petruchio arrives and asks for Kate's hand. After a stormy courtship she agrees. Meanwhile Bianca's suitors, in disguise, press their claims under pretence of giving a music lesson. She favours Lucentio.

Scene 4: A street. Neighbours on their way to Kate's wedding find the matter a huge joke. Bianca's suitors gleefully join them.

Scene 5: Baptista's house. Petruchio arrives late and behaves outrageously at the wedding. After the ceremony he carries off the bride without waiting for the feast.

ACT II, *Scene 1*: A country road. The newlyweds travel through a storm towards Petruchio's house.

Scene 2: Petruchio's kitchen. Kate arrives hungry and soaked through. Petruchio prevents her from eating under the pretext that the food is not good enough. She refuses to go to bed with him and spends a hard, cold night on the kitchen floor.

Scene 3: A carnival. Lucentio, bribing the two ladies of the streets to wear cloaks and masks like Bianca's, tricks his two rivals into marrying them.

Scene 4: Petruchio's kitchen. Still cold and starving, Kate is further provoked by Petruchio. Eventually she capitulates and they admit that they love each other.

Scene 5: A country road. Travelling to Bianca's wedding, Petruchio indulges in some more whims but Kate has learnt how to humour him.

Scene 6: Bianca's wedding. Bianca, like the wives of Gremio and Hortensio, treats her husband disdainfully, but Kate shows them how a wife is expected to behave. Left alone, she and Petruchio revel in their new-found love.

John Cranko loved to make people laugh with his ballets. From his early *Children's Corner*, his very first choreography in London in 1946, through such works as *Pineapple Poll, Bonne Bouche*, and his version of *Sweeney Todd*, he delighted in delighting us with eccentrics, zany caperings and all the myriad amustments his fertile wit could conceive. It is fiendishly hard to make jokes in ballet which survive beyond a first viewing; at his best Cranko rooted his comedy firmly in his characters – Captain Belaye a fine example – and then the fun is durable.

In *The Taming of the Shrew*, Cranko's comedy sense triumphs over certain obstacles: a fragmented score which twitches and pecks at Scarlatti sonatas like a maddened canary; an elision of Shakespeare's play which is speedy if not particularly sensitive in scissoring out incident. But the piece works very well because of the helter-skelter vivacity of Cranko's comic invention: the story swings along at tremendous pace; the characters are always beguiling. His method is to set the central Kate/Petruchio relationship against two complementary views of love: the sincerity of Lucentio and Bianca and the wild antics of Gremio and Hortensio with the whores. The Kate/Petruchio relationship shares elements of the other two views, from broad farce to real passion, and Cranko's skill lies in showing us at the end how they may be reconciled in a happy marriage. In the process he and his characters have a very jolly time, and so do we. One cannot pretend that *Shrew* is a completely satisfying ballet; its incidents are sometimes mere padding and there is a good deal of scampering by the supporting cast. But Cranko's ability to suggest the variety of love, in its most outrageous as well as its sweetest manifestations, gives the ballet a true and touching heart. The work was created for Marcia Haydée and Richard Cragun: their performance with the Stuttgart Ballet, the play between the characters – Haydée hurling blows at Cragun, Cragun pulling Kate unceremoniously to the ground; both artists battling and loving and playing tricks – shows a dance partnership unrivalled in our time in sensitivity of rapport, and completeness of artistry.

While preserving the essentials of Shakespeare's plot, Cranko's ballet departs from it in most of its details, although his inventions (the weddings of Gremio and Hortensio, for instance) often have a decidedly Shakespearean flavour. Apart from its lively humour (rare in a full-evening ballet),

144

the work is notable for its many spirited characterizations and above all for the two leading roles, created by Marcia Haydée and Richard Cragun. These are both virtuoso parts, with many leaps, high lifts in the *adagios* and such rare steps for the man as triple *tours en l'air* performed with nonchalant perfection. Even more important is the fact that they seem credible characters, whose genuine love for each other (visible even beneath the sparring of their early scenes together) gives richness and humanity to the ballet.

Brouillards

Choreography: John Cranko. Music: Claude Debussy; piano preludes. First performed by the Stuttgart Ballet, 8 March 1970. First given by the Sadler's Wells Royal Ballet, 3 May 1978.

> Mist, snow, heather and sails are passing pictures in Debussy's music; the mist dissolves, the snow melts, the heather blooms and the sails flutter, leaving behind no more than sadness and memories of transient beauty. Each day disappears into the past like all human endeavour.
>
> John Cranko

Set against plain black curtains, his dancers wearing simple white leotards, Cranko brings on his ensemble of eighteen dancers to *Brouillards*, the first of the nine piano preludes (performed by a pianist in the orchestra pit) which comprise the musical text for this sensitive, simple-seeming but potent work. The dancers enter in a chain which breaks up into wisps and curls of activity. Then in *La Puerta del Vino* a very Spanish lady is courted by three men; *Voiles* is a duet for a man and woman; *General Lavine-Eccentric* is a trio for three boys, doll-like figures who caper, collapse and display a typically Crankoesque muscular humour, and *Bruyères* is an incident in which a young man disports himself while trying to impress a girl on a park bench. At the end she walks off, disregarding him totally. *Les Fées sont d'exquises danseuses* offers a pair of long-limbed girls dancing, suddenly bumping into each other, and momentarily seized with fatigue; *Feuilles Mortes* is an intense and passionate interlude for a man and a woman; *Homage à S. Pickwick* hymns the indomitable Englishman with bowler hat and rolled umbrella (which provides his gravestone) and the trio of *Des pas sur la neige* is a minuscule but potent drama of a woman torn between two men. Finally *Brouillards* is played again and the cast curl and curve over the stage. For all its brevity and brief incidents, *Brouillards* says much about Cranko's gifts: his sensitivity to human emotion, his fluent dance-making, his humour; it is a small but enduring work.

145

KENNETH MACMILLAN (b. 1929)

Born in Dunfermline, Kenneth MacMillan was trained at the Royal Ballet School, and graduated from there to the Sadler's Well Theatre Ballet on its formation. For this company he danced many leading roles, and then moved to the Covent Garden company in 1948. He returned to the Wells company in 1952, and made his apprentice ballets – *Laiderette* and *Somnambulism* – for the Wells Choreographic Group. Three years later he staged his first professional ballet, *Danses Concertantes*, whose dazzling, spikily witty inventions revealed that an extraordinary new choreographic talent had been found. That same year he made his first dramatic work – *House of Birds* – a version of a Grimm fairy tale, following this in the next year with his first work for the Covent Garden company: *Noctambules*. This was a dramatic work, concerned with a magician in a back-street theatre who hypnotizes his audience so that they reveal their innermost feelings and desires: a Faded Beauty recaptures her youthful loveliness, a Soldier revels in slaughter, an innocent girl is loved by a rich young man, and at the end the Magician is trapped in his own bizarre fancies. All three ballets indicated an original talent, blessed with fluency of invention, and a refreshingly different – though entirely classical – choreographic manner. All three ballets were also marked by an excellence of their design by Nicholas Georgiadis, introducing a collaboration which still continues.

In these works MacMillan was concerned to consolidate his knowledge of his craft (he described *Noctambules* as a dramatized version of the last act of *The Sleeping Beauty*). He returned to working for the Sadler's Wells Theatre Ballet with two more ballets – the dramatic *The Burrow* (1958) which portrayed a group of people hiding from oppressors and the light-hearted *Solitaire* (1956) 'a kind of a game for one'. There followed another work for the Royal Ballet at Covent Garden, a version of Stravinsky's *Agon* (1958) which extended his earliest faceted dance style in a study of a house of pleasure; it was a mysterious and beautiful piece, but it failed to find much favour with the public at the time. He also made two ballets for American Ballet Theater in this year: *Winter's Eve*, a story of a blind girl, and *Journey*, which treated the theme of death with considerable success. A major change in his style was announced with *Le Baiser de la Fée*, for Covent Garden in 1960. Here, working with three lyrical dancers – Lynn Seymour (who was to become the Muse for many of his greatest ballets thereafter), Svetlana Beriosova and Donald MacLeary – his choreographic manner became softer and more expansive. The ballet was notable for the skill with which MacMillan overcame the problems of staging what has

146

always been considered a difficult work to realize, and also for the acutely sensitive way in which the choreography echoed Stravinsky's homage to Tchaikovsky by offering a parallel homage to Petipa – particularly in the Mill Scene for Seymour and MacLeary. The ballet was further distinguished by Kenneth Rowell's décor, which arguably ranks as the most beautiful and poetic ballet designs seen at Covent Garden since the war.

Baiser was followed in December 1960 by MacMillan's most assured and compelling dramatic work, *The Invitation* (q.v.), and in the following September he made a piece of pure dancing: *Diversion*. With *Rite of Spring* in May 1962 (q.v.) he showed a new mastery in manoeuvring large masses of dancers, and his next ballet, staged for the Stuttgart Ballet, was *Las Hermanas* (q.v.). Another plotless work – and one of his finest – came in 1963, when *Symphony* (to Shostakovich's first symphony) was staged at Covent Garden. It was a beautiful piece, one of his most personal statements on what he felt about dancing, having a profusion of choreographic invention. He returned to working with the Royal Ballet's Touring Section in January 1964, making a pop-art version of Milhaud's *La Création du Monde*, and for the Shakespeare quatercentenary celebration in June of that year he produced *Images of Love*, a series of dance incidents, each inspired by a quotation from Shakespeare. The work was uneven, but in two sections for Lynn Seymour (with Gable and Nureyev) he indicated a new plasticity of manner that was extremely impressive, and the ballet also provides an interesting hint of his reaction to a written text, which was to be extended in his *Romeo and Juliet* (q.v.) the following year. In June 1965 he created a work that he had long been contemplating, a ballet that has been recognized as one of his finest, *The Song of the Earth* (q.v.). It was first staged in Stuttgart, and was enhanced there – as it was at its later staging for the Royal Ballet – by the presence of Marcia Haydée as the woman.

In 1966 MacMillan was released for three years by the Royal Ballet to take up the post of Director of the Ballet of the Deutsche Oper, West Berlin – where he was joined by Lynn Seymour as ballerina, and where he staged a variety of works, many designed to help shape and train his company: works like *Valses Nobles* and *Concerto* (1966), and *Olympiade* (1968) were all basically exercises in setting a somewhat raw company dancing with clarity and precision. While in Berlin he also created two fine dramatic ballets: *Anastasia* in 1967 for Lynn Seymour, and *Cain and Abel* (1968). He also mounted two classic stagings: a tremendously opulent *The Sleeping Beauty* (which preserved all the Petipa choreography but aimed at a more sensitive and logical production) in 1968, and a *Swan Lake* in 1969, his last gift to the company before returning to London preparatory to taking up the directorship of the Royal Ballet in 1970.

During the next seven years MacMillan maintained an exceptional flow of new ballets in addition to his time-consuming duties as director of a major company. Eventually, in 1977, he was impelled by the need to devote all his energies to creativity, to give up the administrative post of Director of the Royal Ballet, remaining since then as chief choreographer. During these years, though, MacMillan produced three major full-evening ballets – *Anastasia* (1971), *Manon* (1974), *Mayerling* (1978), and a series of works which displayed the varied facets of his company's talents: *Rituals* (1975), *Elite Syncopations* (1974), *Four Seasons* (1975), *Triad* (1973), *The Seven Deadly Sins* (1973), *La Fin du Jour* (1979), and several works for the Sadler's Wells Royal Ballet: *The Poltroon* (1972) *6.6.78* (1978) and *Playground* (1979) as well as such brief pieces as *Sideshow* for Seymour/Nureyev and *Pavane* for Sibley/Dowell (1973), and supervising the staging of *The Sleeping Beauty* (1973). Further, he produced two major creations for the Stuttgart Ballet, the tremendous setting of Fauré's *Requiem* in memory of John Cranko (1976), and the darkly erotic *My Brother, My Sisters* (1978).

MacMillan's whole creative approach is concerned with the revelation of feeling through movement. He can, because he is a master of his craft, produce brilliantly effective neo-classic choreography, as *The Four Seasons* testifies. He can also make startling extensions of the academic dance, inspired by Japanese themes in *Rituals*, or by the imagery of the sporting life of the *beau monde* of the 1930s in *La Fin du Jour*. In *Elite Syncopations* he produced a ragtime frolic which set his Covent Garden cast dancing with ebullience and wit, and in the two major pieces made for Stuttgart – *Requiem* and *My Brother, My Sisters* – MacMillan could provide, in the first, a work of greatest sensitivity in the face of grief and death, and in the second, a macabre and thrilling exposition of sexual tension within a family. For MacMillan is supremely the poet of passion, of dark unhappy desires and frustrations and self-deceits. He can show us the gnawing appetites and needs, the loneliness and the sexual drive, that society most usually masks behind superficial good manners. MacMillan exposes it in burningly clear movement, acting as a psychoanalyst to his characters, forcing them inexorably into dramatic situations in which the truth of their feelings and sorrows must burst forth in expressive dance.

His *Romeo and Juliet* is as much a ballet about passion as *The Invitation*.

Marilyn Rowe and Joseph Janusaitis in the Australian Ballet's production of *Onegin*

(*above*) *Manon*, with Natalia Makarova and Anthony Dowell. (*below*) Lynn Seymour as Natalya and Derek Rancher as Rakitin in *A Month in the Country*

Rite of Spring showed a primitive community obsessed by the sexual urgency of a tribal ritual which must placate its divinities and guarantee the earth's fruitfulness by the Virgin's first orgasm, which is her death and the earth's life. In his two historical ballets, *Anastasia* and *Mayerling*, he was concerned with extending the range of the three-act ballet to encompass real events rather than merely literary sources or fairy tale, and in *Mayerling* he combined this with a piercing and detailed study of a man's descent into despair and suicidal depression. But one overriding fact must be stated: MacMillan's only means of communicating his view of the world is movement, and movement based upon the classical tradition in which he grew up. This provides him with an inbuilt formal discipline which shapes, canalizes and guides his dance imagination. All his ballets are classical, in that they develop and extend the range and possibilities of the academic *danse d'école*, no matter how far-ranging or extreme may seem their language, as in *Rite of Spring*, or *Rituals*. In this lies the strength of MacMillan's craft, and the necessary foundation for his adventurous and highly poetic ballets.

Danses Concertantes

Ballet in one act. Choreography: MacMillan. Music: Stravinsky. Décor: Nicholas Georgiadis. First performed by Sadler's Wells Theatre Ballet, Sadler's Wells Theatre, 18 January 1955, with Maryon Lane, Donald Britton and David Poole. Redesigned by Nicholas Georgiadis, 1979.

When the curtain fell after the first performance of *Danses Concertantes*, the excitement of the occasion must have been obvious to the whole audience. This first professional work by a young Royal Ballet dancer was an amazing piece, glittering with inventiveness, intensely personal in its expression. It seemed a kaleidoscope in which all the old, accepted dance ideas had been thoroughly shaken up by this new talent, to form fresh and intriguing patterns. Not many first ballets can retain their place in a repertory year after year, but whenever it has been revived, *Danses Concertantes*' interest seems to increase, for here are many of the qualities that have been so richly extended in MacMillan's later work. This cool view of a hothouse was full of unexpected allusions: dancers are as interesting sitting down on chairs as they are when working in class; fingers can make mysterious masks; dancers are like horsemen and gymnasts and movie sirens. It was an explosion of bright dance ideas that never lost sight of those fundamental truths of the classic tradition that had produced and educated MacMillan, and nothing he has created since has departed from this basic belief in the academic dance. This ballet lives because it perennially suits young dancers in a young company.

Solitaire

Ballet in one scene. Choreography: Kenneth MacMillan. Music: Malcolm Arnold; Eight English Dances. Design: Barry Kay. First performed by the Sadler's Wells Theatre Ballet, 7 June 1956.

The choreographer called this very early work 'a kind of a game for one' and its theme is that of a lonely girl who dreams of companions who seem called up from her imagining by the choreography. The texture of the ballet is light, by turns wistful or merry, and it was early evidence of MacMillan's gift for making dances that fixed a mood with charming sincerity. The role of the girl has never been better danced than by its creator Margaret Hill. For a recent revival by the Sadler's Wells Royal Ballet the ballet was redesigned by Barry Kay.

The Invitation

Ballet in one act. Choreography: MacMillan. Music: Matyas Seiber. Décor: Nicholas Georgiadis. First performed by Royal Ballet Touring Section, New Theatre, Oxford, 10 November 1960.

In a wealthy household in some warm climate at the turn of the century a house party has been arranged by a wealthy widow with three daughters. The two eldest girls are of marriageable age, and are carefully guarded from the world by their mother. The youngest girl plays with her boy cousin and their friends, who, with their parents, are guests at the house. She is revolted by the sly, sexual innuendoes of the other children, and is unable to understand the gentle, budding sexuality of her cousin's affection for her. At the afternoon reception we see the guests arrive, among them an unhappy husband and wife; when the guests go to watch the children at their dancing lesson, the husband manifests an interest in the girl which flatters her, though it angers the girl's mother.

That night, the guests are watching a group of acrobats who have come to entertain the house-party; as the guests disperse through the gardens, the husband and wife quarrel yet again, and the husband angrily leaves. The young boy, disturbed by his own feeling of urgently awakening sexuality, comes into the garden, and the wife, sensing his needs, seduces him. The girl, innocently intrigued by the husband, steals out of the house and seeks him out in the garden. He misinterprets her presence, and unable to resist her virginal beauty, savagely rapes her. Aghast at what he has done, he goes back to the house, where his wife, realizing what has happened, still finds strength and understanding to support him. The girl, shattered by her experience, returns distraught to the house, and her cousin endeavours to console her. She believes that his tender passion is exactly the same as the husband's brutality, and with fierce energy drives him from her; as the curtain falls she walks with frozen gaze and rigid gait away from all chance of future happiness.

The Invitation is a ballet about sex; from the moment the curtain rises and we see the young boy gazing at the naked female statue, the theme is plain. In setting his ballet in some unspecified warm climate at the turn of the century, MacMillan was able to use certain recognized social attitudes and conventions to underpin his dramatic structure. The ballet was inspired indirectly by two novels: Beatriz Guido's *The House of the Angel*, and Colette's *Le Blé en Herbe* – these provide, respectively, germs of the girl's and the boy's characters. But the extension of the incidents is entirely MacMillan's. He is concerned with the sexual needs of adolescence, the sexual greed of the husband, and the sexual frustration of the wife – whose seduction of the boy is her only answer to her husband's neglect. It is the particular quality of *The Invitation* that the characters seem to have a life that extends far beyond the stage action; we can sense both their past (notably the reason for the disintegration of the marriage between husband and wife) and their future, in which the boy will be unaffected by the night's events, while the girl will freeze into a spinsterhood as embittered as that of her governess. The hectic sexual air of the ballet becomes more and more intense as the action progresses: the acrobats impersonate two cocks in rivalry for a hen; the flashing trajectories of the guests in the night scene show men and women bent upon gratification – one of the men, rejected by a girl, makes a brief pass at a male acrobat. But lest this seem lurid and overemphatic, it should be stated that MacMillan's expressive choreography is remarkably sensitive and beautiful. In the dancing lesson, the man's increasing interest in the girl is suggested by the gradually wider arcs in which he lifts her; when he attacks her the physical act of rape is portrayed with such subtle symbolism that it is beautiful but never offensive. *The Invitation* is supremely a ballet in which glances and slight gestures play a vital role. At the afternoon reception we can see the moment when the husband is first aware of the girl and sizes up her youthful beauty; a moment later when the wife greets the young cousin the husband's jealousy is sharply stated as he interposes his body between them. At the dancing lesson the husband eyes the girl, and she, aware of his gaze, darts sudden, shy glances at him; when they start to dance the wife's embarrassment and her nervous excuses are tellingly shown. The young cousin's characteristic action at the start of the ballet when he tries to lay his head on the girl's breast, is a leitmotiv that returns when he essays the same gesture with the wife. *The Invitation* is compact with such small, revelatory detail: it is they which give such truth and intensity to the principal characters.

The original cast – Lynn Seymour as the Girl, Christopher Gable as her Cousin, Anne Heaton and Desmond Doyle as the Husband and Wife – were superb; in particular the ballet announced Lynn Seymour as one of the most beautifully expressive dramatic dancers of our time.

The Rite of Spring

Ballet in one act. Choreography: MacMillan. Music: Stravinsky. Décor: Sydney Nolan. First performed by Royal Ballet, Covent Garden, 3 May 1962.

The action of MacMillan's version is, in outline, very simple. The first tableau, *The Adoration of the Earth*, presents a tribe in a rocky setting; groups of adolescents, men and women, dance in a frenzy preparatory to the choosing of the maiden who is to be the central figure of their fertility rite.

For the second tableau, *The Sacrifice*, a backcloth featuring an enormous gold phallus shape is revealed, and the tribe are first seen sitting in a semi-circle round the edge of the stage. Six maidens move into the centre and one is chosen as the sacrificial figure. She is ritually daubed on the face by the Elders, and then she dances with the tribe, sometimes held aloft, sometimes moving among their prostrate bodies. Gradually her dance becomes more ecstatic and frenzied until she collapses dying on the ground; the tribe cluster round and her lifeless body is tossed high in the air as the curtain falls.

The first performance of *The Rite of Spring* by the Diaghilev Ballet in Paris on 29 May 1913 has passed into the annals of theatrical history as one of the most celebrated brawls in a theatre. The shock administered by Stravinsky's score to the decorous eardrums of *le tout Paris* and the originality of Nijinsky's choreographic conception, all produced howls of outrage that still echo down the years. The score is now recognized as one of the most influential masterpieces of this century's music – in it Stravinsky was inspired by 'the violent Russian spring' when the whole earth seems to crack open into life. He noted that he 'saw in imagination a solemn pagan ritual; wise elders, seated in a circle, watching a young girl dance herself to death. They were sacrificing her to propitiate the god of spring'. Diaghilev produced a second version, with choreography by Massine in 1920, and other choreographers – including Maurice Béjart – have also been attracted by the score, notable among them being Kenneth MacMillan, whose staging was made for the Royal Ballet.

MacMillan has noted, 'In *Rite* I wanted the movement to be primitive, but with a "primitiveness" of my own invention rather than an attempt at an imagined prehistory. It does not deal with any specific race, and I believe that the actions and feeling that are shown may still be observed in people today.'

In thus delocalizing the score MacMillan's choreography manages to dominate Stravinsky's massive creation so that the Russian flavour of the music does not obtrude through being unrealized. In the first section he presents an image of the tribe as a single entity through his use of blocks of dancers who move almost in unison; these people have no individuality, only a corporate existence at this crucial moment of their year. Their movement is frenzied; their desperate couplings, their arms thrust forward or up, the blind urgency, the almost animal intensity with which they move – faces and bodies hideously daubed – is extraordinarily communicative of primitive society. At the pause in the music that precedes the final crescendo which ends part one, the three Elders, lion-masked, move forward to lie flat on the ground at the very edge of the stage, preparatory to the choosing of the Virgin.

The second section finds the tribe sitting in a semi-circle awaiting the appearance of the six maidens from among whom the sacrificial victim will come. The Elders wait at the back as six girls, seemingly impelled by the music, move into the centre of this arena, and then one of them is singled out and collapses to the ground. From that moment she ceases to be a girl and becomes a tribal symbol. She is passed, prostrate, over a long column of males, she forms the central, hierarchic figure held high above the outstretched hands of the tribe, like an Egyptian goddess; she dances a solo among the prostrate figures of her people, and her movements become more and more excited. The tribe joins in agitated and eagerly anticipatory dances, and suddenly she collapses again in an orgasm that is her death and the renewed life of the earth for the tribe. They gather round the body and toss it exultantly up to the sky as the curtain falls. The ballet is compact of fierce imagery in which MacMillan has admirably suggested the urgency of the ritual and the girl's terror, submerged in a resolute acceptance of her fate. The choreographic manner was the freest and least classical that MacMillan had made to date, and yet it was possible to see in the shaping of the work and in much of the dance outlines a strong classically trained intelligence at work. But what distinguishes this version from any other is the intellectual approach of the choreographer to his score. The central role of the Virgin was first interpreted by Monica Mason, whose ability to invest her dancing with a superhuman grandeur and an outstanding muscular weight was wonderfully revealed in the role. Her performance has never been equalled for sheer power. Eyes gleaming with terror, driven seemingly by forces outside herself, she gave an unforgettably moving interpretation.

Las Hermanas

Ballet in one act. Choreography: MacMillan. Music: Frank Martin (Concerto for harpsichord and small orchestra). Décor: Nicholas Georgiadis. Based on Lorca's play, The House of Bernarda Alba. First performed by Stuttgart Ballet, 13 July 1963. Marcia Haydée: the Eldest Sister. Ray Barra: the Man. First performed Western Theatre Ballet, New Theatre, Cardiff, 22 June 1966. First performed by the Sadler's Wells Royal Ballet, 2 June 1971, and by the Australian Ballet at Sydney Opera House, 10 May 1979.

The curtain rises in silence to reveal a claustrophobic white and grey interior of a house; the mother limps down the staircase, her walking stick thumping out each step. Her five daughters sit in rocking chairs, aimless, despondent; they move towards the mother and sit in a line springing from the old woman's belly. Gradually the characters of three are revealed; the eldest is an agonized spinster; the middle sister (hunch-backed in Lorca's play) is envious and embittered; the youngest, still a girl, first comes to our attention when she tries on the bridal veil from a wedding dress draped over a dummy in the corner of the room. The eldest sister, for whom it is intended, puts it on next and the three other sisters dance with it; all the while we are made conscious through the taut and almost desperate dancing of the eldest sister that she is declining unhappily into spinsterhood. Now the mother brings on the prospective husband for the eldest – marriage must go by seniority – and we meet a man who reveals, under the stiff best suit, a brutal sensuality. The eldest sister goes out with him, leaving the others rocking and fanning themselves in their chairs as the light fades. The second scene takes place by night. The man returns, freed of his constricting coat, to an assignation with the eldest sister. He tosses gravel to her window, she comes down and they commence a *pas de deux* which is to reveal much of their characters: the man is coarsely sensual, the sister, at first frigid, is yet eager for love though she has to conquer

154

years of repression. Her clenched fists and tense arms indicate how great are her fears; just as it seems that she is warming to her lover, she realizes that the middle sister has been watching them from a balcony. Swiftly she kisses the man, shakes his hand formally and goes indoors. Almost at once the youngest sister rushes out to meet the man and they embark on a frankly sensual duet culminating in a sexual embrace. The middle sister again has been watching and she at once arouses the household, showing the eldest sister with relish just what her future husband is like. The elder sister eddies over the stage in agony of mind while the mother raises her stick and tries to strike the man, but the youngest girl snatches the stick from her. The mother flings the girl to the ground, and drives the man from the house, while the eldest sister expresses her suffering in a solo. The youngest girl rushes upstairs, the mother gathers her family of women about her, and the eldest sister takes one terrifying look out of the window at her lost freedom and happiness. The mother locks the door with a ferocious finality, and climbs the stairs in search of her youngest child. She pulls back the curtain at the stair head and reveals the swinging body of the youngest girl who has committed suicide. The curtain falls.

As with each of his dramatic ballets – from *The Burrow* up to the latest *Playground* (Edinburgh, 1979) – MacMillan is concerned with the inter-action of personalities, and the resolution (often the explosion) of tensions that bring about a final tragedy. His habit is to take a dramatic theme, and sometimes by changing and compressing it extensively, to extract what he feels is its emotional essence. In the brief, concentrated *Hermanas* he pre-sents a claustrophobic house of women where passions, desires and long-ings are firmly controlled by clearly defined social and sexual conventions. There are feline jealousies among the girls, and a terrible sense of frustra-tion in the personalities of the eldest sister and the embittered middle sister. Dominating and controlling is the watchful presence of the mother, a wardress/matriarch presented in rigid, menacing dance images. Each of the principals is sharply characterized: the eldest sister cuts tense, frus-trated arcs of movement with her arms, and when the man comes to court her she undergoes a curious blossoming. With the destruction of her hopes we witness the turning inward of her emotions – one last despairing run towards the window, and then isolation and total despair freezes her body. The man is depicted in equally powerful manner: the ape-like stance, the pungent sexuality, are brilliantly shown – MacMillan always contrives imagery that is entirely apposite and revealing: nothing could be more succinct than the chain of sisters, each sitting on the other's lap, springing

155

from the old mother's body; nothing could better suggest the sense of frustrated waiting than the row of girls rocking in their chairs as the ballet begins. *Hermanas* is tight in structure – MacMillan compresses the very detailed action with entire success into the brief space of the Martin Harpsichord Concerto – and the result is an excellently shaped work whose tensions never slacken.

Romeo and Juliet

Ballet in three acts after Shakespeare. Choreography: MacMillan. Music: Prokofiev. Décor: Georgiadis. First performed by Royal Ballet, Covent Garden, 9 February 1965.

ACT I, *Scene 1*: The market place. It is early morning; Romeo enters with Mercutio and Benvolio, and declares his love for Rosaline who is walking through the square. Gradually the town awakes, and among the market activity are three whores who dance playfully with the three young men. Tybalt, Capulet's nephew enters and provokes a quarrel with the Montague faction which develops into a street fight; Capulet and Montague enter with their wives and followers and a pitched fight ensues, with many slain, but the arrival of the Prince of Verona with his guards ends the slaughter. He orders the two families to live peaceably, and commands them to lay their swords in front of the pile of the slain.

Scene 2: Juliet's ante-room. Juliet runs in and plays with a doll while her nurse watches fondly. Her parents enter with Paris, who is destined to be Juliet's husband. He pays his respects to her, but as he leaves Juliet tries once more to play childishly with her doll, until her nurse shows her that her childhood is over and that she is a woman. A final pose shows Juliet standing with her hands on her breasts.

Scene 3: In front of the gates of the Capulet palace. Romeo and his two friends are amusing themselves as masked guests arrive for a ball at the Capulet's house. Romeo flirts with Rosaline, though the watchful Tybalt tries to drive him away. As the guests enter, Romeo and his friends, masked and carrying lutes, decide to run the danger of attending the ball, too, so that Romeo may see Rosaline yet again.

Scene 4: The ballroom. The guests are moving in a stately dance as Romeo and his companions arrive. Juliet enters, a shy child at her first ball, and dances with Paris. Suddenly, for an eternal second, Romeo and Juliet see each other. Juliet sits and plays a mandoline as six of her friends dance, but Romeo bursts among them and dances for Juliet. She dances again with Paris, but Romeo manages to dance with her too; Tybalt intervenes,

156

and as the guests leave Juliet pleads an indisposition so that she is alone in the ballroom when Romeo appears. He takes off his mask and reveals who he is, and they dance ecstatically together. Tybalt observes this and provokes a quarrel with Romeo but Capulet enters and makes Romeo welcome to the party.

Scene 5: Outside the Capulet house. The guests depart, and Tybalt follows Romeo, and would pursue him were he not restrained by Capulet.

Scene 6: The Capulet garden. Juliet appears on her balcony. A sudden noise in the garden tells her that Romeo is there, and she runs swiftly to him. They express their passion and love in a *pas de deux*.

ACT II, *Scene 1*: The market place. The market is bustling with activity; through it passes a wedding procession, but Romeo is caught up with thoughts of his new love. The Nurse enters, bringing a letter from Juliet, proposing a secret marriage; Romeo, delirious with joy, rushes out.

Scene 2: Friar Laurence's church. Friar Laurence enters and prays and then Romeo arrives; a moment later Juliet and her nurse enter, and the Friar unites the two while the nurse sobs.

Scene 3: The market place. The celebrations and bustle of the market are continuing as Romeo returns from his marriage. Tybalt endeavours to pick a quarrel with him, but Romeo, determined that the ancient strife between the two families shall cease with his marriage to Juliet, refuses to fight. Aghast at what he thinks is cowardice, Mercutio joins battle with Tybalt. Romeo begs him to stop, and Tybalt stabs Mercutio in the back: in his death agonies Mercutio still makes a gallant figure but as he collapses he curses both houses. Romeo, unable to restrain his anger, seizes his sword, fights Tybalt and kills him. Lady Capulet enters, frantic with grief at Tybalt's death; Romeo holds pleadingly to her skirt, but she rejects him and rocks the dead body of Tybalt in her arms.

ACT III, *Scene 1*: Juliet's bedroom. As dawn breaks, the lovers are in bed; Romeo tries to steal away, but Juliet rushes to him and seeks to delay his departure in a passionate embrace. But he must leave as sounds indicate that someone is stirring. The nurse enters, followed quickly by Juliet's parents and Paris. Their marriage must now take place; Juliet frantically rejects Paris, and her father driven to anger, orders her to marry the husband he has chosen and stalks out. Juliet sits for an agonized moment on her bed, then seizes a cloak and rushes to consult Friar Laurence.

Scene 2: Friar Laurence's chapel. Juliet begs for help from the Friar and he gives her a phial containing a drug that will produce a cataleptic trance when she swallows it; her parents will think her dead, and she can then be rescued from her tomb by Romeo. Friar Laurence says that he will ensure that Romeo is told the plan.

Scene 3: Juliet's bedroom. Juliet hides the phial under her pillow; when her parents enter she pleads once more not to be married to Paris, but then yields to their insistence. She dances with Paris moving like a ghost in his arms, and content that she will comply with their wishes, her parents leave with Paris. Juliet knows that she now must take the potion; she delays for a second, then swallows it; as the drug courses through her body she creeps to her bed and lies there. Her friends enter, ready to prepare her for her wedding; as they dance they are puzzled that Juliet should still sleep, and when they go to touch her they find her cold and apparently lifeless. The old nurse, bringing the wedding dress, is distraught with grief, and Juliet's parents, entering soon after, are heartbroken at the tragedy.

Scene 4: The Capulet family crypt. Juliet lies on a central bier while monks and the Capulet family pass in front of her, black-cloaked in mourning. Paris remains behind to bid farewell to her. Romeo, unaware of Juliet's stratagem, reveals himself, throwing off the black cloak he has worn so that he may see Juliet for the last time. He kills Paris, then lifts Juliet's body from the bier in an agony of grief. He dances briefly with it, then placing it back on the cold stone, he takes out a phial of poison, swallows it, and dies at her side. Now Juliet awakes from her sleep, and as she surveys the crypt she sees Paris's body, and then comes upon Romeo's corpse. She snatches up the dagger with which he has killed Paris, and stabs herself, stretching her arms out in a final embrace to Romeo.

MacMillan's Juliet *is* Lynn Seymour, in the same way that Fonteyn *is* Ondine and Chloe and every other role that Ashton has written for her. This identification with a character is one of the most fascinating aspects of the marriage between a choreographer and his chosen ballerina, in which the dancer's gifts are a challenge to the creator and are in turn challenged by his creation. For twenty-five years Ashton and Fonteyn worked in such a partnership; since 1958 (when he made *The Burrow*) MacMillan has been similarly exploring the qualities of Seymour as a glorious and highly dramatic dance instrument.

This production reflects her dramatic gifts, for Juliet is the machine that drives the ballet along; wilful, reacting with extraordinary passion against her world, she has the temperament to try to change her destiny. MacMillan sees the character as a 'positive' girl whose tragedy lies in her defiance of all the conventions of the society she lives in, and his concern is with the psychology of this central characterization.

158

In each of his major dramatic ballets – *The Invitation, Las Hermanas, Anastasia* come to mind – MacMillan has sought to explore the springs of behaviour, to catch those images of love and lust that are all-revealing of personality. (How right that the ballet in which he brought this Freudian approach first to Shakespeare should have been called *Images of Love*.) It is almost as if MacMillan becomes an analyst to his characters, forcing them to delve into their psyches and bring out their fantasies into the light of day – this was, in fact, the whole action of his early *Noctambules*, where the cast relived their dreams under the Hypnotist's spell. In MacMillan's version, *Romeo and Juliet* becomes as much a ballet about sex as *The Invitation*, and there are even parallels to be observed between Juliet and the Young Girl in that earlier work. Both are first seen on the brink of sexual awareness, rejecting their logical partner (Paris in *Romeo*, and young cousin in *The Invitation*) and succumbing to another and ultimately destructive lover – the Husband and Romeo. Juliet is shown first as a child; the crucial moment at the end of the second scene when she stands, hands on breasts, suddenly aware that she is now a woman, is the clue to the sudden expansion of her personality from that of a girl playing with her doll to that of a woman overwhelmed by her first great passion.

Juliet is self-willed; it is she who suggests and engineers the marriage; she is a personality at odds with her surroundings, in rebellion against her parents and the conventions they represent. Romeo takes his colour from her – his arrival in the garden can best be interpreted as another example of that youthful dalliance that finds him serenading Rosaline at the start of the ballet. The ballet exists as an increasingly close observation of the two lovers; MacMillan's choreography bears down on them like a lens, revealing more and more of their passion. As always with MacMillan there is an underpinning of psychological understanding that inspires the intense revelations of the choreography; Juliet when she is taking the sleeping draught curls in foetal position on the bed; awakening in the tomb her hand moves across the bier as if searching for Romeo's body in bed. The relationship between Tybalt and Lady Capulet is seen as having a strong emotional basis: Tybalt's actions throughout show him as if trying to supplant Capulet's authority, and Lady Capulet's frenzy at his death is to be explained by the strong, though unexpressed passion she feels for him. The role of Romeo, of necessity, comes second in this production; the character is something of a roaring Veronese boy, caught up in a love far greater than he could have imagined; if the dramatic opportunities are less exciting than Juliet's the technical demands of the role are great, and have been admirably met by most of the Royal Ballet's interpreters, especially Christopher Gable on whom it was created. Of the subsidiary roles, two are particularly satisfactory: Mercutio, debonair, dashing and wonderfully interpreted by David Blair, and Tybalt, icily fierce, a role taken with total rightness by Desmond Doyle.

The Song of the Earth

Ballet in one act. Choreography: MacMillan. Music: Mahler (Das Lied von der Erde). *First performed by Stuttgart Ballet, 6 November 1965. First performed by Royal Ballet, Covent Garden, 19 May 1966. Both with Marcia Haydée as the Woman.*

Das Lied von der Erde is strictly speaking Mahler's Ninth Symphony, but superstitiously (because ninth symphonies had been final symphonies for Beethoven and Schubert) he refused to give it the title. This symphony for tenor and alto voices and orchestra was composed in 1907–8, using recently published translations of Chinese poems as text, and to the final poem, *The Farewell*, Mahler added the following lines:

> The dear Earth blossoms in the Spring and buds anew
> Everywhere and forever the luminous blue of distant space!
> Forever . . . forever . . . forever . . . forever . . .

These are the clue to the work, which is Mahler's farewell to the joy and beauty of the world, which are all transitory, but which are always renewed. MacMillan's realization of Mahler's work is in no sense a literal translation of words into dance; as in *Images of Love* (where he took phrases from Shakespeare's sonnets as a springboard for his imagination) and in *Romeo and Juliet*, where he seized on the sense of a speech or a scene, he has sought out an imagery that catches the essence of the poems. The ballet is ultimately about death, not as a menacing and dreadful figure, but as the inevitable companion and participant in all human activity: the masked figure who is one of the trio of central characters in the work was called in Germany *der Ewige* – the eternal one – though in England he is named the Messenger of Death. The ballet's subject is that of a man and a woman: Death takes the Man and then they both return to the Woman, and in the last song, *The Farewell*, there is a promise of renewal.

The first song, 'The Drinking Song of Earthly Sorrow', shows the Man running on with five other boys, leaping and soaring, celebrating the brief joys of the world. At the end the Messenger of Death claims the Man. The slow movement, 'The Lonely One in Autumn', is written for the

Woman with three other girls; at first they are partnered by four men, but these leave and there follows a *pas de deux* for the Woman and the Death figure, which ends with the woman solitary and sorrowing: 'O sun of Love, never again wilt thou shine, gently to dry my bitter tears?'

Then come three *scherzi*: the first, 'Of Youth', shows a group of young people enjoying themselves in games and chatter around a green and white porcelain pavilion (there are no sets in the ballet: costumes are simple leotards and tunics, with the Messenger of Death wearing a half-mask; but so vivid is MacMillan's imagery here – and throughout the work – that we seem to see the settings and locations). When the poem speaks of everything mirrored in the smooth surface of the quiet pool that surrounds the pavilion, MacMillan shows his soloist momentarily inverted. It is a fresh, youthful scene filled with innocent joy – and at the end the Messenger enters to carry off the principal girl soloist.

The second *scherzo*, 'Of Beauty', shows a group of girls picking lotus flowers by the river's edge; on dash young men on horseback. 'The loveliest of the maidens send the rider glances of yearning' – and MacMillan shows us just this; passion and happiness are perfectly expressed.

The following 'Drunkard in Spring' finds the Man carousing with two cronies, but there is a fourth member to their party, the Death figure, and at the end – as spring comes with the chatter of birds – he claims the Man.

The final section, the heart of the work, is a long sequence (lasting nearly thirty minutes) which brings together the Man, the Woman and the Messenger of Death. It is a marvellous sequence of dancing that captures everything of the intensity and beauty of the theme. Death brings back the Man to the Woman; they dance, and at the end the promise of renewal is miraculously suggested when the three figures move slowly forward as the curtain falls.

Song of the Earth is a very great ballet – arguably MacMillan's finest. In it his inspiration catches and matches all the elegiac beauty of Mahler's symphony; the dance language (which owes something to the manner of *Symphony*, of *Images of Love* and of *Diversions*) is freely shaped, though entirely classical, and utterly and magnificently revelatory and moving. It also enshrines a superlative role for a ballerina: in this case for Marcia Haydée, the Stuttgart ballerina, one of the most poetic and thrilling of dancers. Her interpretation has the complete rightness of genius; in a ballet where any attempt to 'act' is fatal, she makes the Woman a figure of the utmost beauty and grace.

Concerto

Ballet in one act. Choreography: MacMillan. Music: Shostakovich, Piano Concerto No. 2. Décor: Jürgen Rose. First performance: November 1966, Deutsche Oper Ballet, Berlin, with Lynn Seymour and Rudolf Holtz. First performed by Royal Ballet Touring Section, Covent Garden, 26 May 1967.

Musicality is a clumsy word, but inescapable when talking about ballet. It implies that quality of harmonious accord between dance and music, a feeling for what the score is about, that is – somehow unexpectedly – one of the prime gifts of English dancers. Naturally enough it is also highly characteristic of our best choreographers. Kenneth MacMillan has intense 'musicality' – he had it as a dancer, too; attracted predominantly to the music of this century (he has created a few ballets to music dating before 1900) he is sensitive to both mood and structure of his scores. His chief concern is always to realize as much as he can of these factors in movement, and 'the finer the score, the finer the ballet' is a not imprecise yardstick with which to judge his works.

Like Balanchine and Ashton he seems able – in Martha Graham's phrase – to refract music into dancing, as naturally as a prism breaks up light into the spectrum. This is clear in *Concerto*, which is set to the joyous youthful second piano concerto which Shostakovich wrote for his son and the Moscow Youth Orchestra. The ballet has a fresh, open style that matches the airy textures of the score with neat assurance. The opening movement is set for a principal couple with attendant soloists and *corps*; movement is bright, dashing, with the principals often identified with the piano while the *corps* impersonate the orchestral *tutti*; at the end of the movement, as the cheery opening theme sounds for the last time, the dancers march off in formation, and then the two leading dancers march back on stage for the final chord in a merry, inconsequential fashion.

The lighting dims for the second movement, a sun blooms on the mottled pearl grey of the backdrop and as the piano starts its long, elegiac theme the ballerina and her partner walk on from opposite sides. The *pas de deux* – for this *adagio* is an extended and radiant duet – starts with the ballerina bending and unfurling her arms in slow *ports de bras* (the *pas de deux* has its inspiration in the sight of Lynn Seymour warming up in class, and it evokes her presence in marvellous fashion). The duet is lyrical, flowing effortlessly and beautifully, with occasional reflections of its movement in three couples of dancers who appear at the back of the stage, echoing and underlining certain movements of the principle couple (rather as MacMillan did in *Diversions*). At its close, the sun fades, the lights come

162

up and we are whisked into the jollity of the last movement. One leading girl opens this rondo with a sprightly solo, and gradually the other principals, the soloists and the *corps* are also involved; the dancing is laid out in blocks of movement for wheeling and turning squads of dancers, and at the close the whole cast are involved in a joyous finale.

Kenneth MacMillan staged this happy, lightweight work for his Berlin dancers when he took up his post as director of the Deutsche Opera Ballet: its form and style are dictated by the need he felt to train these dancers in clean, academic choreography, and give his troupe a cohesive and classical style. It entered the Australian Ballet repertory in 1973.

Anastasia

Choreography:Kenneth MacMillan. Music: Tchaikovsky, Symphonies No. 1 and No. 3; Bohuslav Martinu: Fantasies Symphoniques. Scenery and costumes: Barry Kay. First performed by the Royal Ballet at Covent Garden on 22 July 1971. Lynn Seymour: Grand Duchess Anastasia/Anna Anderson. Derek Rancher: Tsar Nicholas II. Svetlana Beriosova: Tsarina Alexandra Feodorovna. Adrian Grater: Rasputin. Antoinette Sibley: M. F. Kshessinskaya. Anthony Dowell: her partner. David Adams: Anna's husband.

ACT I: August 1914: in the countryside. The Imperial family are at a picnic on the Baltic coast with their guests, who include the Tsarina's great friend, Mme Vyrubova, and a group of naval officers from the Imperial yacht. The party is broken up as the Tsar receives news of the outbreak of war.

ACT II: Petrograd 1917. Despite rapidly growing social unrest the Tsar is giving a ball in the Winter Palace to celebrate the coming-out of his youngest daughter, Anastasia. He has invited the ballerina M. F. Kshessinskaya – with whom he had a liaison before his marriage – to dance with the guests. Anastasia is puzzled by the relationships which she observes between various members of the court. The ball is invaded by revolutionaries.

ACT III: Some years later. For the woman who believes she is Anastasia, past and present intermingle. She relives incidents from the years since the massacre of the Imperial family at Ekaterinburg by the Bolsheviks; her rescue by two brothers; the birth of her child; her marriage; the death of her husband; the disappearance of her child; her attempted suicide and the confrontations over the years with the surviving members of the Imperial family who deny her identity as the Grand Duchess Anastasia.

Anastasia, as a three-act ballet, developed from a one-act work which MacMillan staged in Berlin in 1967 while director of the Deutsche Oper

Ballet. Set to Bohuslav Martinu's *Fantaisies Symphoniques*, with a specially composed electronic passage to introduce the bemused figure of Anna Anderson in her Berlin hospital bed, the work starred Lynn Seymour in an unforgettable portrayal of a woman desperately trying to recall her own identity and then persuade an inimical world of the fact that she was a survivor from the Bolshevik massacre of the Russian Imperial family in 1918.

On his return to London to direct the Royal Ballet, and with Lynn Seymour also returned to the company, MacMillan decided to extend the ballet 'backwards', to provide the portrait of the woman in the Berlin hospital as she believed herself to be. The result was a grand company ballet, deploying the full forces of the Royal Ballet as a troupe of dancers and dance actors, and a major work of art, innovative in suggesting how history might be converted into poetic truth, no less truthful in its deepest sense for being in some way a fantasy upon historical fact.

Anastasia works on two levels. Its surface is an evocation, in the first two acts, of the world as seen through the eyes of the young Grand Duchess Anastasia (her view of the world is the ballet's view – an important factor in considering the relationships which are shown to us throughout). The opening scene is idyllic, the Tsar and his wife and children picnicking on the Baltic Coast, the formalities of court life relaxed, and the Imperial family free to be a family first, and imperial second. But even here the second level of the ballet is important. MacMillan is not concerned with a literal representation – though the child Anastasia enters on roller-skates; her games with her sisters and the young officers delightfully truthful – rather he is concerned with the inner landscape of the emotions which has always attracted his narrative gifts.

The first act is almost plotless on naturalistic terms, until the last pages of Tchaikovsky's first symphony ('Winter Daydreams': the musical text for Act I) when the news of the outbreak of war is brought to the Tsar. Instead we are offered a study in human relationships: the extraordinary emotional world of the Imperial family. Straight narrative, of course impinges, or rather, is cunningly integrated. There are ebullient sequences for a group of naval officers; sweeping dances for Anastasia and her three sisters; a lilting folk dance-like number for the Tsarina, her friend Anna Vyrubova and her daughters. With the added weight of MacMillan's poetic drama, they seem irresistibly touching, and accentuate the dramatic highlights of the act: the Tsarevich's fall, and the fear that his haemophilia will strike; the duet in which the Tsar's reliance upon his wife is so clearly

Christopher Bruce as Pierrot in *Pierrot Lunaire*

(*above*) Elaine McDonald, Graham Bart and Sally Collard-Gentle in *Jeux* with the Scottish Ballet. (*below*) Members of the Ballet Rambert in *Ancient Voices of Children*

shown, and the arrival of the telegram that announces the outbreak of war.

In the second act MacMillan's concern with the surface of events and their inner relevance to the drama and to the emotional world of Anastasia is no less strong. Anastasia, on the brink of womanhood, is caught up in the splendour of a court ball – magnificent dances for the *corps de ballet* here – but also aware of undercurrents of feeling and hidden dramas between her parents, and between her father and his erstwhile mistress, Kshessinskaya. Outside in the wintry street filled with starving workers and wounded soldiers we know the Revolution is brewing: inside the warm, gleaming palace we watch a doomed society, and at the end we see the mob burst in. In both these acts MacMillan's use of his symphonic scores is most sensitive. Inevitably they dictate the placing of dramatic effect, but MacMillan has not been a slave of his music (save in having to fight against Tchaikovsky's tendency to drop into a *fugato* as if to show his academic credentials). Very skilled is his setting of a grand *pas de deux* of tremendous bravura to the *alla tedesca* of the third symphony (the score for Act II): it is like the diamond *grand pas* from Petipa's *Sinbad*, a ballet which never existed but seems intensely probable in this duet. Skilful, too, the way the little three note theme of the *andante elegiaco* seems to epitomize Anastasia's wondering contemplation of events.

With the third act, and Anna Anderson's quest for identity, we understand fully the relevance of the events and incidents we have seen earlier in the ballet. Personalities, suffering, time itself, form part of a psychic labyrinth through which Anna Anderson wanders in search of herself and recognition by the world. The drama, as Andrew Porter observed in the *Financial Times*, is about 'much more than the plight of one wronged, or possibly deranged, woman. It is about a changed world; a ballet about security and violence, happiness precariously embraced, loneliness.' At the end, Anna Anderson seems to grasp all her courage of spirit, and sitting on her hospital bed she circles the stage, sure of herself now, and defiant of the world's incredulity. We have seen a considerable work of art.

As Anastasia/Anna, Lynn Seymour gives one of the greatest dance performances of our time. The role is vastly challenging, from beguiling fourteen-year-old child to crop-haired and distraught woman. At every moment Seymour's dancing bespeaks truth, beauty, total identification with the character, entire sympathy with the being she is playing – or rather, has become for us. Among the other Royal Ballet performances, Derek Rencher's impersonation of the Tsar, weak, charming, vacillating at every crisis, and Svetlana Beriosova's assumption of the Tsarina's part, were of great sensitivity and dramatic skill. The décor by Barry Kay, a permanent set of spiralling parchment-like shapes which become in turn a Baltic forest, a palace and a landscape of the mind, are among the best designs British ballet has had. His costuming is of similar quality. Yet *Anastasia*'s importance transcends all these contributory factors. MacMillan has, in this beautiful work of art, extended the capabilities of the three-act ballet. For the first time in the West, there was a work which escaped from the restrictions of its form, finding in recent history a theme that permitted lengthy treatment, and one which transmuted history's truth into a no less truthful poetry.

Triad
Ballet in one act. Choreography: Kenneth MacMillan. Music: Prokofiev Violin Concerto No. 1. Design: Peter Unsworth. First performed by the Royal Ballet at Covent Garden, 19 *January* 1972. *With Anthony Dowell, Wayne Eagling, Antoinette Sibley.*

The theme of *Triad* is the emotional conflict between two brothers following the appearance of a young girl in their lives. The elder boy is attracted to her; the younger senses the break that this will bring in the companionship existing between him and his brother, and also seeks to emulate his sibling in feeling an emotional attraction to the girl. The girl is, essentially, an excuse for the inevitable separation between the brothers: their rivalry over her results in the younger boy being thrown to a gang of youths who attack him, although the elder boy eventually rescues him.

This psychological anecdote is told with commendable simplicity of means, and with an allusive poetry which catches something very touching about the sexual awakenings of boys, their rivalries and sorrows. The relationship between the brothers is complex, the focus of the work falling on the younger, whose grief and incomprehension at life are suggested at curtain rise by the tears we see him shedding, and at the end by his seeking to interpose his body between his elder brother and the girl with whom he has fallen in love. He must try to supplant one or other of them in the relationship: his tragedy is that he fails on both counts.

Elite Syncopations
Ballet in one act. Choreography: Kenneth MacMillan. Costumes: Ian Spurling. Music: Scott Joplin, Paul Pratt, James Scott, Joseph F. Lamb, Max Morath, Donald Ashwander, Robert Hampton. First performed by the Royal Ballet at Covent Garden, 7 *October* 1974.

166

The ragtime craze has had no happier manifestation than this romp for the Royal Ballet. It is set on a stage in a state of undress with odds and ends of equipment and settings still in place and a ragtime band ensconced on a rostrum. They, like the dancers, are dressed by Ian Spurling in clothes of exuberant fantasy. In costuming his dancers Spurling has poured out most daring caprices of patterning and colour on to all-over tights. The result is a phantasmagoria of fashion at its most absurd and most witty. And the dances, like the costumes, are fun. The pace is fast and nicely contrasted in a sequence of twelve variations that have no other purpose than to make us laugh and delight in the ebullient good humour of the dances and their interpreters. At times it looks as if Marius Petipa has been caught larking in a bawdy house. There is a solo that is the apotheosis of the cakewalk; a duet that mocks sincerity and romantic passions and yet manages to be sincere and romantic; there are other duets which explore the idea of movement turned in on itself; and in the most frantic coupling, a tiny male dancer has to cope adoringly with a very tall and elegant girl.

But if *Elite Syncopations* is light-hearted – which it is – it is not lightly made. Structure and invention are sure, and the marriage of ragtime and academic dance is neatly effective in this cascade of happy choreographic ideas.

Manon

Ballet in three acts. Choreography: MacMillan. Music: Jules Massenet orchestrated and arranged by Leighton Lucas with the collaboration of Hilda Gaunt. Designs: Nicholas Georgiadis. First performed at the Royal Opera House Covent Garden by the Royal Ballet on 7 March 1974. Antoinette Sibley: Manon. David Wall: Lescaut. Anthony Dowell: des Grieux. Monica Mason: Lescaut's Mistress. Derek Rencher: Monsieur G.M.

ACT I, *Scene 1*: The courtyard of an inn near Paris. The courtyard at the inn is frequented by actresses, gentlemen and the *demi-monde* from Paris. Among them are des Grieux, a young student, the wealthy Monsieur G.M. and Lescaut, who is there to meet his sister Manon on her way to enter a convent. A coach arrives bringing Manon and an old gentleman who has been very much attracted by her. Lescaut notices this and takes the gentleman into the inn to come to an arrangement with him over Manon. Manon remains outside and meets des Grieux. They fall in love and decide to escape to Paris with the help of the money that she has stolen from the old gentleman. Lescaut and the old gentleman come out of the inn, having made a bargain, and to their dismay see that Manon has disappeared.

Monsieur G.M. tells Lescaut that he too is interested in Manon and because of G.M.'s wealth Lescaut promises to find Manon and persuade her to accept G.M.

Scene 2: Des Grieux's lodgings in Paris. Des Grieux is writing a letter to his father but Manon interrupts him by declaring her love for him. Des Grieux goes to post the letter and in his absence Lescaut arrives with Monsieur G.M. Manon yields to G.M.'s advances and, when des Grieux returns, Lescaut persuades him that there will be great wealth for all of them if he, des Grieux, will sanction the liaison between Manon and G.M.

ACT II, *Scene 1*: A party at the *hôtel particulier* of a madam. Manon arrives at the party given by Monsieur G.M. and is clearly torn between the wealth of her companion and her love for des Grieux, who is also there with Lescaut. Des Grieux tries to persuade Manon to leave with him but she tells him that the time is not right and only will be when he takes more of Monsieur G.M.'s money at cards. Des Grieux is caught cheating and he and Manon rush away.

Scene 2: Des Grieux' lodgings. Manon and des Grieux once again declare their love for one another but Monsieur G.M. arrives with the police and Manon is arrested as a prostitute. In the ensuing struggle Lescaut is killed.

ACT III, *Scene 1*: New Orleans, the port. The gaoler of the penal colony awaits the arrival of the convicts from France. Manon has been deported to America as a prostitute and des Grieux has followed her there by pretending to be her husband. The gaoler now turns his interest towards Manon.

Scene 2: The gaoler's room. The gaoler has arrested Manon but offers her rewards in the hope that she will desert des Grieux and live with him. Des Grieux, however, breaks in and kills the gaoler.

Scene 3: The swamp. Manon and des Grieux have escaped into the swamp of Louisiana. All her former ambitions of wealth and splendour have been renounced for her love for des Grieux. While eluding their pursuers Manon collapses and dies in his arms.

It is small wonder that *Manon* is so popular with audiences. It combines, in prodigal terms, almost all that public taste can demand of a spectacle in the theatre: passion; the tensions of that immemorial battle between wealth and true love; the guilty and gilded splendours of a singularly vicious period, the Régence. It offers two romantic roles for Manon and des Grieux; for Lescaut, there is a character probably more deeply considered than that of the hero; two murders; a whorehouse in full cry; cheating at cards; fine design by Nicholas Georgiadis – there is little omitted that might hold an audience enthralled.

It seems almost incidental that *Manon* also contains some of MacMillan's most fluent and inventive choreography. His ability to convey the emotional roots of a situation, to chart its beginnings as well as its depths, is very evident in the first scene in which the identity of Manon as a negotiable piece of flesh is brilliantly stated, as Lescaut in turn offers her to a lecherous old man, to Monsieur G.M. and then to a madam. The love affair between Manon and des Grieux is told in a sequence of ecstatic, impassioned duets, which are among the best that MacMillan has created; the character of Lescaut – a magnificent creation by David Wall – is clear from the *coup de théâtre* that starts the ballet, when we see the cloaked figure seated on the stage, and as the life of the inn courtyard begins, his contemplative, vulpine features emerge from below his hat. In Sibley and Dowell the ballet found two exultant, lyric performers; in David Wall and Monica Mason, as Lescaut and his mistress, two artists able to extract the ultimate comic effects from the drunken duet, which is a convulsing study in balances just held, arms caught in only the last nick of time. The ballet has, since its first performance, invited and received a remarkable series of cast changes: Jennifer Penney and Wayne Eagling all youthful ardour as the lovers; a compelling performance in which Lynn Seymour and Dowell, as Manon and her brother, seemed almost incestuously close, so alike did they appear in feature, as in their amoral view of the world. There has been a fascinating exchange of roles between Wall and Dowell, in which the reversal of characterization gave the work a sharp new impetus in drama; and a uniquely satisfying impersonation of Manon by Natalya Makarova who, in this role as in *Romeo and Juliet* and *The Song of the Earth*, showed herself a perfect interpreter of MacMillan choreography.

Rituals

Ballet in one act. Choreography: Kenneth MacMillan. Design: Yolanda Sonnabend. Music: Bartok Sonata for two pianos and percussion. First performed by the Royal Ballet at the Royal Opera House, Covent Garden, 11 December 1975.

The Royal Ballet's visit to Japan in 1975 provided the starting point for *Rituals*. Fascinated by the procedures of the Japanese theatre and its attitude towards the human body, as exemplified particularly in Kabuki drama and Bunraku puppets, MacMillan made a ballet in which this alien manner has been rethought in the terms of academic dance. The result was more authentically Japanese than might have been expected, MacMillan fixing the physical flavour of Japanese theatre with great daring upon a musical masterpiece. The ballet is in three scenes. The first is a male ceremony in which two neophytes are prepared for initiation into a company of athletes. A Grand Master supervises and guides the ceremony; its progress is the proving of aspirants in battle. Movement is strongly muscled, often contorted, in positions that recall Sumo combat. The second movement finds a group of attendants bringing on two gorgeously clothed puppets. Under the direction of a Bunraku master, they are stripped and there follows a disturbing sequence in which they are manhandled in grotesque and unhappy pairing. Reclothed, they stand for a moment, then collapse to the ground. The section is disturbing, macabre, a commentary upon human fate, even on the forces that direct and impel the actions of our unclad bodies. The final movement finds a woman immediately after childbirth with a midwife and two celebrants who are a chorus to the mother's travail.

Rituals was a page from the travel sketchbook of a choreographer and as such it showed how quick MacMillan's eye was to preserve in this elusive and mysterious ballet something essential about the Japanese theatre.

The Four Seasons
Ballet in one act. Choreography:Kenneth MacMillan. Music: Verdi. Design: Peter Rice. First performed by the Royal Ballet at the Royal Opera House, Covent Garden, 5 March 1975.

For a classical choreographer, directing a major classical company, there comes a moment when the restatement of this classic identity, in its clearest and purest form, is a task worth undertaking. Hence *The Four Seasons*, which is set to the ballet music Verdi was obliged to write for his Paris Opéra *Les Vêpres Siciliennes* in 1855 with additional pieces from *Don Carlos* and *Jérusalem.*

MacMillan provided a pyrotechnic display of steps designed to tax, inspire, and show off his company; a virtuoso ensemble that framed virtuoso principals. 'Winter' is a group of shivering dancers who give way to a trio of two girls and a boy; 'Spring' is a quartet for a girl with three boys; 'Summer' a lazy duet that finishes with its interpreters yawning and half asleep; 'Autumn' a bravura trio for two boys and a girl.

170

Mayerling

Ballet in three acts. Choreography: Kenneth MacMillan. Music: Franz Liszt. Arranged and orchestrated: John Lanchbery. Design: Nicholas Georgiadis. Scenario: Gillian Freeman. First performed by the Royal Ballet at Covent Garden, 15 February 1978. David Wall: Crown Prince Rudolf.

PROLOGUE: The cemetery at Heilingenkreuz before dawn.

ACT I, *Scene 1*: Vienna. The ballroom at the Hofburg, the Imperial Palace. At the ball to celebrate his wedding to Princess Stephanie of Belgium, Crown Prince Rudolf offends his parents and bride by flirting openly with Princess Louise. Left alone, Rudolf meets Countess Larisch and Baroness Vetsera who introduces her young daughter, Mary. They are interrupted by four Hungarian officers, friends of Rudolf, who forcefully plead the separatist cause of their country. Countess Larisch returns and tries to revive the intimacy of her past relationship with Rudolf. The Emperor discovers them and angrily orders Rudolf to return to his wife.

Scene 2: The Empress's apartments at the Hofburg. Elisabeth has retired from the ball and is enjoying the company of her ladies-in-waiting. Rudolf visits her before going to his bride. He is unhappy at his enforced marriage and attempts to engage the sympathy of the Empress.

Scene 3: Rudolf's apartments at the Hofburg. Stephanie is prepared for the wedding night. Rudolf finds her alone and before making love to her, terrifies her with a revolver.

ACT II, *Scene 1*: A notorious tavern. Accompanied by Bratfisch, Rudolf and Stephanie arrive at the tavern in disguise. Seeing that Stephanie is unhappy, Bratfisch does his best to amuse her. The whores are resentful and try to recapture the attention of their clients. Stephanie leaves in disgust, and Rudolf devotes his attention to his mistress, Mitzi Caspar, and to his Hungarian friends. There is a police raid, during which Rudolf, Mitzi and the Hungarian officers hide. Arrests are made and the police leave. In a mood of despair brought about by the constant surveillance, Rudolf proposes to Mitzi that they should commit suicide together. Count Taafe enters, having been informed that Rudolf is in the tavern. Rudolf again conceals himself, but Mitzi indicates his presence to the Count, with whom she departs.

Scene 2: Outside the tavern. As Rudolf leaves his friends, Countess Larisch, aware of his identity, contrives to present Mary Vetsera whom she is ostensibly chaperoning.

Scene 3: The Vetsera house. Countess Larisch calls and finds Mary absorbed by a portrait of Rudolf. She takes a pack of cards and tells Mary's fortune, assuring her that her romantic dreams will come true. Mary gives her a letter for Rudolf.

Scene 4: The Hofburg. During Franz Josef's birthday celebrations Count Taafe confronts Rudolf with a political pamphlet. At the same time 'Bay' Middleton offers the Prime Minister a joke cigar, greatly amusing Rudolf. Elisabeth presents the Emperor with a portrait of his 'friend', Katherina Schratt. A firework display diverts everyone except Elisabeth and 'Bay'. Rudolf observes their amorous exchange and is bitterly resentful. Katherina Schratt sings sadly of loving and parting. The resumption of the fireworks gives Countess Larisch the opportunity to tease Rudolf with Mary's letter.

Scene 5: Rudolf's apartments at the Hofburg. Mary and Rudolf meet in secret for the first time.

ACT III, *Scene 1*: Countryside: a royal shoot. The pleasant day is shattered when Rudolf unaccountably fires wildly, killing a member of the court and narrowly missing the Emperor.

Scene 2: Rudolf's apartments at the Hofburg. The Empress discovers Countess Larisch with Rudolf and dismisses her, unaware that Mary is waiting outside. Mary joins Rudolf who asks her to die with him.

Scene 3: The hunting lodge at Mayerling. Rudolf, drinking with Count Hoyos and Prince Philipp, indicates he is unwell and they leave. Bratfisch arrives with Mary, and Rudolf commands him to entertain them. Bratfisch realizes he has lost their attention and withdraws. In a mounting frenzy of passion Rudolf makes love to Mary. Calming his nerves with an injection of morphine, he embraces her once more then shoots her. Loschek, Hoyos and Philipp, disturbed by the shot, are reassured by Rudolf who, left alone, shoots himself.

EPILOGUE: The cemetery at Heiligenkreuz before dawn.

(*Reproduced by kind permission of Gillian Freeman.*)

The tragedy at Mayerling in 1889 is best known to us through the cinema versions, which have cheapened and sentimentalized a mysterious incident that seemed a terrible symptom of the degeneracy of the Austro-Hungarian empire. In his three-act *Mayerling* for the Royal Ballet, Kenneth MacMillan has made use of the cinema's procedures while resolutely deromanticizing its view of events. By inviting the novelist Gillian Freeman to provide him with a scenario he benefited from her understanding of scriptwriting for films to create a fluidly cinematic form, making use of the equivalent of the camera's 'dissolves' and swift narrative devices. At the same time he has rejected the popular, cinema-bred idea of the Crown Prince Rudolf and Mary Vetsera as a grander, Viennese, Romeo and Juliet, to show us something much nearer the historical and psychological truth of the characters.

In *Mayerling* MacMillan returns to a major concern of his large-scale choreography: the reshaping and developing of the form of the three-act ballet, moving away from nineteenth-century structure and its conventional fantasy figures, to forge a manner able to deal with the harsher realism suited to late twentieth-century taste. (An interesting case can be made out for seeing *Mayerling* as *Swan Lake* one hundred years on: love in death, royal duty, emotional instability are common to Prince Siegfried and to Prince Rudolf.) *Anastasia* suggested MacMillan's way ahead, as a study of a real woman caught at a moment of crisis: as in Grigorovich's *Spartacus*, and more especially his *Ivan the Terrible*, the stuff of history nurtures the development of ballet, and substitutes fact for convenient fiction. The result, in *Mayerling*, is a tense, searing ballet in which a tragic figure is seen in his very special and dramatically fascinating social setting, his motives and his psychology explored in dances of rare power, his destiny explained in terms of political, family and social pressures. The central character of Rudolf is not a new one in MacMillan's ballet. He is the outcast, the victim, whom we know as the girl in *The Invitation*, Anastasia/Anna Anderson, *Rite's* Chosen Virgin, Juliet, the younger brother in *Triad* – all driven to isolation or death by events they cannot or will not control. But Rudolf is the most complex, and most fully extended in analysis, and as a result the ballet provides what one assumes to be the lengthiest role yet created for a male dancer – more demanding even than Spartacus or Ivan the Terrible. As Rudolf, David Wall is superb: in the role of a lifetime he gives the performance of a lifetime.

The ballet charts the eight years which begin with Rudolf's loveless marriage to Princess Stephanie of Belgium, barely out of the schoolroom, and which culminate in the double shooting at his Hunting Lodge at Mayerling where he first kills Mary Vetsera (his mistress of but two weeks) and then ends his own life. *Mayerling's* hero is never heroic, but he wins all our sympathy, and this without distorting historical fact. His every demand upon his parents rejected, he turns to a life of compulsive womanizing and to debauchery – the Rudolf who lies dead at the ballet's end is venereally diseased, a morphine addict, a prince trapped in political and sexual intrigue, a gun fetishist obsessed with the idea of death, heir to a throne which cannot be his for years to come. And unlikely as it may seem, MacMillan and Wall show him as a man infinitely pitiable, authentically tragic.

To achieve a portrait of such depth and resonance, the action follows

Rudolf's journey to Mayerling by way of the claustrophic, faction-ridden court of the Hapsburgs (Nicholas Georgiadis' settings are admirable in catching the enclosed and stuffy world of the Hofburg, as, too, a seedy tavern and the Vetsera house). Central to the development of the character is a sequence of duets for Rudolf with the woman in his life, and in them MacMillan's mastery of the *pas de deux* has never seemed more complete. In none of them is there a suggestion of conventional romantic love; rather each stresses the isolated lovelessness that drives Rudolf deeper into despair.

We see him with his mother, the Empress Elisabeth, reluctant to become involved with Rudolf's plight. The wedding night encounter with his new bride was illuminated by Wendy Ellis's sensitivity as a girl terrified and brutalized. Earlier we find Rudolf flirting cruelly with his young sister-in-law at the wedding ball. We watch him take Stephanie to a *louche* tavern where he returns to a liaison with his mistress Mitzi Caspar. And recurring throughout the ballet is the woman who seems crucial to his unhappiness, the Countess Larisch. Once his mistress, now a procuress and evil genius, she is yet the only person who offers him any sympathy or understanding. As Larisch, Merle Park gave a performance that called her best qualities to full use; bravura dancing, assured acting, made the role glitter with life as bright as the diamond Larisch wears. To Lynn Seymour fell the role of Mary Vetsera to which she brought a luscious physical presence as a girl recklessly in love with the idea of love. In the duet for Rudolf and Mary, MacMillan is at his most persuasive as an erotic poet, exploring passion with images of dark beauty – the final coupling at Mayerling combining lust and despair. And at the ballet's heart is David Wall. From his earliest performances as a very young and very gifted *premier danseur* Wall knew how to hold the stage. In his maturity he demonstrates complete authority. He has the strength, both emotional and physical for this unique role. Tireless throughout a most taxing series of *pas de deux*, assured in solos, he entered into the soul of the Crown Prince and the degeneration of the character was displayed with terrible inevitability.

It is some comment upon the Royal Ballet's richness of male dancers that two other interpreters of the role of Rudolf – Wayne Eagling and Stephen Jeffries – have been most effective and entirely individual in their readings.

La Fin du Jour

Ballet in one scene. Choreography: Kenneth MacMillan. Music: Ravel (Piano Concerto in G Major). Scenery and costumes: Ian Spurling. First performed by the Royal Ballet at the Royal Opera House, Covent Garden, 15 March 1979.

The choreographer provides the following programme note: '*La Fin du Jour* draws its inspiration from the style of the thirties; the designs and choreography are inspired by fashion plates of an era and a way of life shattered for ever by the Second World War.'

La Fin du Jour is set to the Ravel G Major piano concerto, a work made in 1931 which the composer at first considered calling *Divertissement*. This alternative title, and the score's date, are keys to what MacMillan has achieved. He offers us a series of photographs of the 1930s that might have come from the pages of a fashion magazine of the period – figures caught in the amber of time, sportsmen and women, cinema idols, matinée stars, all seen in that innocent, bright light before the night of the Second World War. It is not a literal portrait. The work's flavour comes from the juxtaposition of elements of play that we, from the other side of the abyss of the war, know was doomed, as was the society that nurtured it. The first movement of the concerto finds a *corps de ballet* of marionette figures who frame a double *pas de deux* of great complexity. The slow movement with its serene *cantilena* becomes a long-breathed *adagio* for two leading ballerinas each attended by five men. For the last movement, the cast who have hitherto been seen in sporting clothes, reappear in evening dress, with the leading women evoking the elegance of Jessie Matthews or Ginger Rogers. The choreography impels the dancers high over the stage but gradually the light dims in the garden that we glimpse in the back of Ian Spurling's creamy setting. The door into the garden is closed to shut out the night. The party is over.

MacMillan's choreography may seem quirky at moments, even frivolous. It does not presume to impose any political attitudinizing upon the refinements of the Ravel score. It makes its point by hints and quick suggestions to provide a requiem for the *douceur de vivre* of an era.

Playground

Ballet in one act. Choreography: Kenneth MacMillan. Design: Yolanda Sonnabend. Music: Gordon Crosse; Playground for orchestra. First performed by the Sadler's Wells Royal Ballet in The Tent, Edinburgh, 24 August 1979. Marion Tait: the Girl with Make-up. Desmond Kelly: The Young Man.

Playground finds Kenneth MacMillan working at his most intense in studying the human psyche. It is a disquieting ballet, making no concessions to conventional attitudes of airiness and bodies beautiful: instead is offers distress and violence of spirit. Yet because it takes a human condition, without romanticizing or fudging its subject, it achieves a certain uncompromising beauty. The classic dance is taken a further step along a path of truthful precision in revealing depths of feeling and suffering.

The playground of the title is a wire-meshed courtyard, more prison than place for games. Behind it we see the walls of an institution with barred windows, and a mural of caricatured figures. Here we find the inmates of a mental hospital grotesquely got up as children, their games making macabre comment upon their wounded personalities. Certain figures stand out: a vicar and his wife; a girl who daubs herself with make-up; another inmate who assumes the role of her mother. The play-acting is dislocated, satiric. Outside the enclosure, a young man watches, then enters the playground. For all his apparent normality, we sense violence that is suppurating just below the surface of his personality. He is attracted to the girl, and they embark upon a *pas de deux* which conveys the extreme tension of their feelings. The girl is driven through excitement into an epileptic fit – a haunting choreographic *tour de force* – and her collapse occasions another game as her companions mourn over her apparently dead body. The young man is attacked by the rest of the cast. At this, three white-coated doctors enter and the man is restrained in a straitjacket. Playtime is over. The patients doff their children's clothes, put on institutional garb and leave. The girl is the last to go: in a scene done with unforgettable pathos by Marion Tait, she stands riven with grief, hands drawn down her tear-stained face to smear the make-up that has been her erstwhile identity. She trails away. The man, straitjacketed, lies abandoned as the gate closes. Kneeling, head against the gate, he seems like Petrushka beating against the door of his cell.

Gloria

Ballet in one scene. Choreography: Kenneth MacMillan. Music: Francis Poulenc (Gloria in G Major). Scenery and costumes: Andy Klunder. With Jennifer Penney, Wayne Eagling, Julian Hosking, Wendy Ellis, Antony Dowson, Ross MacGibbon, Ashley Page. First performed by the Royal Ballet at the Royal Opera House Covent Garden, 13 March 1980.

Death and the afterlife have been an inspiration for MacMillan's choreography since the early *Journey*, which he made for American Ballet Theater in 1957, and two major works of his maturity – *The Song of the Earth* and *Requiem* – have shown how potent is the response that this theme excites in his choreography. The immediate pretext for *Gloria* is that 'lost' generation who felt the full brunt of the First World War. As a programme

176

note MacMillan quoted a poem by Vera Brittain from her portrait of this generation: *Testament of Youth*. The lines which seem to fix the mood of *Gloria* run:

But in that song we heard no warning chime,
  Nor visualized in hours benign and sweet
The threatening woe that our adventurous feet
  Would starkly meet.

The setting – a fine achievement by a new young designer – is of a skeletal metal frame placed on a rising slope of ground. The cast appear, breasting this slope. They are revenants; the girls ghost-grey, in fluttering relics of dresses; the men in leotards that seem rotted, vestigial uniforms, wearing tin hats. The ballet's progress is the contemplation of lost hopes, lost joys, lost selves. The action seems to take place at the very edge of the world, and MacMillan makes stirring emotional and theatrical capital from the fact of the soldiers standing gazing out into the nothingness from which they have returned, or reclining on the slope – like corpses, or sleepers – to provide a counterpoint and commentary upon the central matter of the ballet, which is the writing for a trio (first taken by Jennifer Penney, Wayne Eagling and Julian Hosking) and a quartet originally comprising Wendy Ellis, Antony Dowson, Ross MacGibbon and Ashley Page.

The choreography does not seek to comment upon the text of the Gloria, save in general and incidental terms of responding to the words as prayers. It is the music's atmosphere and structure which inspire the dance, and it is the choreographic images through which MacMillan unites score and theme that catch and hold the imagination.

The lighter, more joyous sections allow the quartet of dancers to explore the idea of a happy, carefree past; the darker and more solemn sections are given to the trio of principals and encompass a wide range of emotion, from a gentle, trusting duet (set to the soprano soloist's 'Domine Deus') to an anguished response to the futility of their sacrifice and the horrors of war itself.

It would be unwise to seek too specific an action in *Gloria*. MacMillan's achievement lies in creating choreography – which owes something to *Requiem*'s manner and to the innovations of *La Fin du Jour* – that combines a retrospective consideration of a tragic generation with a more universal commentary upon the effects of war and of the irreparable loss that speaks in Vera Brittain's poem. The result is a ballet of great seriousness and of profoundly moving imagery.

PETER DARRELL (b. 1932)

Darrell was trained at the Royal Ballet School, danced with Sadler's Wells Theatre Ballet for three years, and then joined Festival Ballet, working later with several continental companies before taking up choreography. His first creations were seen in Ballet Workshop at the Mercury Theatre, and he also worked extensively in television, but his career is chiefly linked with that of Western Theatre Ballet, of which he was joint artistic director with its founder Elizabeth West, and now with Scottish Ballet. For the Western Theatre Ballet he made several ballets which did much to crystallize its early style – pieces as diverse as *The Prisoners*, *Non-Stop* and *Chiaroscuro*. The ideals of the company were implicit in its title: *theatre* was to be as important as *ballet*. The company, originally Bristol based, surmounted extraordinary difficulties in its early days, and gradually gained a reputation for a lively and firmly contemporary view of what ballet should do. Darrell's gifts for dramatic ballets were seen also in *A Wedding Present*, and his comic range extended to works like *Salade* and *Mods and Rockers*.

In 1962, the tragic death of Elizabeth West meant that Darrell became sole artistic director: but he continued to choreograph, creating *Home*, *Sun into Darkness* in 1967, *Francesca* and *Ephemeron* in 1968. In 1969 Western Theatre Ballet, who four years earlier had been invited to take over responsibility for the Sadler's Wells Opera Ballet and share seasons at the Sadler's Wells Theatre, took another and even more important step in their progress, by moving to Glasgow and assuming a new identity – though retaining all their former prestige – as Scottish Theatre Ballet.

Scottish Theatre Ballet has now become Scottish Ballet, with its own headquarters and rehearsal studios in Glasgow. Peter Darrell, choreographer and once inseparable from the image of Western Theatre Ballet, has become Peter Darrell, creator of the image of Scottish Ballet, and now, perhaps more director than choreographer. Already, when director of Western Theatre Ballet, he established the practice, generous and rare among director-choreographers, of enlarging the company's range by commissioning work from other choreographers. Thus Kenneth MacMillan, Peter Wright, Flemming Flindt and Walter Gore were some of those who contributed to the company's repertory. Darrell has continued the same practice with Scottish Ballet, balancing productions of classics like *Giselle* and *Swan Lake* (which national classical ballet companies need) against new ballets in which the particular qualities of his dancers can shine. Darrell himself stages most of the classical productions – always reworked

178

and rethought to suit his company, *Giselle* being an excellent example – and often creates new ballets. But the company has benefited, as usual, from his introduction of creative talent from outside. Sometimes it is also from the past, like a number of ballets by the Danish choreographer, Bournonville, including *La Sylphide* which, of course, is set in Scotland. In the same way he has revived Andrée Howard's *La Fête Etrange*, Fokine's *Le Carnaval*, *Paquita* by Mazilier and Petipa, and Flemming Flindt's *The Lesson*. Among his own original works are *Jeux* and the full length *Tales of Hoffman* and *Cinderella*, described below. He has also created ballets abroad in North America, Denmark, Holland, Germany and Switzerland, and for television as well as the theatre.

Darrell's particular aim as a choreographer has always been to enlarge classical ballet's appeal. To accomplish this he often chooses for his ballets the sort of subjects more often associated with films or televison drama. To the same end he has commissioned scenarios from well-known playwrights like John Mortimer and David Rudkin and involved stage producers like Colin Graham. 'His dramatic ballets,' wrote the critic John Percival, 'are notable for showing recognizable human beings in conditions of stress, characters with the sort of problem an audience would identify with, or at least understand from their knowledge of life today. His comedies, too, have a lively, contemporary humour.'

It is probably as director, however, that Darrell has made his principal contribution to the creation of Scottish Ballet during the last decade. He has always been good at spotting and developing talent, always been able to lead dancers and command their loyalty. Consequently classical ballet is beginning to put down roots in Scotland which it never had before. In due course, perhaps, a Scottish school will emerge using and blending the traditions of Scottish national dance. Already the Scottish Ballet has appeared on the international stage, touring Australia and New Zealand with Margot Fonteyn as guest artist, dancing in Madrid, Barcelona and Paris with Rudolf Nureyev, and in San Sebastian, Biarritz and St Jean de Luz with Bessmertnova and Lavrovsky. Many other internationally established dancers have appeared with the company on its home ground.

Jeux
Ballet in one act. Choreography: Darrell. Music: Debussy. Décor: Harry Waistnage. First performed by Western Theatre Ballet, Citizen's Theatre, Glasgow, 7 March 1963. Clover Roope, Sylvia Wellman, Simon Mottram.

'A Black Comedy: three people have been playing tennis but the game

179

continues after the match is over.' So says the programme note for this intriguing ballet which conceals menace and mayhem beneath the sunniest of exteriors. At curtain rise we see the stage bare save for a table and four chairs. We then meet the three characters – whose relationship is never made clear – a man and two women (is one his wife and the other his mistress ? We shall never know). The man and one of the women have been playing tennis, and they are joined by the second woman who brings on a tray of drinks. The man goes into the house (we must imagine it lies just offstage) to change; in his absence there is a certain feeling of tension between the two women; the man returns, and his partner exits also to change, leaving him alone with the other woman, who proceeds to flirt mildly with him. The first woman returns, and there follow a series of polite but plainly insincere exchanges between the trio. The second woman slips something into the other woman's glass; and she, in her turn, feeling in the man's jacket for a cigarette case, brings out a revolver, which she promptly hides in her handbag. All three go off and there is a pistol shot – but a moment later they all return unharmed, thought slightly jittery in manner. The man hands drinks to each of the women and picks up his glass: they toast each other, and we realize suddenly that one of the glasses has poison in it. But which one ? The curtain falls . . . we shall never know.

This is a consummate tease-piece; nothing happens, yet everything happens – there are undercurrents of hatred, love and frustration that are stated with a subtlety and an atmospheric delicacy that seems entirely in accord with the shimmering sensuous quality of the score. The very mystery that surrounds the identity and relationships of the three is part of the ballet's strength: we return to see it time and again, determined that *this* time we shall solve the enigma – though we never do. The dancing is nicely shaped and entirely suited to the music – more than compensation for our failing to elucidate the basic puzzle of this very mixed treble.

Tales of Hoffmann
Ballet in three acts. Scenario (after Barbier and Carré) and choreography: Darrell. Music: Offenbach, arr. Lanchbery. Décor: Alistair Livingstone. Lighting: John B. Read. First performed by Scottish Theatre Ballet, King's Theatre, Edinburgh, 6 April 1972. Peter Cazalet: Hoffman. Gordon Aitken: Counsellor Lindorf. Hilary Debden: Olypia. Marion St Caire: Antonia. Elaine McDonald: Giulietta.

PROLOGUE: La Stella. A tavern outside the Opera House. Hoffmann is drinking with his friends while awaiting the arrival of La Stella, his latest love, who is appearing at the opera house. He is asked to explain the sig-

nificance of three souvenirs which are on his table but at first refuses. La
Stella arrives and gives her maid a note for Hoffmann which, unseen by
him, is intercepted by Counsellor Lindorf. Hoffmann, now a little drunk,
agrees to tell the stories behind the three souvenirs.

ACT I: Olympia (the first tale). The conservatory in Spalanzani's house.
Spalanzani has invited some friends to see his latest creation – the lifelike
doll, Olympia. The adolescent Hoffmann sees Olympia from afar and tries
to meet her. Spalanzani announces that Olympia will dance for his guests,
but first insists that Hoffmann wear some magic spectacles. Hoffmann
immediately falls in love with Olympia and asks for her hand in marriage.
Spalanzani is delighted with his deception. He agrees, and Hoffmann
whirls Olympia into a dance during which he loses the spectacles. The doll
falls apart and Hoffmann realizes he has been tricked.

ACT II: Antonia (the second tale). The music room of Antonia's home.
Ten years later. Hoffmann, in love with Antonia, is taking music lessons
from her father. Behind her father's back, Antonia flirts with Hoffmann
while dancing to his playing. When they are discovered her father dismisses
Hoffmann and warns Antonia that too much exertion will be fatal to her.
Doctor Miracle suddenly appears. He promises to cure her and hypnotizes
her into believing that she is a great ballerina. Hoffmann returns and
Antonia, enthralled by her vision, implores him to play so that she may
dance again. Urged on by Doctor Miracle, Hoffmann reluctantly does so
until, overcome, she dies in his arms.

ACT III: Giulietta (the third tale). Dapertutto's *salon*. Hoffmann, now an
older and more serious man, has turned to religion for comfort from his
earlier disappointments. He finds himself in the *salon* of Dapertutto, who
tries to lure him again to the enjoyment of sensual pleasures but without
success until the arrival of the courtesan, Giulietta. Goaded by Dapertutto
she so seduces Hoffmann that he renounces his faith but realizes, when his
reflection disappears from the mirror, that he has lost his immortal soul.
In this anguish he prays that he may be forgiven and as his reflection reappears Giulietta and Dapertutto are drawn into the mirror and vanish.

EPILOGUE: La Stella. The tavern outside the opera house. Hoffmann, his
stories told, is offered more drink by the sinister Counsellor Lindorf. La
Stella emerges from the Opera House looking for Hoffmann and finds him
in a drunken sleep, her note crushed on the ground. Sad and disappointed
she is led away by Counsellor Lindorf. Hoffmann, roused from his stupor,
realizes that again he has been duped by the evil presence that has pursued
him throughout his life.

Thus the ballet follows roughly the course of Offenbach's opera with the Antonia act placed between the Olympia and the Giulietta acts, and with Antonia having ambitions to dance rather than to sing. A popular success when first presented in Scotland, the ballet was revived in 1973 for American Ballet Theatre with new décor by Peter Docherty and one ballerina dancing all three heroines. John Lanchbery's arrangement of the Offenbach score includes other sources of Offenbach as well as the opera and amounts almost to a new score. 'Hoffmann's four ages of a poet,' wrote Noël Goodwin in *A Ballet for Scotland*, 'calls for a corresponding range of character sustained on a firm basis of classical technique.'

Cinderella

Ballet in three acts. Scenario and choreography: Darrell. Music: Gioacchino Rossini; arr. Bramwell Tovey. Design: John Fraser. Lighting: John B. Read. First performed by the Scottish Ballet, His Majesty's Theatre, Aberdeen, 7 December 1979. Elaine McDonald: Cinderella. Donald MacLeary: Prince Ramiro. Paul Russell: Dandini his equerry. Gordon Aitken: Don Magnifico. Sue Carlton-Jones: Arabella, his wife. Wendy Roe: Clorinda. Sally Collard-Gentle: Tisbe, his stepdaughters. Patricia Merrin: the Statue Fairy.

ACT I, *Scene 1*: The stone terrace outside Prince Ramiro's palace. Preparations for a masked ball are in progress. Servants, chefs, a tailor, a mask-maker and the major-domo create a busy scene. But Prince Ramiro is bored by the proceedings. The Statue Fairy appears and suggests he changes costume and mask with Dandini. He does so and the deception is successful.

Scene 2: The ante-room of Arabella. After a great deal of bustle and fuss, assisted by maids and the Housekeeper, Arabella, Don Magnifico, Clorinda and Tisbe depart for the ball forbidding Cinderella to go with them. Alone, Cinderella is visited by the Statue Fairy bringing her an invitation and a magnificent dress so that she also may attend.

ACT II: The garden of the palace. Guests arrive and the ball begins. When it is at its height Cinderella arrives, is admired by everyone and unrecognized by her family. Although Dandini (still disguised as the Prince) is infatuated with her, she has eyes only for Ramiro.

ACT III, *Scene 1*: Arabella's ante-room. The family squabbles over breakfast and the memory of the previous night. Dandini arrives with the slipper Cinderella has lost at the ball, seeking its pair. Thus Cinderella is discovered. The Statue Fairy causes Prince Ramiro to arrive, revealing his true identity.

Scene 2: The Land of Eternal Dawn. Accompanied by Dew Fairies and Cavaliers, the lovers enter the land of Eternal Dawn.

As so often in his work, Darrell has taken a well-known story but completely retreated it in his own way. In this case he has returned to the pre-pantomime, pre-Perrault origins of the tale. Cinderella is not a downtrodden scullery-maid but the daughter of Don Magnifico, a pompous fool who has remarried and acquired in the process two beautiful but spiteful stepdaughters. Prince Ramiro, host at the ball which Cinderella would like to attend, is not really interested in the social scene, unlike Dandini his equerry. The result is instant attraction between the two principal characters, thwarted on the one hand by narrow social convention, but assisted on the other by the world of the supernatural. Darrell's concern for the underdog and thwarting of convention appears in many of his ballets mingled with a recognition that audiences like to see rich productions and dancing in the classical style. *Cinderella* is the Scottish Ballet's most lavish production in the company's first ten years of life. Its music draws on Rossini's late piano works and some of his early ballet music; incorporates five numbers adapted from *La Cenerentola* and material from two overtures, *La Cambiale de Matrimonio* and *Il Turco in Italia*.

BARRY MORELAND (b. 1943)

Born in Melbourne, Moreland studied at the Australian Ballet School and joined the Australian Ballet in 1962, the year of the company's foundation. Coming to Europe, he danced with the Hamburg Ballet and in musicals, studied at London Contemporary Dance School, then joined the Contemporary Dance Theatre. His choreography reflects this very broad training. For London Contemporary Dance Theatre he created a number of interesting works, including *Nocturnal Dances, Summer Games* and *Kontakion*, to a religious theme later translated successfully on to television. In 1971 he was appointed resident choreographer to London Festival Ballet, creating for them in 1972 *Summer Solstice* to a commission from the Gulbenkian Foundation, then *In Nomine* the following year. *Prodigal Son (in ragtime)*, perhaps still his best-known work, was created in 1974. He has continued, however, to develop his reputation in Australia as well as UK. Since ceasing to be attached permanently to London Festival Ballet he has created new works for the Australian Ballet as well as Festival Ballet and other companies.

Prodigal Son (in ragtime)

Ballet in two acts. Choreography: Barry Moreland. Music: Scott Joplin, Grant Hossack and others. Décor: Michael Annals. Lighting: John B. Read. First performed by London Festival Ballet, London Coliseum, 7 May 1974. Paul Clarke: the Prodigal. Patricia Ruanne: the Siren. Kenn Wells: Master of Ceremonies.

ACT I: The overture reveals the Prodigal, resplendent in top hat, white tie and tails, tap dancing with a high-kicking chorus against a Hollywood art-deco pink and silver summery backcloth. Plainly, the ballet bears no relation to Balanchine's biblical treatment. From this beginning we move back in time with Scott Joplin, to the days before 1914 when ragtime was being born in New Orleans barrelhouses. We meet the Prodigal as a member of a family oppressed by a sanctimonious father. Rejecting this home life, including a sorrowing pair of sisters, the Son sets out into the world. He comes to New York, meets a girl with whom he wins a dance competition at a nightclub ruled by a snake-hipped Master of Ceremonies who, in many guises throughout the ballet, becomes the Prodigal's evil influence. At the nightclub the Prodigal meets the Siren for the first time. She, in many guises, represents temptation throughout the ballet.

The next scene finds the Prodigal thumbing a lift under a poster of Lord Kitchener declaring, 'Your King and Country Need You!' He joins the army, learns to drill, becomes involved with patriotic wives, sweethearts – and the Siren – goes to war and is last seen at the end of the first act walking among the dead bodies of his companions.

ACT II opens with victory posters and waiting wives and sweethearts. The Master of Ceremonies, now a war profiteer, pins on the Prodigal a row of medals, the Soldiers return and waltz away with their girls returning in mufti. With tap dancing and the charleston, we move through the 1920s into the Depression. Rescued from the breadline by the Siren, the Prodigal is taken to a nightclub where the Master of Ceremonies is head-waiter and pimp of the Siren. Thus through the Hitler era to the Second World War, where the Prodigal becomes a cadet from West Point, and into a post-war world where white-coated people with newspapers go mad as the world revolves. The Master of Ceremonies fights the Prodigal and leaves with the Siren. Left alone, the Prodigal returns home to be welcomed by a forgiving father.

Moreland has always had an ability to create striking roles for his leading dancers. These he creates again particularly for the late Paul Clarke as the Prodigal, Terry Hayworth as the Father and Patricia Ruanne and Ken

184

Wells as Siren and Master of Ceremonies. There is fun, some satire and a hint or two of Brecht – not to speak of the influence of American musicals – but the structure of the ballet cannot carry everything imposed upon it, particularly in Act II. The attempt to compress too long a period of time with too much incident produces a series of scenes so short and rapid they lack dramatic impact and climax. There are many good moments, however, and from the first night onwards, Paul Clarke established the Prodigal as his particular role, forever identified with it. In creating the Prodigal Moreland capitalized on Clarke's radiant good looks and youthful assurance, his gift of quick, fluent movement and unforced charm which carried him through the first act in triumph. But it was in the darker scenes of the second act that Clarke showed an unexpectedly wide range of dramatic sensitivity. The charm remained but it was underscored by a sincerity which made the Prodigal's return a natural end. Paul Clarke's identity with the ballet made it the centrepiece of a gala, *All for Paul*, in October 1978. The gala was the climax of two years work through which his fellow dancers and many others helped to establish a memorial fund following the young dancer's tragic death in September 1976, aged twenty-nine.

RONALD HYND (b. 1931)

A graduate of the Rambert School, Ronald Hynd joined the Royal Ballet in 1951 and danced many leading roles, notably in a partnership in the classic repertory with his wife, the ballerina Annette Page. He made his first choreography, a version of *Le Baiser de la Fée*, in 1968 for Dutch National Ballet, and made his first ballet for London Festival Ballet – *Dvořák Variations* – in 1970. In that same year Hynd went to Munich for three years as director of the ballet company there, creating several new ballets, and on his return to London he choreographed *In a Summer Garden* (1972) and *Charlotte Brontë* (1974) for the Sadler's Wells Royal Ballet, and *Mozartiana* in 1973 for London Festival Ballet, who also mounted his version of *Le Baiser de la Fée*. In 1976 Hynd used Elgar's only existing ballet score to create *The Sanguine Fan*, and followed this with a new version of *La Chatte*. He also worked for the Tokyo Ballet, and the New London Ballet, and for Australian Ballet produced the choreography for *The Merry Widow* in 1975, a staging illuminated by Dame Margot Fonteyn's performance, following this with another danced operetta in 1977 – *Rosalinda*, which was first seen in South Africa and then revived for London Festival Ballet in 1979. In this year Hynd also produced his version of Offenbach's *Le Papillon* for the Houston Ballet. His intelligent, Hoffmannesque staging of *The Nutcracker* was mounted for London Festival Ballet in 1976.

Dvořák Variations

Choreography: Ronald Hynd. Misic: Antonin Dvořák. Design: Peter Docherty. First performed by London Festival Ballet, 28 May 1970, Cardiff, with Galina Samsova and Andre Prokovsky.

Hynd's first ballet for an English company was a well crafted and intelligent response to the quick-changing moods of Dvořák's *Symphonic Variations*. Set for a central pair with four subsidiary couples and a group of six girls, it was cast in classic style, for which the elements of Bohemian folk music in the score inspired a matching use of folk dance steps and attitudes. Hynd reflected the light and shade and the strong dynamics of the score in taxing choreography, that was rewarding to watch.

The Sanguine Fan

Choreography: Ronald Hynd. Music: Elgar. Design: Peter Docherty. First performed by London Festival Ballet in Monte Carlo, 6 July 1976, with Manela Asensio, Patricia Ruanne, Paul Clarke and Dudley von Loggenburg.

Elgar wrote his score for *The Sanguine Fan* as a result of a request for some music for a war charity matinée in 1917. The theme of the entertainment was an eighteenth-century idyll which the artist Charles Condor had drawn in *sanguine* on a fan, and the choreography was by Ina Lowther, who also took the leading role with a cast which included Gerald du Maurier, Fay Compton and Ernest Thesiger.

The score was never thereafter used until 1976 when Ronald Hynd took it for a Wildean intrigue of a missing fan at an elegant party in Carlton House Terrace. Twin brothers receive their guests and after some charming toing and froing, a particularly wordly beauty receives a diamond necklace. The ballet is nostalgic, leisurely and agreeably borne along on Elgar's delightful score.

La Chatte

Choreography: Ronald Hynd. Music: Henri Sauguet. Design: Peter Docherty. First performed by London Festival Ballet, London Coliseum, 22 June 1978. Elisabetta Terabust: the Cat. Kenneth McCombie: the Young Man. Manola Asensio: Aphrodite.

In 1927 *La Chatte*, as originally given by the Diaghilev Ballets Russes,

186

was an elegant retelling of an Aesop fable, with a scenario by Boris Kochno, choreography by Balanchine and very modish and effective design by Naum Gabo and Anton Pevsner, featuring talc and mica. Serge Lifar was cast as the young man who falls in love with a she cat, Olga Spessivtseva, obligingly turned by Aphrodite into a young woman. Love's young dream was, alas, ruined by the appearance of a mouse which caused the young woman to revert to her primal state. Balanchine's choreography was much admired, as was Sauguet's score – which attracted Ronald Hynd to making a new version of the piece. The result looks like a homage to the 1920s Ballets Russes, whose image is so well caught in the ballet itself: a fashionable artistic movement (constructivist décor in new materials), a pretty, very French score which evokes Messager and Poulenc; and choreography which, as one may gather from C. W. Beaumont's comment at the time, hymned the male body beautiful. Peter Docherty's new design, chic in white and blue, provides a double staircase at whose central point the cat heroine reposes. The hero has six *sportif* companions who indulge in acrobatic exercises and occasionally toss the hero about and hinder his relationship with the cat. Loie Fuller appears as Aphrodite – imperious and with sleeves like wings – a *dea ex machina* who acts as marriage broker. The story line does not seem particularly clear on first acquaintance but it is perhaps typical of the period which the ballet so stylishly evokes that one does not particularly care. Fluent choreography with suitably art-deco moments; white-clad cast looking handsome; agreeable score; there are the ingredients of a lightweight piece, sensitive to its score and its period.

DAVID BINTLEY (b. 1957)

A graduate of the Royal Ballet School, David Bintley made a great success of his graduation performance as Dr Coppélius in the Royal Ballet School performance of *Coppélia* in June 1976. In September of that year he joined the Sadler's Wells Royal Ballet and was soon recognized as an exceptionally vivid dance actor. At the same time he was making choreography for workshop performances – his début as a creator came while still at the Royal Ballet School – and for the Gulbenkian National Choreographic Summer School. At the age of twenty he made his first professional ballet for the Sadler's Wells troupe: an assured and compelling adaptation of incidents from two Camus works, entitled *The Outsider*, first seen at the Birmingham Hippodrome on 16 March 1978. In that same year he made a brief *pièce d'occasion* for Lynn Seymour and four boys to Dave Brubeck's

'Take Five' as part of the eightieth birthday celebrations for Dame Ninette de Valois. On 16 March 1979 his *Meadow of Proverbs* was presented by the Sadler's Wells Royal Ballet at the Birmingham Hippodrome, using a Darius Milhaud score. This was a series of sharply drawn dance scenes, inspired by Goya's *Proverbios* and by the *commedia dell'arte*, touched with a fine satiric energy. In the summer of 1979 he provided a less successful ballet for his parent company, a version of Lord Berners' *Triumph of Neptune* under the title *Punch and the Street Party*, which was given its first performance in the Royal Ballet's Tent as part of the Edinburgh Festival's homage to Diaghilev on 20 August. On 22 February 1980 he staged his fourth ballet for the Sadler's Wells Theatre Ballet. This was *Homage to Chopin*. As with his three previous one-act ballets it was designed by Mike Becket.

Homage to Chopin

Ballet in one scene. Choreography: David Bintley. Music: Andrzej Panufnik. Design: Mike Becket. First performed by the Sadler's Wells Royal Ballet, Royal Shakespeare Theatre, Stratford-on-Avon, on 22 February 1980. With David Ashmole.

The ballet's title comes from Andrzej Panufnik's score, and without labouring the point, it is possible to see how Bintley's choreography stands in the same relationship to the Fokine of *Les Sylphides* as does Panufnik's writing to that of his artistic forebear. We are aware of a continuity of tradition – spiritual as well as physical – that is assessed in sensitive and thoughtful terms. Gone the evocation of Taglioni in a moonlit glade; instead we see Mike Becket's backcloth that at first seems shadowy, but which reveals itself as a crayoned, shaded mass of colour against which six white-clad girls are caught dreaming, leaning on the night air. (It is typical of Bintley that the ballet should begin with an image which catches and holds the attention.) There, too, is the Young Man; no longer Fokine's 'youth of the Chopin type' but a virile and, as we later observe, slightly amused figure. The writing for the male dancer is brilliant, marked with touches of real originality as movement progresses from the conventional and expected to the unexpected and vividly fresh. For the women there are duets and trios, group dances which find them floating or bounding, colouring movement through Bintley's own homage to polonaise and mazurka – the score is extended by the inclusion of the *mazurek* from Panufnik's *Polonia*. The sum effect is of choreography economical, unfussed, elegant, with innovation happily matched by a respect for tradition.

MICHAEL CORDER (b. 1955)

Michael Corder entered the Royal Ballet after seven years at the Royal Ballet School, and was soon recognized as a very promising classical soloist. He took his first steps as a choreographer with the Royal Ballet's Choreographic Group, and in February 1978 produced a quintet, set to Stravinsky's *Dumbarton Oaks Concerto*, of such interest that it was given an airing for two performances at Sadler's Wells Theatre on 7 October 1978, with Deirdre Eyden, Judith Howe and Jennifer Jackson, Michael Batchelor and Stephen Sherriff (all members of the Royal Ballet) as its cast. Titled *Rhyme nor Reason*, the piece was no more – and no less – than a flow of plotless classical dancing, alert, witty, youthfully exuberant, and full enough of invention and a true feeling for the possibilities of the academic dance to earn a place thereafter in the repertory of the Sadler's Wells Royal Ballet, who staged it on 30 March 1979 in Bournemouth. Corder left the Royal Ballet to dance for a year with the Dutch National Ballet, but in September 1979 he returned to Britain, joining the Sadler's Wells Theatre Ballet, for whom he next made *Day into Night*.

Day into Night

Ballet in one act. Choreography: Michael Corder. Score: Bohuslav Martinu: Sinfonietta La Jolla. Design: Lazaro Prince. First performed by the Sadler's Wells Royal Ballet at the Theatre Royal, Norwich, 28 March 1980. With Sherilyn Kennedy, Carl Myers; Margaret Barbieri, Derek Purnell; June Highwood, Stephen Wicks; Marion Tait, Alain Dubreuil.

Corder provides a brief theme which he has used to give some emotional colouring for what is, in effect, a ballet of bright, plotless dancing. The first movement of Martinu's happy sinfonietta is used to portray the sun; the second movement is a double duet which contrasts the light and dark aspects of the moon; the final section treats of the effects of sun and moon on the earth's daily cycle. Far more important than these excuses for the dancing is the fact of Corder's evident delight in making classical choreography. He has an individual voice as a creator: his manner is elegant, strong in dynamics, demanding much of his dancers – but enhancing them at every moment.

SIX

British Modern Choreography

Historically, 'modern' choreography has two roots. There is that which derives from the rebellion of Isadora Duncan, Ruth St Denis and others in the USA against the artificiality of classical ballet at the end of the nineteenth century; and there is that which derives from the German *Ausdruckstanz* (German equivalent of modern dance) representing a similar rebellion in Central Europe before and after the First World War. The leading figures here were Rudolf von Laban and Mary Wigman with, later, Yvonne Georgi, Kurt Jooss, Albrecht Knust, Sigurd Leeder, Max Terpis, Harold Kreutzberg and others. Modern dance, therefore, is as old as the century. It is no longer modern. Because of this contradiction a variety of other names or categories are being coined, especially in the United States, to identify the periods of its development since Duncan. There is historical modern which covers the early days of modern up to the establishment of Martha Graham in, say, the late 1950s. Later than this is post-modern, new dance, non-literate and post-Cunningham. 'Contemporary' sometimes implies a category including contemporary classical ballet ranging from the very classical Balanchine to the classical/modern Glen Tetley. In the United Kingdom, however, contemporary has come to mean the style of modern dance developed by Martha Graham in the United States and translated on to British physiques and temperaments through the establishment of the London Contemporary Dance Company and School in the late 1960s. We have referred already to the significance of this event for the theatrical dance in Britain. Similarly, we have identified two other areas of modern British choreography, one being grouped around Ballet Rambert, the other independent of either of the two main centres. The latter comprises small groups of dancers or individual dancers in London and the regions, acknowledging few allegiances to anyone but themselves. Beside these areas of choreography is a range of vocational schools teaching various styles of modern dance in the United Kingdom. Many of them are linked with the modern dance branch of the Imperial Society of Teachers of Dancing, one of the largest and liveliest branches in the society.

The complex social and historical reasons for this development need fuller treatment than is appropriate here. Almost all the important influences on early British modern choreography have been American – from Martha Graham through Robert Cohan on London Contemporary Dance Theatre and from Graham and other sources through Glen Tetley on Ballet Rambert. We describe a number of Tetley's ballets later but draw attention in this introduction to his innovative influence in two areas of British choreographic development. First, he was involved from the beginning with reshaping Ballet Rambert in its modern style from 1966 until today. The connection can be traced in the following pages from *Pierrot Lunaire, Freefall, Ziggurat* and *Embrace Tiger and Return to Mountain,* all reproduced for Ballet Rambert in the late 1960s, to his first full evening work, *The Tempest,* created on Ballet Rambert in 1979. Tetley's classically based modern style – as appropriate to the Royal Ballet as to modern Ballet Rambert – was the new company's strongest creative inspiration in its early days and profoundly influenced also the development of the company's recent principal choreographer, Christopher Bruce.

Tetley was also involved from the beginning with the evolution of the Gulbenkian National Choreographic Summer School (now called International Dance Course for Professional Choreographers and Composers). This is a two-week event, held every summer at the University of Surrey, designed for choreographers and composers who have already shown evidence of talent embracing both classical and modern choreographic styles. Tetley's classical and modern training therefore made him ideal as the school's first director in 1975. In that role he not only established the school's high standards, since equally sustained on two occasions by Robert Cohan, but showed himself to be a remarkable teacher, analyst and intellectual of the dance.

Robert Cohan, the other principal choreographic influence upon British modern dance, has concentrated most of his creative powers upon one company, London Contemporary Dance Theatre. Consequently his influence extends deeper into British dance life, disseminated through this company and its dancers. He does not have the catholic training of Tetley but he, too, combines choreographic talent with outstanding qualities as a teacher and leader of dancers, artistic director and communicator to a wide public of dance supporters. In the latter role he was the principal influence in initiating in 1976 the idea of dance residences for London Contemporary Dance Theatre. These took place in Yorkshire and Lancashire, initially for about six weeks, now eight to ten weeks annually, supported by relevant education authorities and regional arts associations. Although well-

191

established in USA, the practice was new to Britain. Its impact has been so deep as to change significantly the relationship of his company with the public outside London, and to establish the idea as a regular element in the services dance companies should provide, and thus involve other companies, too, in the practice. Among other benefits the residences won, and continue to win, new respect for dancers as communicators able to influence the habits and thoughts of people from all walks of life. In this sense, and as choreographer and teacher, Robert Cohan has become the principal creative influence in establishing modern dance as a force in British theatre. One particularly important result has been to introduce new thinking about the traditional relationship between dancers, choreographers, teachers and management. The more relaxed atmosphere of modern dance is a world away from the hierarchies of classical companies where the effect of this new influence is likely to be profound, quite apart from any effect on choreography or technical training.

ROBERT COHAN (b. 1925)

Born in New York, Robert Cohan decided to study dance only after the end of military service in the Second World War. Accordingly he joined the Martha Graham School in 1946, became a member of her company within four months, and her partner in 1950. He studied and danced with the Graham Company 1946–57 and 1962–9. This did not mean, then, the regular year-round employment which can be offered by major subsidized dance companies in the UK today. It meant comparatively short performance seasons interspersed with longer periods when the dancers earned livings as best they might as teachers, dancing in some other form of theatre such as musicals, or in films, or moving into other kinds of employment, often casual and unrelated to theatre. The survivors thus acquired a very wide experience and maturity. Cohan's background is precisely this and undoubtedly helped him to establish a modern dance company and school of good quality – given, of course, the financial backing and vision of Robin Howard. It was not his first company. In 1957 he left Graham to dance on Broadway and in films, then opened his own school in Boston in 1958 while continuing to teach at the Graham School, Juilliard School, Connecticut College and New York University. In 1959 he formed his own group for which he created several works, returning to Graham in 1962. In 1967 he was invited by Robin Howard to become director of the London School of Contemporary Dance and of the associated London Contemporary Dance Theatre.

Although he regularly creates dance works abroad, notably in Israel, it is through London Contemporary Dance Theatre that Cohan has won recognition as a major choreographer. The selection below cannot do justice to his considerable output, largely because he himself makes clear that he does not create for a permanent repertory but as a part of a never ending creative exploration. We can but select, therefore, some of his works which seem at this moment to be part of his company's repertory but also reflect his own creative development.

Eclipse

Work in one act. Choreography: Cohan. Music: Eugene Lester. Lighting: John B. Read. First performed New York, 1959. First performed by London Contemporary Dance Theatre, with costumes by Peter Farmer, Adeline Genée Theatre, East Grinstead, 10 October 1967.

'When two people eclipse each other, in the ensuing darkness their relationship slowly alters.'

Robert Cohan's brief description of one of his earliest dance creations conceals a remarkably acute study of the deteriorating relationship of a man and woman, called Sun and Moon in the original programme. It begins and ends, it seems, with a memory of meetings and partings. The twenty minutes between these moments recreate the relationship through a series of images which amount to one of the clearest portraits of an emotional encounter in contemporary dance. Conceived originally for Cohan's first company in 1959, and today somewhat dated in style, the work has continued to play a significant role in Cohan's creative life, proof of its quality and the challenge it represents to its two characters. He remounted it for the first season of the then new London Contemporary Dance Group in 1967, with Noemi Lapzeson and Robert Powell. Later he restaged it for an important collaboration with the Royal Ballet's Ballet for All company during two seasons 1970–2. This presented a comparative programme of classical and contemporary dance to audiences throughout Britain. The work was re-presented in London Contemporary Dance Theatre's 1979 summer season at Sadler's Wells Theatre.

Cell

Work in one act. Choreography: Cohan. Music: Ronald Lloyd. Design: Norberto Chiesa. First performed by London Contemporary Dance Theatre, The Place, London, 11 September 1969.

Cell moves through three phases. Within a white walled space whose only exits and entrances are one each side upstage, move six characters, three men, three women. They enter falling, sliding, balancing but forever returning to the walls which represent their prison or their support. At first they are in the clothes of today and their relationships are hectic, aggressive, momentary. One by one they leave. In the second phase the outer shell of reality has been peeled away. They appear in tights whose primary colours perhaps suggest the more primary nature of the changing relationship structure, its new tensions behind the more formal structure. Out of this structure emerges one man as a focal character. Again they leave one by one. In the third phase they have no protection, either from formal society and its surface contacts, nor from their own emotional resources and cover-ups. They are almost nude, defenceless. Thus exposed, they panic, leaving the man alone. In a desperate solo he clutches wildly at each wall which lights up, revealing the silhouette of a person hanging. As the sound track becomes more menacing bricks tumble over the stage. Desperately the man tries to build a wall around himself before pitching forward across his useless efforts. Black-out.

Still in the repertory, *Cell* is the most powerful of Cohan's early works created specially for his new company. It brought together two colleagues of long-standing. Chiesa, the designer, and Robert Powell, whose dancing with the Graham Company in London in 1963 gained him a British public. Both gave to the new work a special distinction. Chiesa's use of a raked white floor and white walls at odd angles seemed to suspend the dancers in space, but also in relief emphasizing their isolation. Powell's strong portrayal of the man focused the drama and underlined the skill of Cohan's choreography and production. *Cell* has been likened to a Pinter play, its tensions, pauses and silences reflecting the private loneliness of each character.

Stages

Hero myth in two stages. Production: Cohan. Music for Stage 1: Arne Nordheim; for Stage 2: Bob Downes. Décor: Peter Farmer. Lighting: John B. Read. Film sequences and projections: Anthony McCall. Gymnastic coaching: Pauline Prestidge. First performed by London Contemporary Dance Theatre, The Place, London, 21 April 1971. William Louther: the Hero.

Stage 1: Reality (impression of the world as it seems to be) – Descent – Meeting of the Goddess – Death – Reflections – Interrogation. 'In the first stage the world is seen as the underworld. From the conscious choice of trying to see it as it is, all loneliness, meetings with illusion or Maya, and self-questionings occur.'

Stage 2: Dream (the cartoons of what once was) – A Journey – Meeting with a Monster – the Sirens and another Monster – Still another Monster – Destruction of the Temple. 'In the second stage the myths or trials, that once might have helped us, seem to be of little use. They have become the subject for technicolour movies and comic books. We are left solely with our humanity at whatever stage it may be . . .'

Stages, Cohan's first two-act work, shows him wrestling, as so often, with the meaning of life. It is symptomatic of much modern choreography whether descended from German or American origins, part of the rebellion against what is seen as the triviality of much classical ballet. All the resources of a multi-media production are summoned to create the images and realize the choreographer's intention. The choreography lies in the manipulation and union of these resources rather than in the creation of dance in any formal sense. In Stage 1 the Hero – a splendid role for William Louther, splendidly performed – descends to the underworld, is crucified, tempted, taunted, interrogated, tortured and reaches out to the unattainable, never to succeed. The Hero is the only human, so his movements are natural rather than danced. All other characters are Furies, a Goddess – in a word, parts of his experience. Stage 2 reveals the truth behind the myth. The underworld is what we ourselves create through the mass media. No one is free, neither the young people in their gear, especially not the Hero who suffers the loneliness and exhaustion of pop-stardom, drug hallucinations, ambition hallucinations, success hallucinations, all reduced in the end to a comic strip. The Hero destroys this world and turns to an exit sign flashing on and off in the darkness.

Cohan's approach is one of total theatre, discarding a generally accepted choreographic structure to weld together all his theatrical resources. It was an achievement of staging from a remarkable collaboration of creative artists which represented an advance for all of them and therefore for the company as a whole. Peter Farmer moved beyond the romantic designs which have made his reputation to create a visual satire of the modern world. '[Arne Nordheim's] prerecorded tapes in the first part, and the jazz-extended character of Bob Downes's Open Music in the second', remarked the critic Noël Goodwin in *Dance and Dancers,* 'pointed the different planes of imagination on which the two sequences take place. The reality and the illusion exist as counterparts of each other.' It is a good summary of the whole experience which began, incidentally, a collaboration with Bob Downes, since repeated several times.

Waterless Method of Swimming Instruction

Dance work in one act. Choreography: Cohan. Music: Bob Downes. Décor and costumes: Ian Murray-Clark. Lighting: John B. Read. First performed by London Contemporary Dance Theatre, Théâtre de Beaulieu, Lausanne, 11 June 1974.

A cruise-liner. The swimming pool drained of water. In the empty space six girls and four men posed sedately in groups, dressed in white flannels, smart dresses, parasols. Two men appear, run along the edge of the pool, somersault into it. The others follow suit, change into swimsuits, life jackets, bikinis. Follows a series of dances for couples, groups, solos, all inspired by swimming or the games one plays on beaches and in the water, all, or nearly all comic, the comedy underlined by one lady who surveys it all from the side of the pool, changing into a succession of costumes, collapsing into deck-chairs and finally appearing with a very long, white feather boa.

Cohan extends his creative talent into the world of dotty humour helped by a fine impressionistic jazz score by Bob Downes and Ian Murray-Clark's imaginatively built set of a shipboard swimming pool which somehow creates an illusion that the dancing is actually aquatic. The work is oblique, witty and rich-textured, with a fine piece of clowning by Siobhan Davies as the Lady of the collapsed deck-chair.

No–Man's–Land

Dance work in one act. Choreography: Robert Cohan. Music: Barry Guy (Statements II for double bass). Design: Peter Farmer. First performed by London Contemporary Dance Theatre, 13 November 1974. Robert North: Orpheus. Linda Gibbs: Eurydice. Siobhan Davies: Lethe. Anthony van Laast: Cerberus. Patrick Harding-Irmer: Charon.

No-Man's-Land is a stylized, hard-edged version of the Orpheus myth. It starts with the advantage of a stripped-to-the-bone setting, of bare stage and a bridge holding batteries of stage-lighting, that does more to stimulate the audience's imagination than a clutter of decoration. The gateway to the underworld is this light-bridge and it is manoeuvred about the stage as the action dictates.

Costuming – black and red for the denizens of Hell; white and beige for Orpheus and Eurydice – has an almost Noh play economy of effect: Cerberus has a red-frilled and pendulous tongue; Lethe is clad with hanging loops of coloured cloth. The score, a transcendental exercise for double bass, is played on stage with the executant enclosed in a black cave. The effect of all this 'exposed' music and setting for the drama is both mysterious and

196

(*above*) Marilyn Rowe and John Meehan in the Australian Ballet's production of *Gemini*. (*below*) Members of the London Contemporary Dance Theatre in *Troy Game*

Patrick Harding-Irmer with members of the London Contemporary Dance Theatre in *Waterless Method of Swimming Instruction*

compelling. Cohan's choreography, menacing and implacable for the creatures of the underworld, strong in outline and somehow archaic in feeling for Orpheus and Eurydice, establishes a Cocteauesque atmosphere. Twists on the usual progress of the myth – Lethe's momentary involvement with Orpheus – sharpen the impact of its telling. In its emotional concentration and the economy of movement it has a fine, uncompromising imagery, as the forces of darkness trick and dog the footsteps of Orpheus, and the dance-language is characterized by its harsh cutting edge, as when Lethe kicks Cerberus, or Eurydice is held and turned in hieratic poses. It is a work of clarity of purpose: we sense that the initial image which inspired Cohan has been kept true and sharp throughout the creation of *No-Man's-Land*.

Class

Dance work in one act. Choreography: Cohan. Music: Jon Keliehor. Design: Charter, later Norberto Chiesa. Lighting: John B. Read. First performed by London Contemporary Dance Theatre, His Majesty's Theatre, Aberdeen, 22 September 1975.

Class needs no libretto. Although presented in a choreographed form, all the movements and patterns of this dance work derive from the company's daily technique classes whose primary purpose is to strengthen, coordinate and shape the dancer's body. It is less obvious – indeed only obvious to those who have watched closely the development of London Contemporary Dance Theatre – that the movement material also demonstrates several years evolution from the Martha Graham style and technique, with which the company started, to a more individual style and technique a decade later. Hence *Class* is what it says, and more than what it says, drawn from the daily class which is for every dancer a ritual, a challenge, a reaffirmation and rejuvenation. To Jon Keliehor's apt, largely percussive score, which seems to take its inspiration from the percussive rhythm to which many modern classes are conducted, Cohan has translated a demonstration of dance training into a work of art which shows off splendidly the dance qualities of his company. The structure is largely that of a class. A close and famous comparison in classical ballet would be Harold Lander's *Etudes* (q.v.). *Class* is also something of a memoir.

Forest

Dance work in one scene. Choreography: Cohan. Music: Brian Hodgson. Design: Norberto Chiesa. First performed by London Contemporary Dance Company at Sadler's Wells Theatre, 13 April 1977.

Forest is no more, and no less, than its title. Brian Hodgson's accompaniment presents us with the constant soughing of the wind through trees. The aural life of the forest starts with the first pipings of birds, moves through thunder and rain to the distant howl of animals as dusk falls. The dances offer no specifics of behaviour, but insist only upon a seemless flow of movement for four men and five women. In solos, duets, group sections, Cohan's fluent, highly imaginative writing suggests something of the activity in the forest as the day passes. It is a mysterious and thrilling work; by looking at the dancers we can appreciate something of the essence of Nature – it is as if Fabre were a choreographer. In one section, a solo created for Anthony van Laast, and superbly danced by him, we see a faun, as credible and as beautiful as Nijinsky's creation must once have been.

Rondo

Dance work in one act and six circles. Choreography: Cohan. Music: John Herbert McDowell. Design: Barney Wan. Knitted fabrics designed and executed: Trevor Collins. Lighting: John B. Read. First performed by London Contemporary Dance Theatre, Roundhouse, London, 2 October 1979.

A work to be seen by audiences sitting in a circle around the dancers. The theme, therefore, is circles, in fact six circles linked each time by the whole company or part of it moving round the stage to make an interlude before the next circle. The work begins in this way followed by the first circle, a solo for a man. The second circle is a quartet for women. The third, a trio for two women and a man. The fourth, a duet for a man and woman. The fifth is a quartet for four men. The sixth brings back the whole company.

Rondo was created for a special season of dances in the round at London's Roundhouse. Three choreographers – Siobhan Davies, Robert North and Robert Cohan – made original pieces for the occasion but Cohan's, coming last, appeared as the major work. In structure, imagery and craftsmanship it is a most mature piece showing Cohan's mastery of all his material. Although the central theme is circles he also explores a number of movement themes, a crouching position for the men like discus-throwers, a circling *grand battement* for men and women. He has developed, too, the implications of the audience around so that the public sits as if participating in a ritual, the dancers marking out the dancing area at their first entrance. The choreography suggests athletic competition, ceremony, celebration; it moves one way and the other between the Apollonian and the Dionysian elements of dance. It is a piece one hopes to see in other settings.

198

The work is notable also for an original score by John Herbert McDowell commissioned with assistance from the Gulbenkian Foundation, developing a collaboration which began at the Gulbenkian National Choreographic Summer School in 1977 and 1978 where McDowell was music director and Cohan director. The design explores the use of knitted fabrics for costumes. These work well for the men, naked from the waist up, dressed in trousers of many colours which cling tightly around the waist and pelvis but loose around the legs with a suggestion of the Orient, gathered at the ankles. For the women it is less successful because the material hangs and moves less well for skirts; nor is it so flattering. Music, design and lighting, however, no less than the choreography, re-emphasize and recall a particular significance of *modern* dance for British dance theatre during the last decade. It has explored and stimulated a whole new range of music from British and other composers. In design its innovative influence can be seen especially in the exploration of design for the body, as here, although the set designs of *Cell*, for example, *Waterless Method of Swimming Instruction*, *Mass* and other works have also been notable contributions to British theatre design. The same, not least, must be said for lighting where Cohan himself, and in frequent collaboration with John B. Read, has set an example which has helped establish new standards of lighting as one of the most important creative elements in dance theatre.

CHRISTOPHER BRUCE (b. 1945)

When, in 1966, the Ballet Rambert was reshaped in a more modern fashion, the new style of the repertory was ideally suited to a young dancer in the company, Christopher Bruce. In the choreography of Norman Morrice, and especially in Glen Tetley's *Pierrot Lunaire*, Bruce was revealed as an artist of intense dramatic power. His Pierrot has been recognized as one of the outstanding interpretations in British dance, and it was characteristic of the adventurous policies of the Rambert company that Bruce should also soon make his mark as a choreographer. His first work was *George Frideric* (1969), a plotless realization of Handel music; it was followed by *Living Space* in the same year, and in 1970 he created *Wings* in Cologne, a study in images of flight transferred on to the bodies of dancers, which was acquired by the Rambert company in the following year.

In 1972 and 1973 Bruce made two ballets for the exposed stage area of the Young Vic, where the Rambert company presented seasons of new works – *For these who die as cattle* and *There was a time* – in both of which his concern with war as a fact of our time was manifest. There followed *Duets* in 1973, a work much lighter in manner, and in 1974 *Weekend* looked to the tensions of couples separated for much of the time and only reunited for brief and often unhappy spells. In the same year he made *Unfamiliar Playground* for the Sadler's Wells Royal Ballet, and then, in 1975, he created one of his finest and most assured pieces, *Ancient Voices of Children.* For the celebrations of the fiftieth anniversary of Ballet Rambert he produced the charming tribute to Dame Marie Rambert, *Girl in a Straw Hat,* inspired by an early photograph of the young Rambert as a schoolgirl in Warsaw, carrying the hat that gave the ballet its title, and in the same season produced his *Black Angels. Promenade,* a realization of some Bach flute sonatas came later in the same year, and after working in Israel as part of a sabbatical leave, Bruce choreographed the full-length *Cruel Garden,* a 'spectacle inspired by the work of Federigo García Lorca' which had been conceived by the mime Lindsay Kemp. In 1977 he revived a work originally created for the Batsheva Company in Israel, *Echoes of a Night Sky,* which continued his association with the music of George Crumb (already seen in *Black Angels* and *Ancient Voices of Children*). He renewed this collaboration with *Night with Waning Moon* created in 1979, the year of his *Labyrinth* for Australian Dance Theatre, music by Morton Subotnick.

In all these works we are made aware of Bruce's concern with the human condition. The brutalities and cruelties of war, the tensions in human relationships, seem to evoke the best of his creative talent. As interpreter of his own work, as well as that of other choreographers, he remains one of the most potent and sharply focused dancers in Britain. In 1973 Bruce's contribution as dancer and choreographer to the British scene was acknowledged when he became the first recipient of the London *Evening Standard* Ballet Award for the most outstanding contribution to dance in that year.

Duets

Ballet in one scene. Choreography: Christopher Bruce. Music: Brian Hodgson. Design: Nadine Baylis. First performed by Ballet Rambert at Sadler's Wells Theatre, London, 21 September 1973. With Julia Blaikie, Joseph Scoglio; Sally Owen, Leigh Warren, Marilyn Williams, Jon Benoit.

Duets grows from silence and darkness and embryos of movement to a peak of activity and sound and light, and then fades in a gradual diminuendo to its first state. Nadine Baylis's setting is a green-edged suggestion of lawns, hedges and fields; the electronic score by Brian Hodgson starts

200

from single bell sounds and develops in pitch and intensity; three couples in simple blue costumes are gradually stretched in bolder, stronger movement. The tone of the work is pastoral, serene, tenderly attentive rather than overtly loving in its relationships, a work at peace with itself. Its structure relies upon canonic form; simple curves pass from one dancer to another, are repeated, picked up, embellished. The feeling of *Duets* is harmonious, understated, a green thought in a green place.

Weekend

Ballet in one scene. Choreography: Christopher Bruce. Music: Brian Hodgson. First performed by Ballet Rambert at the Roundhouse, London, 17 April 1974. With Marilyn Williams, Julia Blaikie, Sally Owen, Jon Benoit, Christopher Bruce.

As a dark, angry reverse of the serene *Duets*, *Weekend* is a picture of couples caught in encounters that suggest the pyschic wounds and unease of relationships that have everything except permanence. (The piece can be interpreted as a view of the life of touring dancers: separated during the week by their performance schedule, they return to their homes and their loved ones, and have the task of re-establishing afresh the partnership that is to be broken afresh by the next week's touring engagement.) To the pulsing monotone of Brian Hodgson's score, Bruce evolves a language that moves from a slow and deliberate manner to frenzied aggression. Like *Duets* it is cast in cyclic form, and its closing moments make brilliant use of a canon in which one duet seems an echo, an after-image, of the same sequence performed by another couple. Because of the numbers in the cast there is always an odd-girl-out, whose identity changes with the varying situations of the couples, and this suggests something of the unease and discontent that characterize this powerful work. The choreography has an almost surgical precision in cutting through to the disquiet of body and mind of the quintet; movement seems rooted in physical and emotional truth, a duet for the two men and the canon for the couples being of exceptional power and expressive force.

Ancient Voices of Children

Ballet in one act. Choreography: Christopher Bruce. Score: George Crumb. Design: Nadine Baylis. First performed by Ballet Rambert at Sadler's Wells Theatre, 7 July 1975.

The starting point of Christopher Bruce's choreography is George Crumb's setting of the poems by Federigo García Lorca which give the

201

ballet its title. The children are urchins and Nadine Baylis dresses them in ragged cast-offs, and places them in a setting made of swatches of greyish white cloth that frame the stage. In the games and dances that Bruce gives these children we see the suffering and tragedy that haunts their every step.

At curtain-rise they lie – in a sleep that is also death – under cotton coverlets and these are to be their shelters and their toys. Four girls, three boys, they rise from their slumbers to play out the series of games that are a meditation upon the dreams and make-believe of childhood and also upon the realities of unwanted and unloved victims of an adult world. A tough section of tumbling and fighting for the boys gives way to a slow duet for a boy and a girl, and there follows an agonized solo for another girl. The children's distress increases. Two girls die and a boy grieves over the body of one of them. And because these are children Bruce next shows four of them in macabre capers beneath their protecting draperies, forming a funeral procession that will carry the dead girl away. There follow hints of games, from hopscotch to bullfighting and the nursing of a doll, and after a lyrical section in which the girls are lifted in arabesque – the Lorca text speaks of children going 'very far/farther than those hills/farther than the seas/close to the stars . . .' – the ballet ends with the young bodies stretched out once again under their covers.

Bruce's affection for cyclic form gives the work a satisfying overall shape, but it is his passionate concern that most impresses the viewer, and his ability to fix emotional states with movement of real sensitivity.

Black Angels

Ballet in one act. Choreography: Bruce. Music: George Crumb. Design: Nadine Baylis. First performed by Ballet Rambert, Horsham, 11 May 1976.

Christopher Bruce has demonstrated a rapport with the music of George Crumb which has resulted in choreography of harsh, nervous imagery. His second work to the music of this composer was *Black Angels*, its title, theme and structure coming from a string quartet for amplified instruments and percussion. These 'thirteen images from the Dark Land' are concerned with the soul's journey, with the fall from grace leading through spiritual annihilation to ultimate redemption. It is a most serious and fraught work for three couples who are discovered in hell, where every abomination of spirit and body must be endured. Bruce's dance language, like the music of the quartet's first section, is harsh and agonized. One white clad man must suffer with his companions and be dogged and attacked by another demonic male. Escape is impossible and the choreography has the same

202

despairing force that we can see in the blackest images of Bosch or Goya. Through the fabric of the quartet writing come strains of Schubert's 'Death and the Maiden', and the lightening of the emotional tension finds the central man identified with Christ. The Crucifixion is suggested, the Deposition – with one of the women as the Virgin – and the Entombment. Yet the resurrected figure we finally see is not the triumphant Saviour, but rather an epileptic Holy Innocent, a Prince Myshkin, Christ-like only in his suffering. The ballet is many-layered, intense and unquestionably powerful with, at its first performance, an exceptional interpretation by Zoltan Imre as the hero.

Cruel Garden

Spectacle inspired by the works of Federigo García Lorca. Conceived by Lindsay Kemp. Choreography: Christopher Bruce. Direction: Christopher Bruce and Lindsay Kemp. Sets: Ralph Koltai, assisted by Sue Blane. Costumes: Lindsay Kemp. Music composed and arranged: Carlos Miranda. First performed by Ballet Rambert at the Roundhouse, London, 5 July 1977. Christopher Bruce: Lorca. John Tsakiris: The Bull.

The aim of this 'fantasy' upon the life of the Spanish poet García Lorca is to show the interaction of his life and the imagery of his poetry. As conceived by the mime artist Lindsay Kemp, and choreographed by Christopher Bruce, it offers a series of scenes, inspired by such Lorca works as *El Café de Chinitas* and *Blood Wedding*, which explain his ideals and his tragic fate in terms of his own creativity. In the bold arena of Ralph Koltai's setting, with its doors, grilles and balconies, marked by a huge bloodstain, Lorca's tragedy, his dreams and sensitivities, his visit to America and his personal mythology (which included Buster Keaton) are all displayed. Immensely popular with audiences, despite a mixed critical reception, the piece – which runs without an interval for ninety minutes – was dominated at its creation by Bruce's own exemplary impersonation of Lorca, a portrayal which, in its concentration and imaginative force, provides a strong centre of integrity in a theatre-piece which has elsewhere a flaunting extravagance of production ideas.

ROBERT NORTH (b. 1945)

American by birth but British trained, North was an art student before studying classical ballet with Kathleen Crofton and at the Royal Ballet School, then modern dance at the London School of Contemporary Dance

203

and with Graham and Merce Cunningham in New York. This duality of training is reflected in his versatility as performer and choreographer. He began to dance with London Contemporary Dance Theatre on its formation in 1967, danced some seasons with the Graham Company, then returned to LCDT in 1969 as a principal dancer. His first choreography was for London Festival Ballet's choreographic workshop but his work soon began to appear in the contemporary repertory ranging from drama to comedy, always well constructed, often with an ingenious climax. He was appointed associate choreographer of London Contemporary Dance Theatre in 1975, but his work appears also in the repertory of other companies, classical and modern, as well as on film and television.

Troy Game

Dance work in one act. Choreography: North. Music: Batucada/Bob Downes. Costumes: Peter Farmer. Lighting: Charter. First performed by London Contemporary Dance Theatre, Queen's Theatre, Stoke-on-Trent, 7 October 1974.

'How to turn your frieze into a light relief'.

Troy Game is possibly North's most popular work, an all-male display which pokes fun at muscle-flexing and athletic show-off while at the same time balancing humour with a persuasive statement of excellent male dancing. The piece emphasized at its first production the strength of the company's male dancers and has done a good deal since for the status of men in dance. Batucada, by the way, is neither a composer nor a group but, as John Percival pointed out at the time, a particular South American rhythm from Brazil. Bob Downes' music is from his *Episodes at 4 a.m.*

Still Life

Dance work in one act. Choreography: North. Music: Bob Downes. Design: Peter Farmer. Film: Peter Selby, John Garland, Mike Brewster. Story and coordination: John Dodson, Dave Hall, Joe McAllister. First performed by London Contemporary Dance Theatre, Shaw Theatre, London, 18 February 1975.

A man steps out of a crowd and into a house. A smart party is in progress; he, in jeans and a sweater, is the odd man out. He is attracted to a girl but she eludes him and the party dissolves. He is on an underground railway platform talking to himself. The girl passes, appears on another platform. Before the man can reach her the doors shut and the train leaves. He returns to his family of gluttons, morons, caricatures of humanity, leaves them for

204

the open air of a park, sees the girl again and follows her to an art gallery where a painting gets larger and larger to provide the background as they dance. She runs away, he catches up, reaches out to touch her, she vanishes. His family, the party dissolve into the crowd which his image, growing ever larger, engulfs.

North is a great collaborator. The same year as this piece he collaborated with Lynn Seymour to create *Gladly, Badly, Madly, Sadly,* and with Wayne Sleep to create *David and Goliath.* In *Still Life* he collaborated with film to make a highly successful marriage of two media, film and movement. Like many of North's pieces it is highly original, allowing effects and an extension of choreographic movement – of the stage scene – such as when he talks to himself on film and when the train enters and leaves the underground station – which would be impossible otherwise. This willingness to experiment in new things whatever the risk (here justified) is a characteristic of North as a choreographer and one of his contributions to current choreography.

Scriabin Preludes and Studies
Dance work in one act. Choreography: North. Music: Scriabin. Design: Peter Farmer. Lighting: Francis Reid. First performed by London Contemporary Dance Theatre, Haymarket Theatre, Leicester, 20 February 1978.

A man plays one girl against another. After violent and passionate encounters with one, he leaves her for the other who had rejected him. The relationship is played out within and between other encounters, solos, dances involving also three other couples. The theme is love found and lost with the man central to the relationships.

North's exploration of the relationship between a man and two women is familiar in his work. This version is danced to fifteen pieces of Scriabin, the dances firmly rooted in their music from the gentleness of the early preludes to more tormented and uneasy moods of the later studies. The style is often balletic, but for the later, darker, passages there are moments of expressionist intensity, recalling a Central European style. The psychological drive is provided by the three central characters, one girl rejected, the two lovers moving from passion through rejection to acceptance. The heart of the work is a duet for the lovers of real beauty, set to three of the Opus 11 preludes, in which the movement speaks poetically of love, culminating in an exquisite image as the girl's body coils and curls downward round the man. Nothing is made too explicit but North here shows a marked gift for dramatically expressive movement sharply revealing

205

character. The music extends and underlines the mood of the dancing, complementing the character and style suggested by Peter Farmer's elegant blue costumes. Allied with *Troy Games* and *Still Life* the rather prosaic title *Scriabin Preludes and Studies* shows North to be a choreographer of remarkably wide range. He created the male role himself, as he often does, recalling that all three associate choreographers of LCDT – Davies, Bergese and North – are also very good dancers.

MICHA BERGESE (b. 1945)

Trained as a musician before gaining a scholarship to the London School of Contemporary Dance, Bergese joined the Company in 1970. Almost immediately he began to choreograph for company workshops while at the same time developing his experience and reputation as a performer. In 1975 he attended the first Gulbenkian National Choreographic Summer School under Glen Tetley from which his *Da Capo Al Fine* entered the LCDT repertory, followed by *Hinterland* the same year and *Nema* in 1976. In 1977 he was made an associate choreographer of LCDT and still works closely with the company although no longer dancing with it. He teaches and choreographs extensively in England, Germany and Switzerland, his work appearing in many of the modern dance repertories and television programmes of all three countries.

Continuum
Dance work in one act. Choreography: Bergese. Music: Morris Pert. Design: Norberto Chiesa. First performed by London Contemporary Dance Theatre, Haymarket Theatre, Leicester, 20 February 1978.

A programme note acknowledges inspiration from Camus' *Myth of Sisyphus*. The setting is a structure made of aluminium masts so angled as to form a sequence of slopes up which Sisyphus climbs and forever slides down while below more ordinary people move, rest and dance in secondary importance.

Bergese, then still dancing with the company, created the role of Sisyphus whose ceaseless, fruitless ascents are a constant of the work. Since he was an exceptionally gifted dancer with a highly concentrated physical and emotional presence, the choreographer gave to the central character an almost hypnotic force. The relentlessness of his behaviour, doomed to an eternity of futile climbs and falls, made the extraordinary fate of Sisyphus credible. Camus' argument of Sisyphus happy, fulfilled

206

by the absurdity of his fate, seems sometimes confirmed, sometimes questioned, by group dances for a double trio and another couple. The final image is a singular burst of activity in which Sisyphus pedals frantically, as if trying to make the structure fly.

Solo Ride

Dance work in one act. Choreography: Bergese. Music: Douglas Gould. Design: Liz da Costa. First performed by London Contemporary Dance Theatre, Royal Northern College of Music, Manchester, 18 October 1978.

The hero appears riding a tricycle, behind him a dummy *doppelgänger*, his *alter ego*. Four girls in voluminous shirt tops and baggy pants await his arrival. Within a walled alcove sits a musician. The hero leaps, slouches, flirts and involves himself with each of the girls in turn, finally dancing with himself.

There is an instant sense of surrealism in the relationship between a figure in a gap in a bare wall and two identical figures pedalling by on a tricycle, especially since it takes a while to realize the second of the two figures is a dummy. Part of the success of the work on its creation was the performance of Tom Jobe as the leading cyclist. His relationships with the girls are arbitrary, sometimes very funny, but none seems to satisfy him. He ends dancing with his *alter ego* to conclude a dazzling performance. The choreography is zany, inventive, 'sometimes,' remarked Peter Williams in *Dance and Dancers*, 'appearing to be influenced by Balinese dance movements. It is perfectly integrated with the score (composer Douglas Gould being the figure playing clarinet and percussion in the gap in the wall)' and, one might add, instantly established by the designer's imaginatively, humorous set and costumes. The work is dominated by Jobe's performance but its success lies, in fact, in the exact balance of its collaborators and the conception of Bergese whose invention and clever timing create a genuinely comic dance work.

RICHARD ALSTON (b. 1948)

Richard Alston is one of the generation of young choreographers who was produced by the exceptional surroundings of The Place at the end of the 1960s.

After a student essay, *Transit*, in 1969, Alston started to make dance works for the seasons by the London Contemporary Dance Company: *Something to Do* (to a Gertrude Stein text) in 1970; *Nowhere Slowly* (1971);

and he hit his creative stride in 1972 when he composed *Cold*; *Combines*; the dreamlike and mysteriously beautiful *Tiger Balm*, and the powerful study in flight and falling *Wind Hover*. In 1973 came the short dance piece *The Average Leap Forward*, and the serene *Lay-Out*, which was later re-titled *Blue Schubert Fragments*. By this time Alston had formed his own dance group, Strider, which reflected very clearly his concern with choreography that explored the post-Cunningham tradition of 'white' and unemotional movement, stressing purity and uncompromising austerity. *Headlong* (1973), a first version of *Rainbow Bandit*, and *Soft Verges* (both 1974) were examples of Alston style at its most persuasive – the trappings of costuming, performance area, dance manner all focused attention upon the merits of the dance as dance, and it is significant that in the following year Alston and his company should appear at the Serpentine Gallery in Hyde Park, dancing in the setting of a Jasper John exhibition, and producing *Slow Field* and the solo *Zero through Nine* as a response to the paintings and the gallery.

There followed an extended period of study in New York, where Alston was able to renew contact with Merce Cunningham's work. In 1977 he returned to Britain, and since then has restaged his *Rainbow Bandit* in revised form for the London Contemporary Dance Theatre, has choreographed the dances in *The Seven Deadly Sins* for the English National Opera, and given seasons at the Riverside Studios, Hammersmith, an excellent and newly developed centre for dance in London. At Riverside, Alston's *Connecting Passages* (1977), *Doublework*, *Elegiac Blues*, *Behind the Piano*, *Distant Rebound*, *Home Ground* and *Unknown Banker Buys the Atlantic* (all 1978) have shown his style both increasing its range, and deepening its impact.

On 24 January 1980 Alston created his first ballet for Ballet Rambert, *Bell High*, set to Peter Maxwell Davies' 'Stedman Doubles' and 'Hymnos'. The work was given its first performance at the Royal Northern College of Music in Manchester, and was a prelude to Alston's appointment in May 1980 as resident choreographer for Ballet Rambert.

Rainbow Bandit

Dance work in one act. Music: Charles Amirkhanian (Just). *First performed, ICA Gallery, London, 15 January 1975, by Strider. Revised for London Contemporary Dance Company, London, 8 December 1977. With Patrick Harding Irmer, Anca Frankenhaeuser.*

Rainbow Bandit, originally given in a Strider programme at the ICA

Galleries in 1975, was revised and extended by Alston on his return to London after two years working in New York. It showed how the choreographer had put on considerable creative muscle, producing dances that were brisk, big in dynamics. The work divides into three movements, the first two played in silence. The opening *allegro* is all brightness and power; the succeeding *andante* starts with the appearance of one female dancer, moving in long lines of dance, then builds into a *forte* of dynamics for its cast of ten, before fading into the *pianissimo* of the female dancer alone again. The musical terms seem apt, albeit the score which is only used in the final *presto* comprises Charles Amirkhanian's fantasy upon the words *Rainbow check bandit bomb* – insidiously, unexpectedly pleasing.

At the first 'Rainbow' two male dancers enter, and soon the entire cast are caught up in a texture of brilliant muscular feats set against slower, more contemplative dances. Alston has in the past commented upon his own predilection for ' conversational' rather than 'musical' rhythm; the result throughout *Rainbow Bandit* is a constantly satisfying texture of activity, marked by the emergence of patterns of movement, contrasts, conflicts, agreements, that are shown with a kind of calm bravura. The special qualities of Alston's style – an uncompromising use of extended arms, sudden, quick flexings of the torso – are part of a manner which avoids obvious emotion, but which braces and stimulates the observer by its freshness.

Doublework

Dance in one act. Choreography: Richard Alston. First performed at Riverside Studios, London, 3 April 1978. With Siobhan Davies, Tom Jobe, Michele Smith, Ian Spink, Maedée Dupres, Julyen Hamilton.

From his very earliest work, Alston has concerned himself with 'dances about dancing', for which he has evolved a style that looks stripped, bone-bare. It is also a style rich and reverberant, but sometimes so 'transparent' in its denial of everything except the dance itself that we seem to gaze through the dancers' bodies to the movement imprisoned inside them. It can be compared to the work of Ben Nicholson: there is the same concern for formal arrangement, for subtleties of tone.

In *Doublework* the fact of partnership is central to the dance, Alston making a closely woven but in no way clogged texture of movement that capitalizes upon the physical interdependance of a dancing partnership. Three couples are contrasted, despite an overall unification of choreographic style: movement is orchestrated (there is no score for the work, though the bodies of the dancers seem to create an unheard but perceptible musical pulse) to contrast bold unison work, strong leaping entries for men, and subtle exchanges between pairs. The dancers are shown stretching, curving, bending, turning slowly, caught at that precarious moment when balance topples into a fall, supporting their partners' bodies on their backs, indulging in a fascinating range of activity that has the calculated beauty of juxtaposition found in the best non-representational painting. The movements are symbols of energy rather than of emotion, yet there are sudden odd shifts of emphasis that take the observer into moments of pungent sensuality.

SIOBHAN DAVIES (b. 1950)

Siobhan Davies is one of the first creative talents produced by the London School of Contemporary Dance. After studies at art school, she joined the students at The Place, and was soon recognized as a dance of exceptionally elegant style. But it was her gifts as a choreographer – starting with *Relay* (1972), and continuing with the allusive *Pilot* (1974) – which suggest how sure is her talent. Since *Pilot*, a succession of dance works: *The Calm* (1974); *Diary* (1975); *Sphinx* (1977); *Step at a Time* (1978), have all shown choreography marked by its sensibility, its feeling of control, its delicate and unforced mastery of effects. To describe it as 'feminine' in these days of equality at all costs, may invite the tedious yapping of sexist accusations, but like such choreographers as Twyla Tharp and Andrée Howard, Siobhan Davies produces work that has qualities of perception, finesse and economy of force (with no dissipation of emotional or dynamic energy) that seem essentially feminine and beautiful. With Robert North and Micha Bergese she is now associate choreographer of London Contemporary Dance Theatre.

Pilot

Dance work in one scene. Choreography: Siobhan Davies. Music: Igg Welthy. First performed by London Contemporary Dance Theatre, Shaw Theatre, London, 27 February 1979.

Pilot was an early indication that in Siobhan Davies, the London Contemporary Dance Theatre had produced a new and commanding creative talent. Its theme is simple: a group of travellers shelter from the gloom round a storm lantern. A virtuoso of the Jew's harp and the harmonica provides a musical background. As the choreography progresses the

210

travellers take their suitcases around the stage, but more importantly they dance. There is a a man's solo which bends and stretches with a cool wit; a man and a woman join in a joyful duet; and the choreographer herself usually interprets a 'blues' with a supporting man, in which she suggests an immense weariness. *Pilot* is a short, mysterious, exceptionally effective piece of atmospheric writing. The dances follow one another with rich invention and throw-away humour. Nothing may be said to happen, but at the end we are delighted to have been in the company of the dancers and their dances.

The Calm

Dance work in one act. Choreography: Siobhan Davies. Music: Geoffrey Burgon. First performed by London Contemporary Dance Theatre in Manchester, September 1974. With Siobhan Davies, Namron, Linda Gibbs, Anthony van Laast, Kate Harrison, Patrick Harding-Irmer, Ross McKim.

The Calm is cool, unforced, lucid in texture and feeling. It has a most attractive score for counter-tenor, trumpet, violin and harp by Geoffrey Burgon (a composer whose work has deservedly attracted the attention of choreographers), with sonorities that hang delicately, sweetly in the air. The dance's action develops from a contrast between the restrained, contemplative movement for a couple – originally the choreographer herself and Namron – and five dancers who leap and disport themselves in quietly joyful mood. It is a work of gentle, perfectly judged and sustained atmosphere.

Step at a Time

Dance work in one scene. Choreography: Siobhan Davies. Music: Geoffrey Burgon. Design: Siobhan Davies; photographs: Michael Creavey. First performed by London Contemporary Dance Company, Sadler's Wells Theatre, 9 December 1976.

Step at a Time came as the fruit of sabbatical leave spent in New York, where Siobhan Davies worked with Merce Cunningham and Richard Alston. Not surprisingly it bears the imprint of their thinking about movement, in its 'white' choreography, purged of any emotional clutter. A series of projections are thrown on to a front gauze showing the white outline of a dancing figure which seems an ideal of stripped, clear movement that must underlie the dance that is to come. The final projection is replaced by a female dancer (at the first performance Linda Gibbs) wearing a white leotard while the rest of the cast are gradually presented in billowing white track suits. Thereafter the ballet deals with contrasts and conflicts between movement seen clearly in leotards and bodies obscured in voluminous suits. There is an insistence upon the emergence of precise forms from imprecision. It seems, not accidentally, a comment upon the creative act itself in the refining of stylized movement from the amorphous energy of everyday activity.

Sphinx

Dance work in one scene. Choreography: Siobhan Davies. Music: Barrington Pheloung. Design: Siobhan Davies. First performed by London Contemporary Dance Company at Sadler's Wells Theatre, 17 November 1977.

In each of her dance works Siobhan Davies demonstrates a choreographic intelligence coolly elegant, yet with sudden sharp perceptions about human behaviour and movement. Her dancing is marked by the same qualities, and at the beginning of her *Sphinx* she sets herself a solo which establishes the mood of the subsequent choreography. As Barrington Pheloung's score gets under way – ticking, clanging and rattling with insect clicks that seem a modern equivalent of Bartok's night music – Siobhan Davies stands watchful, then bends and unfolds her body like an animal observing the world round it. It is not a little wildlife study, but oddly reverberant with imagery that recalls film taken of forest creatures. There follows a lengthy section for five dancers in which the bodies are seen immobile after passages of delicately self-absorbed movement. A hopping solo for a male dancer is contrasted with a fluent outburst for a girl and with mysterious progression in which the five dancers are gradually impelled across the stage in a diagonal. At every moment the eye is held by the constant flux of energy and dynamic interest. In a postlude Siobhan Davies returns to restate the opening theme and close the work with a sense of formal completeness.

Siobhan Davies in *Sphinx* for the London Contemporary Dance Theatre

(*above*) Kim Reader and Carl Myers in the Sadler's Wells Royal Ballet production of *Rhyme Nor Reason*. (*below*) Sadler's Wells Royal Ballet production of *Homage to Chopin*

SEVEN

Americans and Europeans

We have emphasized the essential need for international exchange in choreography, as in all arts. It is essential for dancers, choreographers and audiences. British choreography is seen increasingly abroad – classical, in the work of Ashton, MacMillan, Darrell and others; modern, in the work of Cohan, North, Bergese, Alston and younger choreographers now developing.

Historically, choreography and choreographic influences from abroad have always been a part of the evolution of theatrical dance in Britain. This is clear from chapters one to four. It remains true today, the major influence now being American where once it was French, Italian, Russian. We have benefited greatly from this transatlantic contact which has, in fact, been double contact, reflecting the richness of America's own two traditions of dancing in this century. One is the system of free or modern dance which evolved from the example of Isadora Duncan, Ruth St Denis, Ted Shawn and their pupils, notably Martha Graham and Doris Humphrey. This can be seen in the work of Robert Cohan and Glen Tetley for the London Contemporary Dance Theatre and Ballet Rambert – Tetley claiming Ballet Rambert as 'my London home' as if to match Cohan's long commitment to Britain. The other tradition is the classic academic dance as it has been extended by George Balanchine and Jerome Robbins. For these reasons we place the Americans first in our list below.

Britain, though, has a traditional dance relationship with Europe, and European choreographers are, we think, less well represented in our company repertories than they might be. True, this is not a good period for choreography in Europe – not much original work of international quality appears to be emerging in Scandinavia, France, Italy, Spain or Portugal. But in Germany and Holland there is new, interesting work growing from strong roots. (During the next decade, too, we should like to see more exchange with Eastern Europe and, further afield, perhaps with Japan, China and the emerging countries of the Third World.)

Particularly important to the fostering of choreographic exchange

213

between countries and companies might be the annual International Dance Course for Professional Choreographers and Composers now under EEC auspices, drawing together young talent from the countries of Western Europe. It is the young and future talent we need to seek – not failing to acknowledge at the same time the importance of older European traditions represented below by Serge Lifar, Harald Lander and Rudolf Nureyev. First, though, the Americans.

AMERICAN BALLETS

GEORGE BALANCHINE (b. 1904)

George Balanchine was born in St Petersburg. His family was musical – his father a composer – and this inheritance must be seen to lie at the root of Balanchine's creative identity. He attended the Imperial School of Ballet in Petersburg and graduated from that most illustrious academy at the age of seventeen into the State Ballet Company, the 1917 revolution having occurred during his years of study. While a young dancer, he enrolled at the Petrograd Conservatoire for further study as a pianist and composer, and at the same time made his first choreographic essays. In 1924, with three other dancers from the State Ballet – Nicholas Effimov, Alexandra Danilova and Tamara Gevergeva – he received permission to undertake a concert tour in Europe. There followed a decision to remain in the West, and the invitation from Sergey Diaghilev to join the Ballets Russes, for which company Balanchine was to become resident choreographer in succession to Nijinska. For Diaghilev, Balanchine produced dance scenes in operas – these had been Diaghilev's first and most urgent request – and ten ballets. He proved himself able to provide the novelties which Diaghilev's audience needed each season, but in two works – *Apollo* and *Prodigal Son* – he created ballets which have lasted in the repertory to this day.

In *Apollo*, that crucial work, Balanchine's future path seemed clear as advocate for the continuing vitality and relevance of the classic *danse d'école*. Following Diaghilev's death in 1929 and the disbanding of his company, Balanchine worked in Paris, London and Copenhagen, but it was the invitation to the United States, that came in 1933, which was to be the great turning point in his career and in that of American ballet. Lincoln

214

Kirstein, poet, man of the arts, Maecenas, invited Balanchine to form a school and company in the USA which would implant the noblest traditions of training (those of Balanchine's own schooling) and creativity in the New World. With Kirstein's administrative, moral and financial support (and that of certain of his friends), a school was opened, and from it emerged the American Ballet Company in 1934. This was the first incarnation of a series of ensembles which – with interruptions during wartime, or when Balanchine was working in Hollywood – was to result in the company that in 1948 was invited to take up residence at the New York City Center of Music and Drama, and gained its title of the New York City Ballet.

In 1964 a further move brought the company to its present home at the New York State Theater. The sum of Balanchine and Kirstein's achievement over these years is immense. Through Balanchine's creations, through his belief in the classic dance and his ability to extend it, developing its possibilities logically in the context of a new society and a new world, embellishing and refining it, working, supremely, with Igor Stravinsky in whose music he found a response and stimulus vital to his own creative gift, the classic dance has taken root in the USA. Through the great sequence of ballets he has made, Balanchine has extended the possibilities of the classic dance, reshaping it, sometimes speeding up its physical pulse, finding in musical texts a dazzling variety of relationships between step and score, revealing its continued beauty, relevance and spiritual attitudes in the latter half of the twentieth century. Through the School of American Ballet, which has similarly accepted the traditional Petersburg values and adopted them for American ballet, Balanchine and his teachers have produced a generation of dancers able to act as instruments for Balanchine's genius in a company which is the vivid expression of the work of one of the two greatest choreographers of our century.

In Balanchine ballets we are presented with the classic academic dance at its most adventurous and its most varied. Certain matters of taste emerge: Balanchine has been less and less concerned with narrative, and his ballets and those of his company are marked by a decorative style which is entirely acceptable in its starkness, but far less so when 'design' is allowed: few companies in the world, surely, have less appealing costumes or sets to European eyes than New York City Ballet. Yet Balanchine's acute musical sensibility, his ability to create the right physical realization of a score – from the most romantic to the most modern – give his ballets a far more essential variety than can be acquired with clever stage design. Balanchine's ballets look different because of their fundamental variety of physical imagery, where certain western choreographers produce the same ballet time and time again, persuading audiences that there is variety of inspiration by clothing repetitious dances differently.

The Royal Ballet first acquired a Balanchine ballet in 1950, when his *Ballet Imperial* was staged with superlative designs by Eugene Berman. Alas, the designs were abandoned, and later redecoration proved singularly hideous. The *Trumpet Concerto* (to music by Haydn) which Balanchine made for the Sadler's Wells Theatre Ballet in the same year – the time of New York City Ballet's first visit to Britain – was abandoned: inexplicably so in view of the persistence of certain far less interesting works in the repertory. *Serenade, The Prodigal Son, Apollo, Four Temperaments, Agon* and *Liebeslieder Walzer* are still happily (if unidiomatically and sporadically) present in the Royal Ballet repertory.

Apollo (Apollon Musagète)

Ballet in one act, two scenes, Choreography: George Balanchine. Music and libretto: Igor Stravinsky. Décor: André Bauchant. First performed by Diaghilev's Ballets Russes, Théâtre Sarah Bernhardt, Paris, 12 June 1928. Serge Lifar: Apollo. Alice Nikitina (alternating with Alexandra Danilova): Terpsichore. Lyubov Tchernichova: Polyhymnia. Felia Dubrovska: Calliope.

Scene 1: The birth of Apollo on Delos; the young god next appears in swaddling bands, which are unwound by two attendants. They give him a lute, sign of his future greatness, show him how to use it, and Apollo understands his destiny. Black-out.

Scene 2: We see the god radiant in his young manhood. Three Muses – Calliope, Muse of Poetry, Polyhymnia, Muse of Mime and Terpsichore, Muse of Dance, appear, and he sports with them, then presents each with an emblem of her art. In turn they dance, but Calliope's verses do not please the god, and Polyhymnia forgets that mime is a silent art and mouths a shout at the end of her dance. Only Terpsichore pleases Apollo, and there follows a solo for the god which ends with him sitting on the ground, a finger and arm extended. Terpsichore enters, touches his outstretched hand with hers, and joins him in a *pas de deux*. The other muses enters; the god rests his head for a moment on their hands, then hears the voice of his father, Zeus, summoning him to Olympus. Apollo leads the muses like a chariot team, to the staircase which symbolizes the slopes of the sacred mountain. He climbs, the muses lined below him, as Leto his mother appears momentarily at the side of the stage watching her son's departure for the skies.

With *Apollo*, Balanchine found himself in the theatre – although

216

characteristically it was through the music that the revelation came. In *Stravinsky in the Theatre* he wrote:

I look back on the ballet as the turning point in my life. In its discipline and restraint, in its sustained oneness of tone and feeling, the score was a revelation. It seemed to me that I could not, for the first time, dare not, use all my ideas; that I, too, could eliminate. I began to see how I could clarify, by limiting, by reducing what seemed to be myriad possibilities to the one possibility that is inevitable.

It is significant that this revelation should have occurred when Balanchine was working with Stravinsky (*Apollo* was the second Stravinsky score that he choreographed for Diaghilev – the first had been *Le Rossignol*, his first creation for the Ballets Russes, in 1925). The Stravinsky/ Balanchine collaboration was one which was to beget marvels in the dance theatre, culminating in the great Stravinsky Festival given by the New York City Ballet in 1972, when no less than thirty ballets were presented to Stravinsky scores.

The Prodigal Son (Le Fils Prodigue)
Ballet in one act and three scenes. Choreography: Balanchine. Music: Sergey Prokofiev. Décor: Georges Rouault. First performed by Diaghilev's Ballets Russes, at the Théâtre Sarah Bernhardt, Paris, 21 May 1929. Serge Lifar: the Prodigal. Felia Dubrovska: the Siren. Mikhail Fedorov: the Father. Leon Woizikovski and Anton Dolin: servants.

Scene 1: The Prodigal's servants are arranging his provisions for a journey. The Prodigal comes out, excited at the prospect of travel, despite the anxiety of his sisters. Their Father enters, and commands his family to come to him, an order the Prodigal obeys reluctantly. Then, eager to be off, he sends his servants on ahead and leaps over the fence that stands between him and freedom.

Scene 2: The Prodigal and his servants arrive in a city. Revellers, bald-headed and scuttling, are eager to welcome him. They produce a mysterious female, the Siren, whose icy beauty first bemuses then excites the Prodigal. He dances with her and her seductive skills overpower him. He is plundered by the revellers and by the Siren and is left broken and alone. He struggles away in self-loathing; the Siren and her accomplices load the Prodigal's goods on to a ship with the Siren as its prow.

Scene 3: The Prodigal, dressed in rags and clinging to a staff, reaches the gate of his home. Ashamed, he dare not enter, but his sisters discover him. The father appears; the son crawls to his feet, clambers remorsefully up his father's body, and is at last taken in his father's arms, covered with his robe and carried into the home.

The Prodigal Son was Balanchine's last ballet for Diaghilev. It starred Serge Lifar as the hero, and its expressionistic language allowed Lifar to gain one of the greatest successes of his career in a strongly dramatic role. In the scene of the orgy Balanchine created images of extreme eroticism by borrowing from acrobatics, and throughout made use of a language of great stylization: naturalism has no place in this ballet. Typical of the entire work is the skilled use of a single property: the fence-like structure which becomes also a table, a pillar, a ship; in its imaginative adaptability we can sense the entire approach of Balanchine to telling this biblical tale in contemporary yet timeless terms.

Serenade

Ballet in one act. Choreography: George Balanchine. Music: Tchaikovsky; Serenade for strings. Costumes: Jean Lurçat. First performed by the students of the School of American Ballet at the estate of Felix M. Warburg, White Plains, New York, 9 June 1934.

Serenade was the first ballet that Balanchine made in the USA. It is a portent that the lines of girls we see at the curtain-rise, with one arm raised, make their first conscious dance movement by taking up the basic 'first position' in ballet. It must seem to us now that this is a symbolic action, American classic ballet placing itself firmly and purposefully on the path which Balanchine was to show it. The ballet thereafter develops without reference to plot, but each of the four movements can be seen to indicate some emotional state. Because, when he was making the piece, Balanchine was using whatever dancers were available at rehearsals, irregular numbers are involved in each section, and the choreography also incorporates accidental moments that occurred in rehearsal: a girl arriving late, another falling as she came into the studio. Boys appear late in the ballet because they were not available when the ballet was starting to be rehearsed. In the final section an element of tragedy seems implicit, as a man is guided in by one girl to a meeting with another girl, who is finally deserted by him; she is ultimately carried out high above the other dancers in a procession which closes the ballet.

Serenade continues to find great favour with the many companies for whom it has been mounted since its creation, through its sensitive realization of the lyricism of the Tchaikovsky score and the exultant grace of the writing in which Balanchine celebrates the beauty of the academic dance.

Ballet Imperial (Piano Concerto Number Two)

Ballet in one act. Choreography by Balanchine. Music: Tchaikovsky; (Piano Concerto No. 2 – in Siloti's edition, which shortens the middle movement). First performed by the American Ballet in New York, 27 May 1941. Subsequently revived for New York City Ballet. First performed by the Royal Ballet at Covent Garden, 5 April 1950. Designs: Eugene Berman.

Ballet Imperial was created for a tour of South America by Ballet Caravan, an ensemble which was a later manifestation of the American Ballet. Intended as a tribute to the world of Petipa, it refracted the glitter and bravura (and lyrical drive) of Tchaikovsky's second piano concerto into dances of magnificent power and great virtuosity. The outer movements were displays for a ballerina and her cavalier, with an attendant trio of two men and a girl, and a *corps de ballet*; the central *andante* suggesting something of the emotional quest for an ideal beloved that can be found in the ballets of the nineteenth century.

As staged at Covent Garden in 1950, it benefited from noble designs by Eugene Berman – the only example of the work of this great stage decorator in the British repertory – and remained one of the most splendid showpieces for the company. (Nadia Nerina, the outstanding incumbent of the ballerina role for the Royal Ballet, noted how, on visiting the Winter Palace at Leningrad, she at once sensed the world implicit in *Ballet Imperial*.) Lamentably the ballet's designs were changed for the worse, and subsequently changed yet again, very much for the worse: as in New York, where the piece is now given under the title of *Piano Concerto Number Two*, the implied nostalgia, the external evidence of the ballet's choreographic homage to the world of the Imperial Ballet (and to Petipa, its master) was not apparently considered suitable in the 1970s. The result is that the ballet has lost a vital, imaginative springboard for artists and audiences: at its last revival in London it was but a shadow of its former glorious self, seeming to be located in some dire pedestrian underpass, and the necessary brilliance of performance manner was also lost.

Night Shadow (La Sonnambula)

Choreography: George Balanchine. Design: Dorothea Tanning. Music: Bellini; orchestrated and arranged Vittorio Rieti. First performed by the Ballets Russes de Monte Carlo, New York, 27 February 1946. Alexandra Danilova: Shadow. Nicholas Magellanes: the Poet. Maria Tallchief: the Coquette. First performed by London Festival Ballet, 20 March 1967, Venice. Designs: Peter Farmer.

A masked ball is taking place in the gardens of the castle; the host – a baron – greets his guests, and near him his Mistress, the Coquette, watches events. A poet enters unexpectedly, is greeted by the host, and sits with the Coquette while a *divertissement* takes place – a peasant couple dance a pastorale; two blackamoors caper; a harlequin goes through a solo which hints at moments of acute muscular pain – and when the guests move away to dine, the Coquette and the Poet dance an impassioned *pas de deux*. Now the guests return and the Baron jealously claims the Coquette: the guests, sensing some unease, leave, as do the Baron and his mistress, and the Poet is alone in the garden. At this moment a light is seen flickering through the castle windows, and suddenly a white figure emerges, bearing a candle. It is a beautiful young woman in a nightdress, her eyes shut in sleep. She is a somnambulist, and she glides through the garden feeling her way in exquisite *pas de bourrée*. The Poet is at once obsessed by her. He dances round her, and she avoids him; he pushes her and she eddies like a white flower on water; he lies on the ground, encircling her with his arms and she steps through them. By now entirely entranced, the Poet follows the Night Shadow as she drifts back into the castle, and his exit with her is seen by the Coquette. As the Baron and the other guests return, she jealously whispers what she has seen into the host's ear. As the guests dance, he draws a dagger and enters the castle. The guests watch aghast as the Poet emerges, staggering and clutching his heart where he has been stabbed. He dies. A light now flickers through the castle windows. The Night Shadow emerges, eddying once again across the garden. Her foot is stopped by the corpse of the Poet. The entertainers pick up his body, lay it in her arms, and she carries this burden into the castle, and we watch the flicker of her candle mounting upwards through the castle windows.

Night Shadow is a piece of Gothic fantasy, unusual in Balanchine's *oeuvre*, and one which shows him a master of dramatic nuance. It is marked by the hectic, uneasy atmosphere generated throughout. The party-goers have a frantic air in their gaiety; the sense of supressed eroticism, of dark events brooding in the garden, is eminently disquieting. At the heart of the work is the duet for the Night Shadow and the Poet, a masterly example of choreographic economy, built up from the somnambulist's *pas de bourrée* and the Poet's attempts to impede or guide her progress. It is a ballet which has been especially illuminated for European audiences – it has featured in the repertory of several companies – by the interpretation of the Night Shadow herself given during the 1950s by the great Franco-Russian ballerina Nina Vyrubova, a performance of exquisite sensibility and technical beauty.

Four Temperaments

Ballet in one act. Choreography: Balanchine. Music: Hindemith. Décor: Kurt Seligmann. First performed by Ballet Society, New York, 20 November 1946. First performed by the Royal Ballet, 25 January 1973, in practice dress which is now the accepted costuming for the work.

Four Temperaments takes the form of a theme and four variations, in which are exemplified the different moods of classic Greek medical theory: the four 'temperaments' – melancholic, sanguinic, phlegmatic, choleric, which also correspond to the four elements of earth, water, fire and air.

Three couples take the stage to display the statement of the ballet's musical theme. Then follows the Melancholic variation, despondent, for a male soloist, who is eventually joined by two girls, and four more girls stalk mysteriously through the action. For the Sanguinic waltz a couple dance happily, with an attendant group of four dancers. The Phlegmatic male dances disconsolately alone, but then his mood is changed when four happy girls appear. Finally the Choleric girl arrives in a vehement solo, and the final pages find the entire cast assembled for the recapitulation of their dances, and a final magical passage in which the girls are carried high across the stage by their partners in great arcs of movement.

An implied theory in this action is that the melancholic and phlegmatic side of the male, the choleric side of the female, can only be reconciled (in the happiness of sanguinic temperament) when man and woman are together. But the chief merit and importance of this tremendous work is in its ability to evoke the essential manner of New York City Ballet itself as a twentieth-century classic ensemble.

Bourrée Fantasque

Choreography: Balanchine. Music: Chabrier. Costumes: Karinska. First performed by New York City Ballet, New York, 1 December 1949. Revived for London Festival Ballet, 1968. Designs: Peter Farmer.

Like Gaul, *Bourrée Fantasque* is divided into three parts: the opening *bourrée* is a danced burlesque that is witty, and entirely classical. Its humours depends on fans, upon bright, brilliant movements executed with entirely deadpan expressions, and the mismatching of a very tall girl dancer with a diminutive partner. Everything is a joke: the ballerina's attempts to ignore her partner, his enthusiasm for his task, and the sheer strangeness of ballerinas' feet in block shoes (the boys get down on the ground and examine the girls' feet with the seriousness of stamp-collectors studying a penny black). The contrast with the second movement (from *Gwendolyne*)

221

could not be more marked: it is lyrical, concerned with the eternal search for the ideal beloved, as a boy and a girl at first fail to meet and then are joined in a beautiful romantic duet. 'Fête Polonaise' is a bounding joyous finale, built on a crescendo that gathers tremendous momentum as the movement progresses. A ballerina flies across the stage supported by her partner who holds her arm as she curvettes and beats; the ballerina of the second movement enters with her troupe of dancers, and soon all three ballerinas, with their own groups are on stage. Balanchine here devises a breathtaking sequence of patterns: circles, stars and whirling formations, and the movement ends in a final spectacular mêlée as the curtain falls.

Agon

Ballet in one act. Choreography: Balanchine. Music: Stravinsky. First performed by the New York City Ballet, New York, 27 November 1957. Presented by the Royal Ballet at Covent Garden, 25 January 1973.

'The piece contains twelve pieces of music. It is a ballet for twelve dancers. It is all precise, like a machine, but a machine that thinks.' Thus Balanchine commented on the score which was commissioned by Lincoln Kirstein from Stravinsky for the New York City Ballet. The starting point for Stravinsky was a seventeenth-century manual of French court dances, which suggested certain formal ideas – though the score is in no way a duplication of old dance forms. The title, *Agon*, is the Greek word for a contest and is also the root of the English word *agony*, implying here a feeling of struggle. This too was merely a launching pad for the ballet. From these elements emerged a work whose choreography is the ideal visual equivalent of the textures, constructions and spirit of the score – a masterpiece. Balanchine clothes the music in flesh, reveals its form, makes our ears see, in this exploration of a world defined by Stravinsky's score. Like some great *horloger du roi* he has built a clock that measures out the time and rhythm of Stravinsky's music in movement.

One of the greatest ballets of our time, *Agon* makes us live more intensely: watching it we seem caught up in a world of brilliant physical effects, of extraordinarily intense relationships between bodies, movement, time.

Liebeslieder Walzer

Ballet in one act and two scenes. Choreography: Balanchine. Music: Brahms; Liebesliederwalzer *Op. 52 and* Neue Liebesliederwalzer *Op. 65. Design: David Hayes. Costumes: Karinska. First performed by the New York City*

222

Ballet, New York, 22 November 1960. *Revived for the Royal Ballet at Covent Garden,* 19 *April* 1979.

'Never have I moved so lightly. I was no longer a human being. To hold the most adorable creature in one's arms and fly around with her like the wind, so that everything around us faded away . . .' Thus Goethe wrote at the moment when the waltz fever first seized Europe, and aptly, his poems form the text of the *Neue Liebeslieder*, the second set of Brahms' settings for vocal quartet and piano duet. They are also the second part of this heart-stirring ballet which uses both sets of Brahms' songs. The *Liebesliederwalzer* are domestic music, intended for the intimate surroundings of a drawing room where our great-grandparents made harmonious entertainment for themselves. And this is the quality that epitomizes the tone of the first section of the ballet.

Scene 1: A candlelit room, open to the night, wherein the pianists and the singers are found with four dancing couples. They are social beings, not ballet dancers, the girls in long dresses and heeled slippers, the men looking like Max Wall in a nasty approximation of nineteenth-century evening dress (the ballet is, yet again with Balanchine, indifferently designed). The range of their dance is limited to the waltz as a ballroom activity. Good manners prevail; emotion is restrained, behaviour speaks of breeding, and the flirtations, the passages of feeling, the appeals and embraces, are governed by attitudes implicit in the formal dress of the dancers. But the waltz, the irresistible, intoxicating, giddying whirl of triple time, infuses every moment, and Balanchine's genius is never more apparent than in the richness of invention he contrives upon this basis. The variety, beauty, prodigality of the choreography seem to spring with the most ravishing rightness from the waltz itself. Do the four couples just waltz? Yes; but to amend the famous dictum about the minuet: *que do choses dans une valse.*

Scene 2: At the end of the first set of waltzes, the curtain falls; a brief pause; as it rises again, the candles have gone out to be replaced by a starry sky. The women return, dressed now in smoky tulle and ballet shoes, and to the *Neue Liebeslieder* set, the waltz itself takes off. Reality has given place to dreams that the giddying steps inspire in the flirting couples. The move away from the ballroom to the ballet stage, from heeled slippers to *pointe* shoes, frees the dance from the formal restraints of the waltz as a social dance. (It may also, inferentially, imply the freeing of the human body from the confines of social behaviour through the disciplines of the academic dance.)

223

The change also brings a sharpening of emotion. What has been concealed or contained by society manners is now freed by the conventions of ballet. The lovers are franker, more intense, and also more isolated. The choreography treats them more clearly as couples than as a group of friends‘ and – naturally enough – Balanchine's invention soars. If one finds more pleasure in the ingenuities and felicities of the first part because of the way Balanchine sets and solves certain dynamic problems, it is not to deny that the second part of the ballet is as superb as the first in choreographic grace. And at the end, as the quartet sing an 'Envoi' addressed to the muses, the dancers return in their evening clothes; the stars dim, the candles flare up, and the couples rest, listening to the notes of the last song. A beautiful ballet has ended.

JEROME ROBBINS (b. 1918)

Jerome Robbins is widely regarded as the foremost American-born classical choreographer, and in his work we can trace something essential about America itself. This has to do with the combining of European traditions – in a nation which received a vast immigrant influx from the Old World – with those that have emerged over the past century as essentially American. Robbins' concern has often been with the admixture of demotic elements into the fabric of the classic theatrical dance: it was this which gave such superb vitality to his first ballet, *Fancy Free*, a study of three sailors on shore-leave in New York in 1944.

Starting as a dancer in musical comedy, Robbins joined American Ballet Theater in 1940, appearing in much of the repertory. After the initial triumph of *Fancy Free* he produced two further works, *Interplay* and *Facsimile*, which confirmed his stature as a young creator very much of his time, concerned with jazz, with the realities of urban living, bringing them to the ballet stage with uncompromising energy. He also worked on Broadway, but in 1949 he began an association with the New York City Ballet which has continued, with intermittent periods of absence, ever since. He has combined this with a separate but linked career as director/ choreographer of a sequence of highly successful Broadway shows – *Fiddler on the Roof*, *The King and I* among them, and supremely *West Side Story* in which the supremacy of dancing in a Broadway show was made tremendously manifest. In many of his ballets there is a *demi-caractère* flavour which gives a special quality of credibility to the dance; in dealing with themes which relate to American life – from the early *Age of Anxiety* to

Events and even his hilarious *The Concert* – we can see how naturalistic observation is clothed and refined, but not destroyed, by being incorporated into ballet.

At one time in the 1960s Robbins withdrew to work on the creation of a theatrical form which would combine musical, dance and theatrical elements into a new and vital expression. The workshop experiments did not result in any public productions, and in 1969 Robbins marked his return to the ballet stage with *Dances at a Gathering*. This initiated a decade in which Robbins has produced a series of major dance works for New York City Ballet, several of which have entered the Royal Ballet repertory.

Afternoon of a Faun

Ballet in one act. Choreography: Jerome Robbins. Music: Debussy. Costumes: Irene Scharaff. Set and lighting: Jean Rosenthal. First performed by New York City Ballet, New York, 14 May 1953. First performed by the Royal Ballet, 14 December 1971.

Place: A room with a mirror. A young male dance student is found curled asleep on the floor of a dance studio. He stretches. He gazes at himself, staring straight into the audience, for the convention of this piece is that the proscenium arch frames the looking glass that is the essential feature of any dance studio. A girl enters in practice dress. She starts to work seriously at the barre. Boy and girl observe each other only as reflections in the glass. He starts to partner her; suddenly he kisses her lightly on one cheek. She sees him only as a reflection, but slowly raises her hand to her cheek. The spell has been broken, and she leaves. The boy lies down on the floor, arches his body, and sleeps.

Dancers' preoccupation with their bodies is bound up with their ceaseless quest for physical excellence, for the ever-elusive mastery of their muscles and bones. Always in front of their eyes is the image of the body reflected in the looking glass of the classroom; their concentration on this reflection is narcissistic in that it mirrors the progress of their life's work. In a sense the reflected figure has a greater reality for them than anything else: their career is bound up with this *doppelgänger*. This is the world of Robbins' ballet, a brilliant work on many counts: in its rethinking of the Nijinsky original, keeping its sensual warmth but not its dated eroticism; in its relationship to the Debussy score, whereby the shimmering luminosity of the music is not betrayed; in its capturing of an essential truth about dancers by the most delicate of means. The arrival of the girl/nymph is as beautifully managed as in the Nijinsky original, but its eroticism is entirely

225

modern; the tiny drama seems played entirely by the dancers' reflected selves. Only when real emotion breaks in – the boy's giving of the kiss – does the atmosphere shatter, and the girl depart. The boy's final arching of his body is a reference to the end of the Nijinsky ballet.

The Concert

Ballet in one act. Choreography: Jerome Robbins. Music: Chopin; Polonaise in A Major, Op. 40, No. 1; Berceuse, Op. 57; Prelude, Op. 28, No. 18; Prelude, Op. 28, No. 16: Waltz in E Minor, Op. posth.; Prelude, Op. 28, No. 7; Mazurka in G, Op. posth.; Prelude, Op. 28, No. 4; Ballade, No. 3, in A Flat, Op. 47. Costumes: Irene Scharaff. Frontcloths: Edward Gorey (for the Royal Ballet). First performed by the Royal Ballet, Covent Garden, 4 March 1975.

Subtitled *The Perils of Everybody*, and called 'a charade in one act', *The Concert* was created for the New York City Ballet in March 1956, and revised for Robbins' own Ballets USA company which presented it at the Spoleto Festival in 1958. Robbins provides a programme note which explains the initial idea of this hilarious work:

> One of the pleasures of attending a concert is the freedom to lose oneself in listening to the music. Quite often, unconsciously, mental pictures and images form; and the patterns and paths of these reveries are influenced by the music itself, or its programme notes, or by the personal dreams, problems and fantasies of the listener. Chopin's music in particular has been subject to fanciful 'programme' names such as the *Butterfly étude*, the *Minute* waltz, the *Raindrop* prelude, etc.

The result is a sequence of comic sketches in dance which range from the subtle to the slapstick, and always convulse an audience. Earnest music lovers start to live out their fantasies; a man tries to stab his wife to the sacred 'Sylphides' prelude; a sextet of girls always finds one member out of position with their routines; a lady acquires a blue-feather busby with delight, and then is destroyed to find another lady wearing the same bonnet; hussars, butterflies, and a dominant wife are part of the fabric of a glorious comic piece which is sharp, ebullient, and – miraculously – preserves its comic freshness even after repeated viewings.

Dances at a Gathering

Ballet in one act. Choreography: Jerome Robbins. Music: Chopin; Mazurka, Op. 63, No. 3; Waltz, Op. 69, No. 2; Mazurka, Op. 33, No. 3; Mazurka,

226

Op. 6, *No.* 4; *Mazurka, Op.* 7, *No.* 5; *Mazurka, Op.* 7, *No.* 4; *Mazurka, Op.* 24, *No.* 2; *Mazurka, Op.* 6, *No.* 2; *Waltz, Op.* 42; *Waltz, Op.* 34, *No.* 2; *Mazurka, Op.* 56, *No.* 2; *Etude, Op.* 25, *No.* 4; *Waltz, Op.* 34, *No.* 1; *Waltz, Op.* 70, *No.* 2; *Etude, Op.* 25, *No.* 5; *Etude, Op.* 10, *No.* 2; *Scherzo, Op.* 20, *No.* 1; *Nocturne, Op.* 15, *No.* 1. *Costumes: Joe Eula. First performed by New York City Ballet, New York,* 8 *May* 1969 (*gala*). *First performed by Royal Ballet, Covent Garden,* 19 *October* 1970.

The basic premise of *Dances at a Gathering* seems almost too simple: take five male and five female dancers, set them in simple costumes against a cyclorama, and let them move to a chain of eighteen Chopin piano pieces. The work began as a duet to Chopin music, grew in rehearsal to include a *pas de six,* and from then on Robbins seemed to strike a vein of rich creativity which finally encompassed the numbers which make up *Dances,* and then moved on to create *In the Night* (also to Chopin music) as a pendant, and completed the sequence with the later *Other Dances* of 1976 which were his tribute to Natalya Makarova and Mikhail Baryshnikov.

Dances at a Gathering has no plot or excuse other than the dancers on stage – Robbins is very insistent upon this fact – and the choreography seems rooted in the score, flowering from it, expressing its innermost feelings and its formal structure. The ballet begins with one male dancer entering to the sound of a mazurka, his dance acquiring a technical flavour from the steps of the mazurka as a Polish dance. But just as Chopin uses national dances and transforms them through an extremely cultivated sensibility, so does Robbins take mazurka steps and set them in the academic vocabulary, to provide an equivalent of Chopin's pianistic manner. As the other dancers join the man, and the mazurkas give way to waltzes and an *étude,* a scherzo and a final nocturne, the fabric of the dancing becomes richer, the personalities of the dancers and their relationships expand through the choreography. Without drama, but with the dramatic flavour of emotion, Robbins' dances offer contests, displays, jokes, and above all, a flood of wonderful movement that is deeply, ever satisfyingly, a realization of his score. There are highlights: a waltz *pas de six* of extreme virtuosity; a battle between two show-off boys which is like two dogs taunting each other; a drifting solo for a girl in which three men resolutely refuse to dance with her; a number in which a boy and girl seem to challenge each other in 'anything you can do I can do better'. A moment of emotion and darker feeling marks the scherzo; the dancers watch a storm cloud passing across the sky, and at the end the male dancer who first appeared, bends down and touches the ground, and the dancers salute each other as the curtain falls.

227

Dances at a Gathering has won audiences wherever it is performed, and remains one of the major works produced in the decade of the 1970s.

Requiem Canticles

Ballet in one scene. Choreography: Jerome Robbins. Music: Igor Stravinsky; Requiem Canticles. First performed by New York City Ballet, New York, 25 June 1972. First performed by the Royal Ballet, Covent Garden, 15 November 1972.

In 1972, New York City Ballet staged a week-long festival in homage to Igor Stravinsky, performing thirty-two ballets to Stravinsky scores, with *Requiem Canticles* as the final ballet on the final night. Writing of the festival, Mary Clarke observed, 'That last Sunday evening had an almost religious quality. We had been worshipping Stravinsky all the week, and that night we remembered he had been a religious man.' Stravinsky composed the *Requiem Canticles* when he was eighty-four, at an age when a man of faith must inevitably contemplate what the composer himself called 'the celebration of death'. Sparse, epigrammatic, the nine sections of the score seem pared to the doctrinal bones of the *Requiem* text. How, then, to realize this intensity in movement?

Robbins' procedure was to emulate with some exactness the structural devices of the score. The prelude introduces a cast of four soloists with a chorus of fifteen dancers; the *Tuba Mirum* and *Lacrimosa* (both vocal solos) are danced solos; the central interlude is a quartet for the soloists; and the final postlude unites the whole cast again. The four choral sections make use of the dance chorus with the soloists, and in these the words seem to impel the movement, while the orchestral writing brings repose or a preparation for fresh dance activity.

There is little that is conventional or even expected in Robbins' approach. The dancers are clad in severe black leotards; fluttering hands, attitudes of submission, agonized upward thrusts of bodies in the *Dies Irae*, the male soloist's tormented leaps in the *Tuba Mirum*, a mixture of academic movement and highly personal distortion of gesture and step, are all fused into a cohesive language. After each number the tension breaks, the dancers walk quite naturally in preparation for the next section, and in certain passages naturalistic effects – hand slapping, finger snapping – insist upon a contemporaneity (even an Americanness) which shocks and jolts our responses. After the central interlude, the mood of the work becomes more solemn with the *Rex Tremendae*, and the postlude finds the clanging of bells in the score reflected in shifts of the bodies in the massed shape of the

228

chorus, in hieratic changes of hand position, and in a final breathtaking group in which the chorus kneels abjectly while the soloists remain standing, heads raised, and mouths agape at the heavens, in terror and amazement at the awful majesty of what is to be revealed.

GLEN TETLEY (b. 1926)

Born in Cleveland, Ohio, Tetley originally studied medicine and graduated from New York University before deciding to train as a dancer. He trained in modern technique with Martha Graham and Hanya Holm, and in classical ballet technique with Antony Tudor and Margaret Craske, becoming principal dancer in both the Martha Graham Company and Tudor's American Ballet Theater 1958–60. Before that and since, he danced in musical productions and in Hanya Holm's company; with New York City Opera; in John Butler's company; the Joffrey Ballet; and Jerome Robbins' Ballets USA. In 1962 he formed his own company and created *Pierrot Lunaire*, one of his most acclaimed works, the fruit of a long choreographic apprenticeship since 1948. The same year he joined Nederlands Dans Theater as dancer and choreographer, eventually becoming artistic co-director with Hans van Manen. In 1969 he formed his own company with which he toured Europe. He succeeded John Cranko as director of the Stuttgart Ballet 1974–6, since when he has developed his choreographic work which is represented today in many of the major dance companies of the world, classical and modern.

At first uncompromisingly modern, his work now blends the academic and modern vocabularies in a uniquely personal as well as a uniquely balanced manner. In Britain he is represented in the repertory of London Festival Ballet as well as Ballet Rambert and directed the choreographic summer school at Surrey University in 1975 and 1979. Unfortunately, two works for the Royal Ballet, *Field Figures* (1970) and *Laborintus* (1972), seem to have been allowed to lapse. This is a pity because both were interesting pieces specially created for the company. *Field Figures*, in particular, illustrated very well his way of creating out of his dancers and the situation in which he finds them. The ballet was a free-form *pas de deux* continually interrupted by five accompanying dancers. Part of its inspiration came from the hierarchic organization of the Royal Ballet and the distance and tension this creates between groups of dancers, continually influencing their lives.

Pierrot Lunaire

Ballet in one act. Choreography: Tetley. Music: Schoenberg. Décor: Rouben Ter-Arutunian. First performed by Glen Tetley Company, New York, 5 May 1962. First performed by Ballet Rambert, Richmond Theatre, London, 26 January 1967.

'In the antiquity of the Roman theatre began the battle of the white clown of innocence with the dark clown of experience. Pierrot and Brighella are their lineal descendants and Columbine their eternal pawn.' Tetley's programme note serves to introduce us to the theme of his ballet; at curtain rise we see Pierrot swinging high on the white tower of scaffolding that forms the set. He is wide-eyed, innocent, a dreamer, a moody introverted clown, and when Columbine appears he is seized with delight; her appearance is brief, but she returns with a clothesline which she gives him to hold. He is in an ecstasy of delight but when he tries to kiss her, and then puts a hand on her breast, she slaps him, sends the laundry line whisking back into the wings, and leaves him. She returns again, cloaked, and Pierrot grovels, abjectly adoring. The third character appears, announced by the dark sonorities of the eighth poem, 'Nacht'. It is Brighella, clothed in sombre colours; Pierrot plays with him, but Brighella soon achieves a dominance, and Pierrot's innocence is gradually destroyed by this confrontation with experience. Brighella now brings on Columbine, dressed in brilliant scarlet, and they tease and taunt Pierrot, and eventually attach cords to him so that he becomes their puppet. Next Brighella strips Pierrot of his white costume and puts it on over his own dark clothes; Pierrot lies defeated on the ground while Columbine and Brighella dance around the stage. He struggles to his feet and staggers across the stage to lean on the proscenium arch while the other two watch his suffering from the vantage point of Pierrot's tower. Pierrot mimes some fighting gestures, then lies exhausted on the ground. Slowly he gets to his feet, and climbs up his tower to join Brighella and Columbine at the top. They offer him back his hat, but he casts it aside and in a final gesture of strength he puts his arms round Columbine and Brighella, pressing their heads to his breast.

Pierrot Lunaire is an extraordinary and moving ballet – and an amazing first work. As with every Tetley ballet, it is full of allusions and analogies – not least with *Petrushka*, but whereas Fokine's creation triumphed only in death, Tetley's comes to terms with life and its torments. This Pierrot is the eternal victim, the dreamer forever wounded by experience, and the theme of Tetley's work is the education he undergoes at the hands of the bitch Columbine and the tough, worldly-wise Brighella. At the last, after being mocked and derided, after being stripped of everything including the identity of his traditional dress, with his domain (the tower) invaded and taken over, he can still find strength to forgive and to accept the world.

The ballet gains enormously from the beauty of Ter-Arutunian's décor; Pierrot's white suit, white tower, white setting are wonderfully evocative of the moonlit world of Schoenberg's *Pierrot*, and the costumes are admirable in shape.

Tetley uses the score with remarkable freedom, ignoring most of the Beardsleyesque imagery of Albert Giraud's poems, but he associates everything 'white' in the *commedia dell' arte* with Pierrot, and the dark elements and the feminine references serve respectively to identify Brighella and Columbine.

The Anatomy Lesson

Ballet in one act. Choreographer: Tetley. Music: Marcel Landowsky. Décor: Nicolas Wijnberg. First performed by Nederlands Dans Theater, The Hague, 28 January 1964. Jaap Flier as the Man.

The ballet was inspired by Rembrandt's famous painting; at curtain rise we see seven men in dark clothes standing before a high, circular building with part of its upper storey cut away. The central building is turned round and the men take their places in the grouping round the body on the anatomy table that we know from the painting. The Man's body now moves down from the table and bends on to the ground; after a brief moment of activity, the Man returns to the table. The doctors cover the body with a cloth, then hold the cloth so that the body forms a pietà shape as if freshly deposed from the cross of his life. The Man, bare save for a loin cloth, now relives parts of his life; children pass, playing together, and he mingles with them – though never able to touch or communicate with them. His mother and wife appear and dance with him – he holds his mother in his arms so that she seems like a wooden Flemish Madonna – and throughout the ballet stalk two of the doctors who are now identified as the Prosecutor and his Assistant, inexorable judges of the Man's life.

In the final section, a procession of black-dressed men with women carrying gold laurel wreaths moves across the stage and takes up a position in the auditorium of the anatomy-theatre. They then leave the stage, and the body rests entirely alone on the dissecting table under its sheet.

In an illuminating BBC television version of *The Anatomy Lesson* Glen Tetley introduced the work with a brief commentary in which he talked of his desire to make this, his first ballet for the Nederlands Dans Theater, a

231

specifically Dutch work. The movements of the children seen in the early moments of the Man's story were inspired by Dutch tiles; other groupings and poses found their inspiration in Dutch art. The ballet is a bold and extremely successful piece of theatre-craft; Tetley dissolves time, compressing incidents to extract maximum impact, exploring the tragedy of the Man on the table – to whom he gives a much more universal implication – with a wonderful compassion. The ballet was dominated by a superb performance of the central role by Jaap Flier.

Freefall

Ballet in one act. Choreography and décor: Tetley. Music: Max Schubel; Concerto for Five Instruments. First performed by Repertory Dance Theatre, Salt Lake City, 1967. First performed London, Ballet Rambert, Jeannetta Cochrane Theatre, 13 November 1967.

Freefall's title implies matters of weightlessness, of parachutists tumbling through the air, of bodies turning and falling; and Tetley's concern seems to be with setting his five dancers falling, and then observing what happens to them. They move and turn, buoyed up on strong currents, or straining against them, their movements by turns slow, languorous or fiercely energetic. They can seem like figures in a dream, having the curious lethargy of dream walkers; the designs that Tetley has devised, with their use of gleaming white and transparent polythenes, insist on the strangeness of the dancers and their surroundings. The action starts with a mutually complementary duet between a man and a woman (doubled by a reflection behind a sheet of perspex). They are somewhat encumbered as to boots and transparent jackets, but once these are removed, and the two men and three women of the cast are fully involved, there follows a sequence of solos and *pas de deux* that offer intensely stimulating choreographic ideas. There are a series of erotic partnerings that explore the dynamic and dramatic possibilities of male/female, male/male, female/female duets, in which Tetley makes fascinating use of the possibilities of movement slowed down by weightlessness, and by the emotional as well as physical implications of the title – never has the idea of 'falling for someone' been so literally shown. But there is hatred, too, in these encounters, and a tense dramatic quality; at times the ballet seems to undergo a punning alteration from *Freefall* to *Free for All*.

Technically the ballet offered a remarkable view of Tetley's ability to combine – to fuse is perhaps a better word – elements from both parts of his own training – academic and modern dance – to make a language that is entirely communicative of his themes.

232

Ziggurat

Ballet in one act. Choreography: Tetley. Music: Stockhausen; Gesäng der
Junglinge *and part of* Kontakte. *Décor: Nadine Baylis. First performed by
Ballet Rambert, Jeannetta Cochrane Theatre, London,* 20 *November* 1967.

Ziggurats are those Assyrian brick structures which can still be seen in
Mesopotamia, rising like pyramids to the sky. In essence they were temple-
towers whose summit was the meeting of earth and heaven, a place where
man could most nearly offer his sacrifice to God. For Glen Tetley, as his
programme note to this ballet suggests, they are also the Hanging Gardens
of Babylon, the stairway of Jacob's Dream and the Tower of Babel. All
these ideas can be discerned in *Ziggurat,* which like many of Tetley's
ballets, offers cross-references, allusions, dovetailed incidents that elide
present and past, *then* and *now.*

Ziggurat's theme is – arguably, since interpretation of this kind of modern
work is often a very personal thing – man's search for the divine, his
concept of a god, and his rare and terrifying contacts with a deity, his terror
if he finds that there is no God, his attempts even to bolster up his faith by
bolstering up an image of a deity. At curtain rise we are presented with
seven men, naked save for a covering of fine looped thread, grouped in
front of a structure of metal scaffolding, a temple in which sits the God-
figure, the whole dominated by a large metal frame above. The men's pose
recalls Assyrian frescoes, but their movements – agonized, terror-struck, a
series of frantic dashes, mouthings of nausea with fingers to lips – denote a
horror, a flight from dreadful pressures that implies, perhaps, the dilemma
of modern man crushed beneath the ziggurats of his skyscrapers. Their
silent screams, frantic stampings and slappings, brief sequences of turns –
man seen in the terms of animals in flight from disaster – subside as the
Godhead keels over sideways. The men place the fallen divinity on their
reclining bodies, trying to revive him; as they carry him off stage a white
screen descends and tilts over the stage, and the men remove the temple
structure to the side of the stage and crouch within it.

A series of colour-film projections are now shown on the screen and on
the white backdrop (the stage otherwise bare to the back walls of the
theatre) and there follows a series of dances for one of the men and a
group of white-clad girls. This gives way to a duet between the man and
the Divinity, who returns to show the contrast between human and superhuman. The stage is now bathed in red light and another of the men rolls a
sheet of polythene across the stage to form a shining path on which he
dances and where one of the women meets him in a voluptuous duet. After
another group dance for men and women, the Divinity returns to join

another man in the most beautiful section of the work, a struggle between Jacob and the Angel which is also a commentary on the basic father/son relationship. The women go off, the screens disappear, the scaffolding throne for the God is brought back, the men return, alone once more, and the God is propped back into his temple as the men assume the agonized poses of the work's beginning, and the curtain falls.

Ziggurat is by no means an 'easy' work; it is densely written, packed with imagery that speaks directly to us without any literary or dramatic under-tones, though movement and gesture are immensely dramatic in themselves.

Tetley's view of man suffering and disoriented, still like an animal in his desperate frenzy, is moving, and most movingly expressed in dance.

Embrace Tiger and Return to Mountain

Ballet in one act. Choreography: Tetley. Music: Morton Subotnick. Décor: Nadine Baylis. First performed by Ballet Rambert, Jeannetta Cochrane Theatre, London, 21 November 1968.

T'ai-Chi is a system of Chinese callisthenics, thirty-seven exercises in 'shadow-boxing' that were invented 1400 years ago, originally as a system of self-defence, in which an attacker's energy was used to confound him by a delicate appreciation of balance and falls. It later developed into a method of physical and emotional training, intended to create mental as well as physical well-being. Tetley saw a film showing Chinese performing these exercises, and was so intrigued that he studied the method and in *Embrace Tiger and Return to Mountain* (which is the name of the seventeenth of the exercises) he has taken *T'ai-Chi* as the starting point for a ballet. But this is no piece of mock-oriental knick-knackery; Tetley is inspired by the idea of a totally alien code of muscular and intellectual self-betterment brought into contact with western ideas of dance activity. In *Embrace Tiger*, coolness of manner, reserve – the cliché of the inscrutable oriental – are important, as is the electronic score by Subotnick – *The Silver Apples of the Moon* – music as cool and distant as its title.

The fusing of these elements, their translation into Tetley's own very personal movement idiom, makes for a ballet that seems both remote and immediate.

Tetley – and the ballet – starts with a basic *T'ai-Chi* exercise done by a cast of ten who pose, flex and stretch their bodies, and look very handsome in flame-shot leotards under a clear Chinese-white décor, with a silver floor that reflects light upwards and adds to the different 'feel' of the piece. The development of the ballet shows Tetley's extension of the basic attitudes of *T'ai-Chi*; as with others of his ballets, slowness and an unhurried exploration of muscular possibilities mark its style, the unfamiliar starting poses serving as a springboard for Tetley's imagination. It is a ballet about dancers in reaction to one another both in duets and in group work; for much of the time the ballet's style has the kind of time-suspended quality seen in underwater swimming (also manifested in *Freefall*) with the same feeling of a strongly controlled muscular pulse behind it. Emotions are hinted at, balances and falls are as much a manifestation of personality as of physique, and in the closing section, where the score braces itself into a remarkable crescendo, so does Tetley's invention. Four men and a girl become involved in fierce eddyings of energy, like swimmers battling with submarine currents. But calm is at last restored; the exercises reassert their original purposeful control.

Embrace Tiger is a handsome and original work, suggesting more surely than one would have dared hope, that it is possible to make a fruitful cross-breeding between oriental and occidental attitudes to movement; best of all, it abounds in freshness of imagery.

Gemini

Ballet in three movements. Choreography: Tetley. Music: Henze. Design: Nadine Baylis. First performed by the Australian Ballet, Elizabethan Theatre, Sydney, 6 April 1973. First performed by Sadler's Wells Royal Ballet, 5 May 1977.

Gemini is a plotless ballet to Hans Werner Henze's Symphony No. 3 and explores the relationships of two couples through choreography of extraordinary brilliance requiring exceptional virtuosity in performance.

The original dancers of the ballet in Sydney were Marilyn Rowe, Carolyn Rappel, John Meehan and Gary Norman. When the Australian Ballet performed in London in 1973 Alida Chase replaced Carolyn Rappel, who was ill. On that occasion the work was the company's principal artistic success and was regarded as a measure of artistic and technical development since the first visit to London in 1965. When the ballet was first performed by Sadler's Wells Royal Ballet in 1977 the dancers were Maina Gielgud, June Highwood, Desmond Kelly and Dale Baker, an Australian dancer who knew the work and replaced an injured David Ashmole at short notice. It has been revived also for Stuttgart Ballet in 1974 and American Ballet Theater in 1975.

Voluntaries

Ballet in one scene. Choreography: Glen Tetley. Music: Francis Poulenc; Organ Concerto. Design: Rouben Ter-Arutunian. First performed by the

Stuttgart Ballet, Stuttgart, 22 December 1973. Marcia Haydée and Richard Cragun in leading roles. Staged for the Royal Ballet, Covent Garden, on 18 November 1976, with Lynn Seymour and David Wall.

'*Voluntaries* – by musical definition – are free-ranging organ or trumpet improvization often played before, during or after religious services. The Latin root of the word can also connote flight or desire, and the ballet is conceived as a linked series of voluntaries.' Thus Glen Tetley's programme note for a ballet which he created as his first work for the Stuttgart Ballet, of which he became director in succession to John Cranko, following the latter's death in 1974.

Voluntaries opens in silence, its principal couple standing in an embrace that suggests the sharing of some common grief. The poignancy of this initial image, and the fact that Tetley created the ballet in Stuttgart as a memorial to John Cranko in the months immediately following Cranko's untimely death, lend the work a strong emotional colouring. It may be dangerous to ascribe meaning to a work of plotless dance, but the upward soaring lines of the choreography, the implied feelings of desolation and consolation are very powerful in Tetley's writing, and beautiful. Conceived for a central pair, a subsidiary trio of two men and a woman, with an accompanying chorus of six couples, the work has a 'dark' and very arduous choreographic text, with broad-spanning lines of energy contrasted with serpentine convolutions of double work for the principals, all of which sit with remarkable rightness upon the highly charged writing of Poulenc's Organ Concerto. It is a ballet which has invited exceptional performances. The original partnership of Haydée and Cragun with the Stuttgart Ballet inevitably has had an emotional dignity and depth of perception uniquely apposite to the work; but the Royal Ballet performances by Lynn Seymour and David Wall, by Alfreda Thorogood and Wayne Eagling, and by Natalya Makarova with David Wall, have been of the noblest distinction.

Greening

Ballet in one act. Choreography: Glen Tetley. Design: Nadine Baylis. Score: Arne Nordheim. First performed by the Stuttgart Ballet, Stuttgart, 29 November 1975. First presented by London Festival Ballet, Oxford, 10 April 1978.

In several of Glen Tetley's ballets the point of inspiration can come from an event in life which acquires a resonance and a symbolism for him which he later expands and explores in choreography: this is true of his *Rag*

Dances (whose starting point was his hearing Messaien's *Quatuor pour la Fin du Temps* and the death of four friends in a brief space of time: see *Making a Ballet*, Mary Clarke and Clement Crisp) and of *Greening*.

The ballet was created in Stuttgart during the period of his directorate of the ballet, and was provoked by the fact that young dancers, who had recently joined the company, found it difficult at first to become integrated into the close 'family' atmosphere of the Stuttgart Ballet. To provide some necessary bridge, Tetley decided to create a ballet for them, which would also feed upon the idea of waiting that was implicit in their newcomer status:

> . . . a work about waiting for something else, people who are at the beginning of something and are being moved by emotional storms that are beyond their understanding. Only later, when the sky is clear, can they look back and understand these youthful urges of desire for an as yet unrealized partner or whatever may lie ahead. I have always been influenced by Dylan Thomas, as his poetry is full of movement. I think his poem, about the green fuse that drives through everything, must have subconsciously influenced me to drive a green fuse through my ballet. (From Peter Williams' programme note about *Greening* for London Festival Ballet: reproduced by kind permission of Mr Williams.)

For London Festival Ballet the work provided challenging and illuminating choreography, excellently performed by a cast headed by Eva Evdokimova and Kenneth McCombie, Elisabetta Terabust, Nigel Burgoine and Nicholas Johnson.

The Tempest

Ballet in two acts. Choreography. Glen Tetley. Score: Arne Nordheim Design: Nadine Baylis. First performed by the Ballet Rambert, Rokokotheater, Schwetzingen, 3 May 1979. Christopher Bruce: Prospero. Lucy Burge: Miranda. Thomas Yang: Caliban. Gianfranco Paoluzi: Ariel. Mark Wraith: Ferdinand.

The Tempest is Shakespeare's last play, and its attraction has been always to invite commentary, exploration – like Prospero's island. It constantly asks for expansion of its hermetic incidents and quality, almost demanding that we supply explanation and supposition to fill out characters to our own satisfaction, to investigate its power, discover its secret. Since it lays itself so open to interpretation, any interpretation is justified as the proper response to the work itself, and it can be argued that *The*

237

Tempest is better suited to dance realization – by reason of its magical incident, its compression – than many another Shakespeare play.

Tetley had long been attracted to the play; his programme notes for the production provide copious and eloquent evidence to the power he felt in its action as myth and metaphor. In many Tetley works we have been aware of the layers of meaning which invest his choreography; symbols, relationships, which provide an undercurrent of correspondences that we can accept or reject as we choose, but which are self-generating from Tetley's own wide-ranging sensibilities. In his version of *The Tempest* Tetley attempts a skeletal placing of the play's narrative bones in two acts which he fleshes out with his own mythology, finding parallels between Prospero and Leonardo da Vinci, and identifying Caliban as a natural and innocent being, 'curious, full of appetite and lust, childlike and simple' and making him a strong focal point for much of the action. The result is a work that, with the help of Nadine Baylis' distinguished design (which involves a prodigal use of fabric to suggest the magic world of the island, of Ariel's nature, and the sea itself), has excited a wide range of critical comment.

Sphinx

Ballet in one act. Choreography: Glen Tetley. Music: Bohuslav Martinu; Concerto for two string orchestras, piano and timpani. Set: Rouben Ter-Arutunian. Costumes: Willa Kim. First performed by American Ballet Theater. Kennedy Centre, Washington, 9 December 1978. First presented by London Festival Ballet, Bristol, 26 October 1979.

The legend of the young Oedipus' encounter with the Sphinx which guarded the pass above the city of Thebes was adapted by Jean Cocteau in his play *La Machine Infernale*. The myth told of the Sphinx who posed the riddle to passers-by: 'What goes on four legs in the morning; on two legs at noon; on three legs in the evening?' Those travellers who could not answer the question were killed. Only Oedipus was able to give the right answer: 'It is man.' In Cocteau's play, which is the basis for this ballet, the Spinx is weary of immortality and, Tetley observes in his programme note, 'appears in the guise of a young woman who is filled with the overwhelming desire to fall in love with a human. Her companion, Anubis, the jackal-headed Egyptian god of the dead, warns her of the consequences, but she desires Oedipus so greatly that, in order not to risk his life in asking him the riddle, she also tells him the answer. The Sphinx loses Oedipus and her own human form for ever.'

With a handsome setting of a winged platform for the Sphinx, and a cast

238

comprising only the Sphinx, Oedipus and Anubis, the ballet has a strong emotional drive, concentrated in writing for the Sphinx which conveys with entire clarity the combination of desire, weariness and a fatalistic acceptance of the inevitable. The theme also served for an earlier ballet of great distinction: David Lichine's *La Rencontre*, staged for the Ballets des Champs-Elysées in 1948, and starring Jean Babilée and Leslie Caron, with a superlative setting by Christian Bérard, and score by Henri Sauguet.

EUROPEAN BALLETS

SERGE LIFAR (b. 1905)

Born in Kiev, Lifar first saw dancing when he had occasion to watch a class at the school Bronislava Nijinska had opened in that city. He was so overwhelmed by the sight that he knew that he had to become a dancer, and joined Nijinska's classes. Barely a month later Nijinska left for Europe to assist in the Diaghilev staging of *The Sleeping Beauty*, and Lifar was left to work as best he could. Three years later Nijinska sent word to her school that the five best boys should be sent to Paris to join the Diaghilev company. Since one of those selected had disappeared, Lifar pleaded to be the substitute, and in 1923 he arrived in Europe. His rudimentary technique doomed him at first to ferocious hard work to make up for his inadequacy, and after unflagging study with Cecchetti he started to show the beautiful style and prowess that made him one of the greatest dancers of his time. He soon attracted the attention of Diaghilev, and was featured in increasingly important roles – notably in the two Balanchine ballets, *Apollo* (1928) and *Le Fils Prodigue* (1929) – roles which indicate something of his range and qualities even then.

In 1929 he made his début as a choreographer with a revival of Stravinsky's *Le Renard*, which earned considerable praise, but with the death of Diaghilev in that same year, the whole company disbanded. Lifar was then asked to stage a version of Beethoven's *The Creatures of Prometheus* at the Paris Opéra, and the success of this production led to his engagement as *premier danseur* and *maître de ballet* there, a post which he retained until 1959. His reign at the Opéra, and no other phrase will really convey the importance of his reputation and achievement, saw him raise the ballet company to a position of excellence that it had not known since the great days of the Romantic era. He has produced over a hundred ballets, and his work at the Opéra revitalized both the teaching and the reputation of ballet in France. In his most celebrated roles – in ballets he created for himself, like *Icare*, *Joan de Zoarissa* and *David Triomphant*, and in the classics (he was a fine Albrecht in *Giselle*) – he showed himself a performer of magnetic presence, and he worked with two of the greatest ballerine of our time at the Opéra: Yvette Chauviré and Nina Vyrubova, besides creating a fine company of dancers. Political agitation about his wartime activities to keep his company functioning led to his departure from the Opéra for two years after the Liberation in 1944, but he returned in triumph and continued there, with a brief break, until 1959. It is significant that thereafter the ballet company at the Paris Opéra has lacked the sense of creative continuity which is associated with a permanent director.

Noir et Blanc (Suite en Blanc)

Ballet in one act. Choreography: Lifar. Music: Lalo (from his ballet Namouna). *First performed, Paris Opéra, 23 July* 1943. *Revived for London Festival Ballet, Royal Festival Hall, 15 September* 1966.

Suite en Blanc is a display piece, designed to show off the stars and the prowess of a fine company. Its music is taken from Lalo's beautiful score to *Namouna*, a ballet by Lucien Petipa, first staged in 1882. At the Opéra it was given against plain curtains, but with rostra on which the dancers are first seen posed at the beginning; they exit leaving three girls in long tarlatan skirts, who dance the 'Siesta'. Their exit is succeeded by two men who leap on and announce the arrival of a ballerina who joins them in the *pas de trois*, and there follows a 'Serenade' for another ballerina plus eight *corps de ballet* girls. Next comes a *pas de cinq* for a third soloist with a quartet of men, which in turn gives way to 'La Cigarette', a ravishing solo for the chief ballerina with the rest of the women in the company grouped behind. Next comes the big male solo, a mazurka; then a *pas de deux* for the principal ballerina and her partner, to be succeeded by another ballerina solo for yet another star dancer, 'La Flûte'; a final general dance brings the ballet to a close.

Lalo wrote the ballet score for *Namouna* within a period of four months in 1881; alas, despite the enchantment of the score, the ballet was not a success and it was taken off after fifteen performances (Debussy, then aged nineteen, was so vociferous in his enthusiasm for the work that he was forcibly ejected from the theatre). The story had to do with slave girls, pirates and true love in seventeenth-century Corfu. Lifar turned to the score in 1943 to make this grand showpiece of a ballet, retaining many of the titles to the numbers from Lalo's original score (hence the *valse lente* is still called 'La Cigarette' because in the original ballet the heroine, Namouna, snatched a cigarette from the mouth of her lover: the 'Siesta' is a prelude to Act II and showed freed slaves taking what must have been a well-earned rest). The *pas de deux* did not exist in the original, and was put together by Lifar from pages from the score. Lifar's most exciting quality as a choreographer has always been an heroic boldness; as a theorist and apologist for dancing he has written at great length, and in works like *Icare* (which has no score, and is danced to rhythm accompaniment from drums and other percussion) he has made fascinating experiments. *Suite en Blanc* preserves some of the finest of his inventions; it bears all the hallmarks of the Lifarian style: dancers working in parallel formation; feet placed in Lifar's own invented sixth and seventh positions; sharply held bodies; brilliant use of beaten steps. All this gives a very fair view of a notable and influential figure in the ballet of our time.

DAVID LICHINE (1910–72)

Russian born, David Lichine made his début with the Ida Rubinstein company and also worked with Pavlova. When the de Basil troupe was founded in 1932, he joined as soloist and created many important roles in the repertory, and also choreographed ballets, notably *Francesca da Rimini*, *Protée* and *Graduation Ball*. After the war he created two fine works for Les Ballets des Champs-Elysées: *La Création* (which was performed in silence) and *La Rencontre*, which had a superb décor by Bérard, and featured Jean Babilée as Oedipus and Leslie Caron as the Sphinx. He also composed two ballets for Festival Ballet. He was married to the ballerina Tatiana Riabonchinska. His only ballet still in repertory in Britain is:

Graduation Ball

Ballet in one act. Choreography: Lichine. Music: J. Strauss; orch Dorati. Décor: Benois. First performed, De Basil Ballets Russes, Sydney, Australia, 28 February 1940; revived for London's Festival Ballet, 9 July 1957.

The curtain rises to reveal the gilded and chandeliered splendour of a drawing room at a girls' school in Vienna in the 1850s. The junior students are in a fine frenzy of excitement preparing for a ball at which they expect the cadets of a nearby military academy. One girl has discovered a swans-down powder-puff and as the senior girls watch amusedly, the juniors share the delights of random powdering. Suddenly they remember their manners as the Headmistress – a forbidding looking lady (though the role is often danced by a man) – enters; the young cadets now make their entrance, escorted by their headmaster, a whiskery, stiff-jointed though still gallant, general. At first both groups are on their best behaviour but soon the ice is broken – one girl with pigtails shows a lot of merriment – and before many moments the cadets and girls are waltzing joyously. Now the Headmistress and the General return for the formal entertainment: a series of *divertissement* dances. These include a romantic *pas de deux* for La Sylphide and James; a Drummer; and a dance-step competition in which two girls try to outdo each other in brilliant turning steps. There follows a general *perpetuum mobile,* and all this time a flirtation of slightly creaking roguishness has been blossoming between the General and the Headmistress. After a final general dance the cadets take their leave and the girls go up to bed and dream of their conquests. One of the cadets and the junior girl creep back, determined to bid a last farewell – but the Headmistress is there to forestall them and they scuttle off as the curtain falls.

This is an enchanting, high-spirited ballet, with choreography bouncing sweetly along to the delights of the Strauss score. Overenthusiastic playing can spoil it, for Lichine has created a remarkable evocation of innocent and endearing fun; but with sensitive playing it can be an unalloyed delight. It was first seen in London given by de Basil's Original Ballets Russes, to fine effect – and with one unforgettably elegant performance by Nicholas Orlov in his created role as the Drummer in the *divertissement.* Festival Ballet staged the piece with considerable care in 1957, and the Benois set, reproduced under that master's own supervision, looked particularly pleasing. The ballet also features in the repertory of the Royal Danish Ballet where it is given a loving and careful production.

HARALD LANDER (1905–71)

Since August Bournville, now well represented in British repertories, Denmark has produced only one choreographer of international standing, Harald Lander. Born in Copenhagen, Lander trained at the Royal Danish Ballet School under Christiansen, Beck and Uhlendorff, thus inheriting the French tradition which he later did so much to sustain. He studied with Mikhail Fokine in the United States and Russian folk dance in the USSR and became one of the Royal Danish Ballet's most distinguished character soloists. He was appointed ballet master of the company in 1930 and director of the school in 1932. He choreographed about thirty ballets and raised Danish ballet to a height of creativity it had not known since Bournonville. Under him, too, began the Bournonville renaissance from which ballet is still benefiting across the world.

Etudes

Ballet in one act. Choreography: Lander. Music:Knudaage Riisager, adapted from Czery's Etudes. Costumes as for daily ballet class. First performed by Royal Danish Ballet, Royal Theatre, Copenhagen, 15 January 1948, titled Etude. First performed by London Festival Ballet, Royal Festival Hall, London, 8 August 1955.

The ballet is structured on the daily class of classical dancers and develops as a demonstration of the academic style. Therefore it begins with *pliés* at the barre, moves through centre practice and *adage* to *batterie* and *allegro* exercises reaching a climax with steps of virtuosity.

There have been many ballets based on the dancer's daily class, among them Bournonville's *Konservatoriet*, Jerome Robbins' *Afternoon of a Faun* and Robert Cohan's *Class*. Degas, of course, made famous this part of a dancer's life in the late nineteenth century. Lander's ballet is propelled by an irresistible escalation of technical difficulties matched by mounting excitement in the music. Although it is the best known of Lander's ballets and an international success his skill in creating character ballets should not be overlooked. Among them, for example, was *Qarrtsiluni*, also to music by Riisager, an Eskimo invocation of the spirit of spring, created in 1942, in which the Copenhagen audience of German occupied Denmark saw an unmistakable political message.

RUDOLF NUREYEV (b. 1938)

Since his decision, taken during the Leningrad State Kirov Ballet's first visit to Paris in 1961, to stay in the West, Rudolf Nureyev has become an integral part of western ballet. He has danced ceaselessly, tirelessly, with many companies, made and starred in films, been the subject of several books, produced ballets of the nineteenth century, made three choreographic essays (the second his *Romeo and Juliet* for London Festival Ballet) and become the most celebrated male dancer of the age. In his own stagings of nineteenth-century works: *Sleeping Beauty, Swan Lake, Don Quixote,*

The Nutcracker, he has been at pains to reassert the place of the male dancer in these ballerina-vehicles, sometimes to the detriment of the ballet itself (his *Sleeping Beauty*, with its distorted vision scene, a case in point).

Single-handed, he has done much to make the ballet public more conscious of the male dancer as a performer; endlessly newsworthy, he can fill theatres night after night in the marathons of dancing which – at an age when many other dancers are husbanding their strength – find him appearing in three ballets at each performance. He is a brilliant star in an age sadly lacking in such theatrically irresistible figures; he is adored by a huge audience; he is a force of nature.

Romeo and Juliet

Ballet in three acts. Choreography: Rudolf Nureyev. Score: Prokofiev. Design: Ezio Frigerio. First performed by London Festival Ballet, Coliseum London, 2 June 1977. Romeo: Rudolf Nureyev. Juliet: Patricia Ruanne Mercutio: Nicholas Johnson. Tybalt: Frederic Werner.

ACT I, *Scene 1*: The market square. The city of Verona is split by a feud between the Montague and Capulet families. Romeo, a young Montague, is paying court to Rosaline, but she rejects his advances. An encounter between the retainers of the rival families turn into a brawl. Benvolio tries to pacify his followers, the Montagues, but Tybalt encourages the Capulets; Mercutio, who is friendly with both families, joins in cheerfully both sides. The quarrel is interrupted by the arrival of the Prince of Verona and peace is restored.

Scene 2: Juliet's ante-room. Juliet is playing with her companions and her Nurse. Lord and Lady Capulet, arrive with their nephew Tybalt. They introduce Paris, a young man whom they have chosen as a husband for Juliet. He brings a wedding dress as a gift.

Scene 3: Outside the Capulets' house. Guests are arriving for a feast given by the Capulets. Rosaline is still followed by Romeo, but again she spurns him. Mercutio and his friends make fun of Romeo's dejection, caricaturing the effects of love. Lord Capulet invites Mercutio and his party to the feast. They put on their masks and enter, with Romeo following.

Scene 4: The Capulets' ballroom. Tybalt leads off the dancing with Lady Capulet and the whole assembly celebrates its solidarity against the Montagues. Juliet enters and performs a betrothal duet with Paris. Romeo enters with Mercutio and Benvolio and they join in the dance. At the first touch of their hands, Romeo and Juliet fall in love. Romeo is recognized and Tybalt tries to throw him out, but Lord Capulet intervenes. All join in a final 'wheel of fortune' dance.

Scene 5: The Capulets' garden. Romeo is hiding outside where Juliet is preparing for sleep. Mercutio and Benvolio come in search of him but Tybalt's arrival disturbs them. As Juliet comes out into the garden Romeo emerges and they pledge their love for each other.

ACT II, *Scene 1*: The market square. Romeo is waiting for news from Juliet. Her Nurse arrives with a letter but she cannot find Romeo: Mercutio and Benvolio tease them both. The square fills up with market crowds, acrobats and entertainers. The Nurse discovers Romeo and delivers the letter. Romeo reads that Juliet has arranged for Friar Laurence to marry them secretly in his chapel.

Scene 2: A chapel. Romeo is waiting in the chapel. Juliet arrives and the two lovers are married by Friar Laurence.

Scene 3: The market square. The rival factions vie with each other in displays of dancing. Mercutio and Benvolio enter followed by Tybalt, who is angrily looking for Romeo. He tries to provoke Romeo to fight and, when Romeo refuses, accuses him of effeminacy. At this insult Mercutio challenges Tybalt. He jokes as they fight but Tybalt is serious; a knife flashes and the revellers find that Mercutio is dead. The Montagues force a sword into Romeo's hand and he fights Tybalt and kills him. The Prince arrives with Juliet, who finds that her new husband has become her cousin's murderer. Romeo is condemned to leave next morning for exile in Mantua.

ACT III, *Scene 1*: Juliet's bedroom. While Lord and Lady Capulet discuss with Paris his marriage to Juliet, she sits in her room filled with dread. But Romeo steals in by the window and their marriage is consummated. Day breaks and he must leave for Mantua. Juliet's family return and force her to prepare for her wedding with Paris.

Scene 2: A chapel. Juliet runs to Friar Laurence for advice but finds Paris discussing his wedding. Friar Laurence gets rid of Paris and explains to Juliet a way out of her predicament. She is to drink a potion which will cast her into a deep sleep. Thinking her dead, her parents will place her in the family crypt. Meanwhile Friar John will have warned Romeo in Mantua and he will return at night to carry her away when she awakes. Juliet foresees herself reunited with Romeo.

Scene 3: Juliet's bedroom. Juliet pretends to agree to be married to Paris. Left alone, she is filled with doubts. Should she choose suicide with Tybalt's dagger for the family honour, or the device to live for love? Finally she drinks the potion.

Scene 4: Juliet's ante-room. Paris arrives to greet Juliet with his marriage retinue of musicians and dancers. But when her family try to wake her she appears to be dead. The wedding turns into a funeral. Benvolio hurries away to tell Romeo.

Scene 5: The road to Mantua. On the way to Mantua with Friar Laurence's letter to Romeo, Friar John is attacked, robbed and killed.

Scene 6: Mantua. Ignorant of all that has happened in Verona since he left, Romeo dreams of Juliet. He is woken by Benvolio bringing news of Juliet's apparent death. Seized by despair, he leaves for Verona.

Scene 7: The Capulet crypt. Juliet is laid to rest in the Capulet crypt. When the mourners have gone, Romeo steals in to say farewell to his wife. He find Paris there and kills him; then, distracted by grief, he poisons himself. Juliet wakes to find him dead beside her and kills herself.

(*Reproduced by kind permission of London Festival Ballet.*)

From its brilliant opening moment with a quartet of macabre dice-players, the progress of a plague-cart across the stage laden with bodies, and the subsequent fall of a vast crimson and black silk cloth to prepare us for the drama to come, it is plain that Nureyev's *Romeo and Juliet* is to be a 'different' staging. It is compact with theatrical ideas – a flag dance; a 'wheel of fortune' dance; a most effective reading of the role of Mercutio – all of which sit excellently against the fine designs of Frigerio, scrupulous recreations of Renaissance costuming and painterly evocations of town-scapes. The choreography has a strong nervous drive to its energies, and the handling of crowd scenes is efficient; what appears lacking is any sense of lyric effusion for the lovers, or any depth of observation about their feelings. The production pays careful attention to the text of its original in images and incident; it misses the fine ardour of youthful love and tragedy that is the spirit of the play.

HANS VAN MANEN (b. 1932)

Since the Second World War, Holland has become a creative centre of dance more modern than classical – yet its modern dance is classically based. Its dance achievements in the theatre are expressed principally through three companies, the Dutch National Ballet, the Nederlands Dans Theater and Scapino Ballet. The latter, founded in 1945 to entertain and instruct children, is the oldest of the three companies offering a repertory of ballets for young people. Nederlands Dans Theater, the most experimental of the three, was formed in 1959 by the American teacher and choreographer Benjamin Harkarvy. The Dutch National Ballet (Het

National Ballet), largest of the three, was formed in the autumn of 1961 under the direction of Sonia Gaskell but derives from a pedigree and amalgamation of groups going back to 1936. Its exceptionally wide repertory ranges from the nineteenth-century classics and Fokine ballets, to revivals of famous modern works as well as creations by its two principal choreographers, Rudi van Dantzig, director of the company, and Hans van Manen.

Represented in a number of North American repertories (van Manen's *Four Schumann Pieces* entered the repertory of the National Ballet of Canada in 1976), but particularly influential in Australia because the New South Wales (now Sydney) Dance Theatre was established in its present image by Jaap Flier of Nederlands Dans Theater, Dutch choreography has appeared in Britain through ballets by van Dantzig and van Manen, both founder members of Nederlands Dans Theatre. Van Dantzig has created or revived ballets for the short-lived London Dance Theatre in 1965, Ballet Rambert in 1966, and the Royal Ballet in 1970. One of his best known works internationally is *Monument for a Dead Boy*, created in 1965, about the isolation of a homosexual boy which ultimately destroys him. This ballet was produced on Cologne television in 1967, and revived for the Harkness Ballet in 1969, American Ballet Theater in 1973, the Royal Danish Ballet in 1976 and the German Opera, Berlin, in 1976.

The best known Dutch choreographer outside Holland, however, is Hans van Manen. He is now choreographer for Dutch National Ballet, working with van Dantzig but was previously one of the creative inspirations of Nederlands Dans Theater. Born in Nieuwer Amstel, van Manen studied with Gaskell, Françoise Adret and Nora Kiss, thus inheriting the Franco-Russian classical style mingled with Central European and, later, American modern influences. He worked first in Dutch classical companies, then with Roland Petit, before joining the newly formed Nederlands Dans Theater in 1960. This catholic background has given him not only a very wide vocabulary of movement but assisted his necessarily considerable output of ballets, necessary because the economics of Nederlands Dans Theater has always demanded a prodigious schedule of new ballets each year. These include a remarkable series of plotless pieces, offering a novel view of dance as emotion, mirroring human passions and fears. The shape of their dramatic structure and interior logic is dictated by van Manen's feeling for emotional truth revealed in movement. These qualities are seen clearly in the three works he revived for the Royal Ballet's New Group between 1972 and 1974.

Grosse Fuge

Ballet in one act. Choreography: van Manen. Music: Beethoven. Scenery: Jean-Paul Vroom. Costumes: van Manen. First performed by Nederlands Dans Theater, Circus Theatre, Scheveningen, 8 April 1971. First performed by Royal Ballet New Group, the Odeon Cinema, Golders Green, London, 28 April 1972.

Danced to an orchestrated version of Beethoven's Op. 133, the Great Fugue, and the Cavatina from his B Flat String Quartet, Op. 130, the curtain rises on four white, seemingly nude, girls and the immediate entrance of four men, bare-chested wearing long, black oriental-style skirts which open and fan out as the men leap and spin. The work seems conceived as a ritual, particularly in its first section where men and women remain separate until a short dance for each couple in turn. The men remove their skirts to appear in brief black trunks heavily belted. The couples remain together in a series of sensual dances from which the element of ritual never departs and which gives the work a sense of inevitability, exploring the contrasting relationships between each couple until a resolution of harmony is reached.

With *Grosse Fuge* the influence of Dutch modern dance first entered the repertory of the Royal Ballet. The Royal Ballet had disbanded its former large-scale touring company and established the New Group in the autumn of 1970. For this Glen Tetley created *Field Figures* to music by Stockhausen and designs by Nadine Baylis. It seemed to justify in every way the term 'new' and herald a more positive and adventurous, creative policy for the Royal Ballet as a whole. Subsequently *Field Figures* was taken into the repertory of the Royal Ballet's large company at Covent Garden. The New Group reverted to older, tried works such as *Pineapple Poll*, *The Rake's Progress* and *Les Rendezvous*. Van Manen's *Grosse Fuge* in 1972 thus seemed like a second attempt to establish the 'new' concept with regional audiences. It was splendidly danced (as *Field Figures* also had been), suggesting that Royal Ballet dancers could handle very well any modern idiom.

Twilight

A ballet for two dancers in one act. Choreography: van Manen. Music: John Cage. Design: Jean-Paul Vroom. First performed by Dutch National Ballet, the Holland Festival, Stadsschouwburg, Amsterdam, 20 June 1972. First performed by Royal Ballet New Group, Royal Shakespeare Theatre, Stratford-upon-Avon, 2 March 1973.

Against a backcloth of a murky industrial landscape and danced to John Cage's piano solo *The Perilous Night*, played on stage on a 'prepared' piano, the work is a dramatic exploration of a precarious relationship between a man and a woman. It is fought by the woman with unrelenting aggression and provocation, eliciting a range of guarded responses from the man. *Twilight* was created originally for Alexandra Radius and Han Ebbelaar and designed to exploit their well-known dramatic qualities. It had no less success when danced by Patricia Ruanne and Paul Clarke. They had not before been challenged by a work of this kind but went on later, especially in Festival Ballet, to justify and develop the extension of talent van Manen had revealed.

Septet Extra

Ballet in five movements. Choreography: van Manen. Music: Saint-Saëns. Design: Jean-Paul Vroom. First performed by Nederlands Dans Theater, Circus Theatre, Scheveningen, for the Holland Festival, 2 July 1973. First performed by Royal Ballet New Group, Sadler's Wells Theatre, 12 February 1974.

The music is Saint-Saëns' Septet for Strings, Piano and Trumpet plus his Etude in Waltz Form, Op. 52, No. 6. Hence part of the 'extra'. The other part of the extra refers to movements the choreographer could not use in previous ballets. The work is humorous, indicated at curtain-rise by a backcloth of unfinished crossword clues and, in due course, by the continuing surprise of dotty movements and moments throughout the plotless choreography. The first movement is for all five couples who comprise the cast; the next for two trios; the third and fourth for a variety of groupings and increasingly witty exploration of movement often at the expense of conventional ballet. At the end of the very fast fourth movement everyone bows as if the ballet has ended. So comes another meaning of 'extra', an extra section which starts before the applause has finished and is danced to the 'extra' piece of music. It is the wittiest of the five movements.

'There is no doubt about the ballet's charm and fun,' said Peter Williams in *Dance and Dancers*. 'Here is all the mastery of what has now become a very personal style with a loud and clear signature to which the dancers respond with polished enthusiasm.' John Percival, in the same issue, also drew attention to the obvious rapport between choreographer and dancers. It is regrettable, therefore, that *Septet Extra* ended for the time being van Manen's liaison with a section of the Royal Ballet for which his talent seems particularly suited. He created *Four Schumann Pieces* for the Covent Garden company in 1975, and this has remained in the repertory. He continues also to be represented in many other repertories in Europe and North America.

EIGHT

Other Choreographers and the Future

If we have omitted well-known names in the previous pages it is not from lack of a wish to acknowledge talent. There are choreographers, honoured and important in their own country, like Fernand Nault and Brian MacDonald in Canada or Domy Reiter-Soffer in Ireland, who do not have a large international following but who make significant contributions in other ways to the dance affairs of their country. There are choreographers established and beginning to build larger reputations like Jonathan Thorpe in Britain's Northern Ballet Theatre, Graeme Murphy in Australia's Sydney Dance Theatre, and Anna Wyman in her own company in Vancouver. There are choreographers at the beginning of promising careers like James Kudelka in Canada and Michael Corder, Jonathan Burrows and David Bintley in Britain. There is the wide field of musical theatre and new areas of choreographic creation like John Curry's Theatre of Skating. If we had attempted to include all these we would have needed not only a much larger book but an accurate crystal ball. Therefore we have stuck to our criteria knowing that in another decade the choreographic picture will look very different from the one presented here, which itself is different from the way things were ten years ago.

The principal difference between 1970 and 1980 lies not so much in choreographers as in the expansion of choreographic opportunity and the provision to acquire choreographic experience. In Britain, Canada and Australia there has been a significant expansion out of the traditional centres of theatre dance and away from classical ballet. One of the main problems today, in fact, is the shortage of young classical choreographers working in a classical, rather than classical/modern, style. Hence the importance of the Royal Ballet School's new choreographic department and similar developments at the National Ballet School of Canada and the Australian Ballet School.

It is worth reviewing briefly the nature of the choreographic opportunity now provided across the whole field because this is likely to change and expand choreography further during the 1980s. Some of the opportunity arises from long-established practice such as the various choreographic awards and competitions in all countries. Some is a result of adapting established events, such as summer schools, to new or partly new purposes. Most of the opportunity, however, has developed in an organized way only in the last ten years or so. It can be divided into provision for professional dancers and provision for students.

Provision for professional dancers includes company choreographic workshops and the establishment of new companies, and hence an enlarged market for choreography including choreographic experiment. The idea of company choreographic workshops was well-established in 1970, but they were rather rare events in Britain and almost never happened in Canada, Australia and New Zealand. In Britain there was an alternative tradition of central voluntary provision going back to the mid-1940s. Today company workshops are much more regular events and have produced a great deal of new choreography, especially in modern dance. Ballet Rambert workshops – to mention only one series – gave first opportunity to Judith Marcuse, now back in Canada; Jonathan Taylor, Joseph Scoglio and Julia Blaikie now working in Australia; and Lenny Westerdijk, the Australian Leigh Warren, and others working in Britain. The same sort of value derives from other company workshops provided they are regularly organized and properly supported with time and resources.

The second important professional development of the 1970s has been the establishments of new small companies dedicated to the exploration of new ideas, often around the work of one or two choreographers. In Canada one thinks of the Groupe de la Place Royale in Montreal, the Contemporary Dancers in Winnipeg; in Britain, Moving Visions Dance Theatre, Cycles Dance Company, EMMA Dance Company, Extemporary Dance Company, the Maas Movers, and many others working mostly outside London; in Australia, of course, there are not only the state companies but ethnic companies as well as the beginnings of small modern dance companies. All this has changed the climate of choreography and made it more accessible to a wider audience, not least through television.

A third professional development of the 1970s seeks to consolidate and take further these elements. Since 1975, first under the auspices of the Gulbenkian Foundation and now independently, an annual choreographic course for composers as well as choreographers has been established near London to serve Commonwealth and other countries. Directed each year by a leading choreographer of international standing, and maintaining the highest standards, this is now the top institution of its kind for those who have already shown evidence of talent. It completes, as it were, the ladder of professional opportunity short of actually receiving a professional commission.

A similar development for professional dancers has taken place in Canada, first at York University Toronto, in the summer of 1978, directed by Robert Cohan who directed the international course in Britain the same year, and then in 1980 at the Banff Center, Alberta. Parallel to both developments, but independently, a series of choreographic summer schools and workshops for professional dancers and dance teachers have been held at the University of New England, Armidale, in New South Wales during the 1970s. It can be said with some confidence, therefore, that the provision of choreographic courses and opportunities at professional level is becoming institutionalized in all three countries.

Partly these developments in the professional field reflect a considerable expansion of provision in the educational field during the 1970s. Well-known private teachers, like Nesta Brooking in London, have long offered choreographic opportunity and guidance as part of their courses. The 1970s added to this kind of personal commitment the regular organization of choreographic departments at major vocational centres and the development of choreographic departments in institutions of tertiary education as well as occasional provision at secondary level. Out of the Royal Ballet School's choreographic department, for instance, have emerged already the promising talents of Jonathan Burrows and David Bintley. Out of the department at the London School of Contemporary Dance have come many of the young choreographers who have formed small new companies in different parts of Britain.

This development of choreographic training in vocational institutions is being matched on a larger scale in universities, polytechnics and teacher training colleges. In Canada, for instance, there are now three universities with degree programmes in dance and many others with minor specializations or courses in dance. Among the former, York University Toronto, has developed one of the most important university dance departments in North America with choreography as an important element of its courses. In Britain since the mid-1970s many degree courses have been validated in which dance is a major option with choreography a required element. In all three countries the dance composition element of teacher training has been expanded or changed to incorporate higher standards and a wider range of styles. In Australia, for example, the country's first four-year degree programme specializing in drama and dance for the award of bachelor of education at Rusden State College, Victoria, includes choreography and dance production.

All this is bound to stimulate further expansion and experiment during the 1980s. Indeed it has begun to do so. The development of new dance and dance composition courses at secondary level and the formation of many youth dance companies based on individual schools have largely taken place under the guidance of graduates who gained their own first opportunities during tertiary education. This expansion not only provides boys and girls with the opportunity to create their own dances but also provides professional choreographers with the opportunity to work with and help young people as has happened through the London Youth Dance Theatre.

Collaboration between the dance and education professions in this way is a key to further development. If the significant opportunities for choreographic learning and practice now being created in all three countries are to achieve full results they need to be supported in other ways too. First, with regular funding from arts and educational sources at local as well as central level. Next, in professional circles there is a need for better organization, especially of dancers' time to consolidate the opportunities. Third, in general education there is a need to develop dance appreciation so that the audiences of the future see more dance and comprehend choreography as an important area of communication as well as personal expression. Fourth, new choreography needs to be projected regularly on television, like new plays and films, as an art form in its own right, building its own public. But the overwhelming needs in both fields are for more collaboration between the education and dance professions, more international exchange and the encouragement of ethnic and national dancing to provide choreographic roots. We hope that these will be targets for the 1980s.

254

Further Study

During the last ten years a number of institutions have been developed where choreography and dance composition can be undertaken in a learning situation. Among these institutions are the following:

For professional dancers
1 Choreographic workshops organized by professional companies. For details approach the companies but opportunities are usually reserved to company members.
2 The International Dance Course for Professional Choreographers and Composers. Administrator: Gale Law, Creative Dance Artists Limited, 15b Lauriston Road, London SW19 4TJ.
3 The National Choreographic Seminar. Administrator: Grant Strate, 100 Richmond Street East, Suite 325, Toronto, Ontario M5C 2P9, Canada. This is a three-week course initiated in 1980 and co-sponsored by the Banff Centre School of Fine Arts and Dance in Canada Association. It is for composers as well as choreographers and is developed from experience of the international course above and a choreographic seminar organized by York University, Toronto, in 1978.
4 Important choreographic workshops or presentations for professional dancers have been organized from time to time in Australia by the Department of Continuing Education, University of New England, Armidale, NSW 2351, Australia, and by the Australian Ballet.

For vocational dance students
Many vocational dance schools now maintain choreographic departments, organize dance composition courses and provide choreographic opportunities in various ways. Among these institutions are:
1 The Royal Ballet School, 155 Talgarth Road, London W14.
2 The London School of Contemporary Dance, The Place, 17 Duke's Road, London WC1.
3 The Laban Centre for Movement and Dance, Goldsmiths' College, New Cross, London SE14 6NW.

4 The Brooking School of Ballet and General Education, 110 Marylebone High Street, London W1.
5 The National Ballet School of Canada, 111 Maitland Street, Toronto, Ontario M4Y 1E4, Canada.
6 School of the Toronto Dance Theatre, 80 Winchester Street, Toronto, Ontario M4X 1B2, Canada.
7 The Australian Ballet School, 11 Mt Alexander Road, Flemington 3031, Melbourne, Australia.
8 The Victoria College of the Arts, 234 St Kilda Road, Melbourne 3004, Australia.
9 New Zealand Ballet Company, P.O. Box 6682, Te Aro, Wellington, New Zealand.

For other students of dance
Dance and dance composition can be studied in many ways and in many educational situations. Many students in public education at tertiary level study it out of interest; others hope to make it a career in some way. Most tertiary institutions with dance departments include provision for choreographic opportunity. It is usually integral, for example, to specialist dance teacher training courses, so such courses are not listed below. Among other tertiary institutions are:
1 The Dance Department, York University, 4700 Keele Street, Downsview, Toronto, Ontario M3J 1P3, Canada.
2 The Drama and Dance Department, Rusden State College, 662 Blackburn Road, Clayton 3168, Australia.
3 The Laban Centre for Movement and Dance, Goldsmiths' College, New Cross, London SE14 6NW.

For students of dance notation
The study of dance notation is very relevant to choreography for obvious reasons. It can be studied at almost all the institutions listed under the last two categories above, but also at two specialist centres:
1 Institute of Choreology, 4 Margravine Gardens, Barons Court, London W6 8RH.
2 Language of Dance Centre, (business address) 5 Lincoln's Inn Fields, London WC2; (library and personal interviews) 17 Holland Park, London W11 3TD.

Further Reading

In addition to organized study, private reading is essential. Through books one can explore new aspects of dance, or prepare with deeper knowledge to re-see well-known dance works. A small library of dance books could be drawn from amongst the following:

Armitage, *Martha Graham* (New York, 1937/66)

Beaumont (trans.), *Noverre: Letters on Dancing and Ballet* (New York, 1930/66)

Blasis, *The Code of Terpsichore* (New York, 1975)

Brinson, *Background to European Ballet* (Leyden 1966/New York, 1980)

Bruhn and Moore, *Bournonville and Ballet Technique* (London, 1961)

Buckle, *Nijinsky* (London, 1971)

Buckle, *Diaghilev* (London, 1979)

Clarke, *The Sadler's Wells Ballet* (London, 1978, reprint)

Clarke and Crisp, *Ballet: An Illustrated History* (London, 1973)

Clarke and Crisp, *Making a Ballet* (London, 1974)

Clarke and Crisp, *Introducing Ballet* (London, 1977)

Clarke and Crisp, *Design for Ballet* (London, 1978)

Cohen, *Doris Humphrey. An Artist First* (Middletown, 1972)

Crocc, *After Images* (London, 1978)

Denby, *Looking at the Dance* (New York, 1949/76)

Denby, *Dancers, Buildings and People in the Streets* (New York, 1965/76)

Goodwin, *The Scottish Ballet* (London, 1979)

Grigoriev, *The Diaghilev Ballet* (London, 1953)

Guest, *The Dancer's Heritage* (London, 1960)

Guest, *The Romantic Ballet in Paris* (London, 1966)

Gulbenkian Foundation, *Dance Education and Training in Britain* (London, 1980)

Haskell, *Ballets Russes. The Age of Diaghilev* (London, 1968)

Horst, *Pre-Classic Dance Forms* (New York, 1937/69)

Horst and Russell, *Modern Dance Forms* (New York, 1961/67)

Karsavina, *Theatre Street* (London/New York, 1931)

Kirstein, *Movement and Metaphor* (London, 1970)

Kirstein, *Nijinsky Dancing* (London, 1975)

Kirstein, *Thirty Years: The New York City Ballet* (New York, 1978)

Kochno, *Diaghilev and the Ballets Russes* (London, 1970)

Levinson, *Marie Taglioni* (London, 1977)

Makarova, *A Dance Autobiography* (London, 1980)

Martin, *Modern Dance* (New York, 1933/65)

Martin, *Introduction to the Dance* (New York, 1939/65)

Mazo, *Prime Movers* (London, 1977)

McAndrews (trans.), *August Bournonville: My Theatre Life* (London, 1979)

McDonagh, *The Complete Guide to Modern Dance* (New York, 1976)

Pask, *Enter the Colonies Dancing* (Melbourne, 1979)

Payne, *American Ballet Theatre* (New York, 1978)

Percival, *Modern Ballet* (London, 1970)

Ralph, *John Weaver: His Life and Works* (London/New York, 1980)

Roslavleva, *Era of the Russian Ballet* (London, 1966)

Schneider, *Isadora Duncan. The Russian Years* (London, 1968)

Strong, *Splendour at Court* (London, 1973)

Stravinsky and Craft, *Stravinsky* (London, 1979)

Swift, *The Art of the Dance in the USSR* (Notre Dame, Indiana, 1968)

Swift, *A Loftier Flight: The Life of Charles Louis Didelot* (London, 1974)

Taper, *Balanchine* (London, 1974)

Van Praagh and Brinson, *The Choreographic Art* (London/New York, 1963, new edition due London, 1981)

Vaughan, *Frederick Ashton and His Ballets* (London, 1977)

Winter, *The Pre-Romantic Ballet* (London, 1974)

Yates, *Astraea* (London, 1975/78)

Some of the above books are expensive because of their valuable illustrations, or are difficult to obtain. Most of them, as an alternative, should be available through libraries.

PERIODICALS

The last ten years have seen a number of changes in periodical publications, particularly the development of journals published by university and college dance departments and a rise in the standard of house journals published by professional bodies. Attention is drawn particularly to the following:

Britain

Dancing Times, monthly – 18 Hand Court, Holborn, London WC1.

Dance and Dancers, monthly – 75 Victoria Street, London SW1.

New Dance, quarterly – X6 Dance Space, Butler's Wharf, Lafone Street, London SE1.

Dance Studies, annually – Centre for Dance Studies, Les Bois, St Peter, Jersey, Channel Islands.

Canada

Dance Canada, quarterly – Dance in Canada Association, 100 Richmond Street East, Suite 325, Toronto, Ontario M5C 2P9, Canada.

York Dance Review, occasional – Department of Dance, York University, 4700 Keele Street, Downsview, Ontario M3J 1P3, Canada.

USA

Dance Magazine, monthly – 10 Columbus Circle, New York, NY 10019.

Dance News, monthly except August – 119 West 57 Street, New York, NY 10019.

Ballet News, monthly, except bi-monthly July/August and January/February – Metropolitan Opera Guild Inc., Box 918, Farmingdale, New York, NY 11737.

Dance Chronicle, quarterly – Marcel Dekker Inc., 270 Madison Avenue, New York, NY 10016.

Index